## More Praise for RICHER, WISER, HAPPIER

"Endlessly fascinating . . . *Richer, Wiser, Happier* is going to be a classic."
        —Guy Spier, CEO of Aquamarine
        Capital and author of *The Education*
        *of a Value Investor*

"Wonderful . . . a profound, eloquent, and much-needed call for a reassessment of how we build our portfolios and live our lives."
        —Stig Brodersen, cofounder of The
        Investor's Podcast Network and host
        of the podcast *We Study Billionaires*

"Highly recommended . . . a thoroughly engaging book that is brimming with unique insights into investing and life."
        —John Mihaljevic, chairman of MOI
        Global and author of *The Manual of Ideas*

"Invaluable . . . destined to become a timeless classic on lifelong learning, self-improvement, and becoming the best version of ourselves."
        —Gautam Baid, author of *The Joys of*
        *Compounding*

"Edifying . . . William Green draws on history, philosophy, and spirituality to present a meditation on investing. Far more than a book about stock picking, *Richer, Wiser, Happier* is the enlightened investor's guide to life."
        —Nina Munk, author of *The Idealist* and
        *Fools Rush In*

"Fantastic . . . accomplishes what few books ever have, which is to show how to be *rational*."
        —Saurabh Madaan, deputy chief
        investment officer at Markel
        Corporation and former senior data
        scientist at Google

# RICHER, WISER, HAPPIER

## HOW THE WORLD'S GREATEST INVESTORS WIN IN MARKETS AND LIFE

## WILLIAM GREEN

SCRIBNER

New York    London    Toronto    Sydney    New Delhi

Scribner
An Imprint of Simon & Schuster, Inc.
1230 Avenue of the Americas
New York, NY 10020

First Scribner hardcover edition April 2021

SCRIBNER and design are registered trademarks of The Gale Group, Inc.,
used under license by Simon & Schuster, Inc., the publisher of this work.

For information about special discounts for bulk purchases,
please contact Simon & Schuster Special Sales
at 1-866-506-1949 or business@simonandschuster.com.

The Simon & Schuster Speakers Bureau can bring authors to your live event.
For more information or to book an event, contact the Simon & Schuster Speakers Bureau
at 1-866-248-3049 or visit our website at www.simonspeakers.com.

Manufactured in the United States of America

1   3   5   7   9   10   8   6   4   2

Library of Congress Cataloging-in-Publication Data is available.

ISBN 978-1-5011-6485-9
ISBN 978-1-5011-6487-3 (ebook)

For Lauren, Henry, Madeleine, and Marilyn

# Contents

# CONTENTS

# Inside the Minds of
# the Greatest Investors

I've been obsessed with investing for a quarter of a century. At first, it seemed an unlikely passion. I had never taken a class in business or economics. I had no talent for numbers and no grasp of the esoteric mysteries of accounting. After leaving Oxford with a degree in English literature, I reviewed novels for magazines and wrote profiles of fraudsters and murderers. As an aspiring author with high-minded dreams of literary fame, I found it easy to dismiss Wall Street as a casino full of crass speculators who cared only about money. When the *New York Times* landed on my doorstep, I would jettison the business section without even glancing at it.

But in 1995, I found myself with a bit of cash to invest—my half of the proceeds from the sale of an apartment that I owned with my brother. I began to read incessantly about stocks and funds, eager to increase my modest windfall. This reawakened in me a gambling streak that had briefly run wild when I was a teenager in England in the 1980s. At fifteen, when I was a student at Eton, I'd sneak out of school on lazy summer afternoons and spend hours at a local "turf accountant" near Windsor Castle, betting on horses while my classmates played cricket or went rowing. I was meant to become a posh English gentleman like Boris Johnson, Prince William, and six centuries of Etonians before us. Instead, I had an illegal betting account under the name of Mike Smith.

My interest in horse racing was fueled not by the romance of the sport or the majesty of the equine form, but by a desire to make money without working. I took it seriously, jotting down elaborate notes about horses and courses, using multicolored ink pens to highlight my wins and losses. I ruined my sixteenth birthday by fighting with my parents over their refusal to buy me a subscription to Timeform, a pricey system for rating horses. I was outraged that they blocked this obvious route to untold riches. Shortly afterward, following a string of disillusioning losses, I renounced racing once and for all.

A decade later, when I began to read about investing, I discovered that the stock market offered similar thrills. But the odds of success were much higher. Stocks struck me as the perfect way to cash in merely by *outthinking* other people. Of course, I had no idea what I was doing. But I had one inestimable advantage. As a journalist, I could indulge my new fixation by interviewing many of the best investors in the business.

In the years that followed, I interviewed a pantheon of investment legends for *Forbes*, *Money*, *Fortune*, and *Time*, returning again and again to the same overarching questions that fascinate me to this day: What principles, processes, insights, habits, and personality traits enable this tiny minority to beat the market in the long run and become spectacularly rich? More important, how can you and I profit by studying these financial outliers and reverse engineering their winning ways? Those questions lie at the heart of this book.

To my delight, many of the investors I encountered were fascinating and oddly exotic. I flew to the Bahamas to spend a day with Sir John Templeton, the greatest global stock picker of the twentieth century, who lived in a Caribbean idyll called Lyford Cay. I traveled to Houston for an audience with Fayez Sarofim, an enigmatic Egyptian billionaire nicknamed the Sphinx. In his office, he displayed paintings by El Greco and Willem de Kooning, along with a fifth-century mosaic floor imported from a Syrian church. I spoke with Mark Mobius (the Bald Eagle), who flew around the developing world in a Gulfstream jet adorned with gold-plated fixtures and iguana-skin upholstery, purchased from a Middle Eastern tycoon who had fallen on hard times. I interviewed Michael Price, a polo-playing centimillionaire who terrorized underperforming CEOs and came to be known as "the scariest SOB on Wall Street." I met Helmut Friedlaender, who had fled from Germany in the 1930s, stopping only to pick up his teenage sister and buy a hat "because a gentleman does not travel without a hat." He drank Château Pétrus, collected precious medieval books, and traded everything from coffee futures to the Empire State Building. In his nineties, he told me, "I have lived uproariously."

It was a priceless education. Jack Bogle, the index fund icon who founded Vanguard, which now manages $6.2 trillion, talked to me about the formative investment lessons he'd learned from his mentor and "hero," a mutual fund pioneer named Walter Morgan: "Don't get carried away. Don't take excessive risk. . . . Keep your costs low." And: "The crowd is always wrong." As we shall see, Bogle also explained why "you don't need to be great" to thrive as an investor.

Peter Lynch, Fidelity's most famous fund manager, talked to me about how he'd won by outworking everybody else. But he also spoke about the wild unpredictability of markets and the need for humility: "You get a lot of A's and B's in school. In the stock market, you get a lot of F's. And if you're right six or seven times out of ten, you're very good." Lynch recalled one of his first failures: a high-flying apparel business went bust "all because of the movie *Bonnie and Clyde*," which altered women's fashions so unexpectedly that the company's inventory became "worthless." Ned Johnson, the multibillionaire who built Fidelity into a behemoth, laughed and told Lynch, "You did everything right. . . . Things come out of left field every now and then."

In the tumultuous days after 9/11, when financial markets were suffering their worst week since the Great Depression, I headed to Baltimore to visit Bill Miller, who was in the midst of an unprecedented streak of beating the S&P 500 index for fifteen years running. We spent a few days together and traveled in his Learjet, which he'd bought in part so that his 110-pound Irish wolfhound could fly with him. The economy was reeling, war was brewing in Afghanistan, and his fund had tumbled 40 percent from its peak. But Miller was relaxed and cheerful, coolly staking hundreds of millions of dollars on beaten-down stocks that subsequently soared.

One morning, I was standing beside him when he rang his office to check in. The analyst on the other end of the line broke it to him that AES, a stock that Miller had only just bought, had announced terrible earnings. The stock halved, costing him $50 million before lunchtime. Miller instantly doubled his bet, calmly assuming that irrational investors had overreacted to the company's dismal news. As he explained to me, investing is a constant process of calculating the odds: "It's all probabilities. There *is* no certainty."

And then there was Bill Ruane, one of the most successful stock pickers of his generation. When Warren Buffett closed his investment partnership in 1969, he recommended Ruane as a replacement for himself. Until his death in 2005, Ruane's Sequoia Fund generated stunning returns. He almost never granted interviews, but we spoke at length about the four guiding principles he had learned in the 1950s from "a major star" named Albert Hettinger. "Those simple rules have been of enormous importance to me," said Ruane. "They formed the basis for a large part of my philosophy ever since. . . . And they are the best advice I can give people."

First, warned Ruane, "Do *not* borrow money to buy stocks." He recalled an early experience when, by using leverage, he "took six hundred dollars and multiplied it many times." Then "the market cracked" and he was hit so hard that he sold out and was "back almost to square one." As he discovered then, "You don't act rationally when you're investing borrowed money." Second, "Watch out for momentum." That's to say, proceed with extreme caution "when you see markets going crazy," either because the herd is panicking or charging into stocks at irrational valuations. Third, ignore market predictions: "I firmly believe that nobody knows what the market will do. . . . The important thing is to find an attractive idea and invest in a company that's cheap."

For Ruane, the fourth principle was the most important of all: invest in a small number of stocks that you've researched so intensively that you have an informational advantage. "I try to learn as much as I can about seven or eight good ideas," he said. "If you really find something very cheap, why not put fifteen percent of your money in it?" For regular investors, there are safer paths to success. "Most people would be much better off with an index fund," said Ruane. But for investors aiming to beat the market, concentration struck him as the smart way to go: "I don't know anybody who can really do a good job investing in a lot of stocks except Peter Lynch."

When we spoke in 2001, Ruane told me that 35 percent of Sequoia's assets were riding on a single stock: Berkshire Hathaway. It had fallen out of favor during the dotcom craze, and Buffett, its chairman and

CEO, was lambasted for losing his touch. Yet Ruane saw what others missed: "a wonderful company" with superior growth prospects run by "the smartest guy in the country."

What I began to understand is that the greatest investors are intellectual mavericks. They're not afraid to question and defy conventional wisdom. They profit from the misperceptions and mistakes of people who think less rationally, rigorously, and objectively. In fact, one of the best reasons to study the investors spotlighted in this book is that they can teach us not only how to become rich, but how to improve the way we think and reach decisions.

The rewards for investing intelligently are so extravagant that the business attracts many brilliant minds. But there can also be a devastating price to pay for being wrong, which is rarely the case for professors, politicians, and pundits. The stakes involved may explain why the best investors tend to be open-minded pragmatists who search relentlessly for ways to improve their thinking.

This mindset is embodied by Buffett's frighteningly clever partner, Charlie Munger, who once remarked, "I observe what works and what doesn't and why." Munger, who is one of the central figures in this book, has roamed far and wide in his quest for better ways to think, borrowing analytical tools from disciplines as diverse as mathematics, biology, and behavioral psychology. His role models include Charles Darwin, Albert Einstein, Benjamin Franklin, and a nineteenth-century algebraist named Carl Gustav Jacobi. "I learned a lot from a lot of dead people," Munger told me. "I always realized that there were a lot of dead people I ought to get to know."

I've come to think of the best investors as an idiosyncratic breed of practical philosophers. They aren't trying to solve those abstruse puzzles that mesmerize many *real* philosophers, such as "Does this chair exist?" Rather, they are seekers of what the economist John Maynard Keynes called "worldly wisdom," which they deploy to attack more pressing problems, such as "How can I make smart decisions about the future if the future is unknowable?" They look for advantages wherever they can find them: economic history, neuroscience, literature, Stoicism, Buddhism, sports, the science of habit formation, meditation, or anything else that can help. Their unconstrained willingness to explore "what works" makes them powerful role models to study in our own pursuit of success, not only in markets but in every area of life.

Another way to think about the most skillful investors is as consummate game players. It's no coincidence that many top-notch money managers play cards for pleasure and profit. Templeton used his poker winnings to help pay for college during the Depression. Buffett and Munger are passionate about bridge. Mario Gabelli, a billionaire fund mogul, told me how he earned money as a poor boy from the Bronx by playing cards between rounds as a caddy at a fancy golf club. "I was eleven or twelve," he recalled, "and everybody *thought* they could win." Lynch, who played poker in high school, college, and the army, told me, "Learning to play poker or learning to play bridge, anything that teaches you to play the probabilities . . . would be better than all the books on the stock market."

As I've come to realize, it's helpful to view investing and life as games in which we must *consciously and consistently seek to maximize our odds of success*. The rules are elusive and the outcome uncertain. But there are smart ways to play and dumb ways to play. Damon Runyon, who was besotted with games of chance, once wrote that "all life is six to five against."\* Perhaps. But what captivates me is that Templeton, Bogle, Ruane, Buffett, Munger, Miller, and other giants whom we'll study in the chapters to come have figured out shrewd ways to stack the odds in their favor. My mission is to show you how.

Consider Ed Thorp, who is probably the greatest game player in investment history. Before he became a hedge fund manager, he achieved immortality in gambling circles by devising an ingenious scheme to beat the casino at blackjack. As Thorp explained to me over

---

\* One of Runyon's greatest short stories is "The Idyll of Miss Sarah Brown," which inspired the musical *Guys and Dolls*. The hero, a high-rolling gambler nicknamed the Sky, receives invaluable advice from his father about the perils of overconfidence—a warning that every investor would do well to internalize. " 'Son,' the old guy says, 'no matter how far you travel, or how smart you get, always remember this: Some day, somewhere,' he says, 'a guy is going to come to you and show you a nice brand-new deck of cards on which the seal is never broken, and this guy is going to offer to bet you that the jack of spades will jump out of this deck and squirt cider in your ear. But, son,' the old guy says, 'do not bet him, for as sure as you do you are going to get an ear full of cider.' "

a three-hour breakfast of eggs Benedict and cappuccino, he refused to accept the "conventional belief" that it was mathematically impossible for players to gain an edge over the dealer. Thorp, the father of card counting, gave himself an advantage by calculating the change in probabilities once certain cards were "gone from the deck" and "no longer available." For example, a deck packed with aces offered him better odds than one without them. When the odds favored him, he bet more; when they favored the casino, he bet less. Over time, his modest advantage became overwhelming. Thus, he transformed a loser's game of luck into a lucrative "game of math."

For his next trick, Thorp figured out how to beat the casino at roulette. He and a partner, Claude Shannon, created the first wearable computer, which Thorp activated furtively with a big toe inside his shoe. The computer, which was the size of a cigarette pack, enabled him to "measure the position and velocity of the ball and rotor very accurately," so he could predict where the ball was likely to land. For centuries, roulette was a mug's game in which players had no edge, since the ball has an equal chance of falling in each of thirty-eight pockets. "But by adding some knowledge and some measurement, we get a little better grasp on the probabilities of what's going to happen," said Thorp. "You won't get it right every time, but your forecast will be somewhat better than chance. . . . So we were turning what seemed like a game of pure chance into a game where we had an edge. And the edge was provided by the information that we were adding."

Unless you own a casino, Thorp's subversive genius is irresistibly appealing. It was never the money that excited him so much as the joy of solving "interesting problems" that all of the experts insisted were insoluble. "Just because a lot of people say something is true, that doesn't carry any particular weight with me," said Thorp. "You need to do some independent thinking, especially about the important things, and try to work them out for yourself. Check the evidence. Check the basis of conventional beliefs."

As Thorp's adventures suggest, one critical way to improve our financial lives is to avoid games in which the odds are stacked against us. "As far as gambling is concerned, if I don't have an edge, I don't play," said Thorp. Applying that same principle, the rest of us would be wise to face reality as honestly as possible; for example, if my knowledge of technology is flimsy or I lack the basic financial skills required to value a business, I should resist any temptation to pick individual tech stocks for myself. Otherwise, I'm like the patsy at the roulette wheel, hoping that fate will smile kindly upon me despite my delusions. As Jeffrey Gundlach, a coldly rational billionaire who oversees about $140 billion in bonds, remarked to me, "Hope is not a method."

Another common mistake that tilts the odds *against* many unsuspecting investors is to pay lavish fees to mediocre fund managers, stockbrokers, and financial advisers whose performance doesn't justify the expense. "If you're paying tolls as you go and trading costs, advisory fees, all kinds of other charges, you're swimming against the current," said Thorp. "If you're *not* paying all these things, you're swimming *with* the current." One obvious way, then, for regular investors to boost their odds of long-term victory is to buy and hold index funds that charge minuscule fees: "You don't have to do any work and you're ahead of maybe eighty percent of the people who do otherwise." An index such as the S&P 500 will "probably" rise in the long run, added Thorp, driven by the "expansion of the American economy." So, unlike gamblers in a casino, "you have an automatic edge" by merely participating in the market's upward trajectory at a minimal cost.

By contrast, Thorp's hedge fund crushed the indexes over two decades without a single losing quarter by focusing on more obscure investment opportunities that "were not well understood." For example, his exceptional math skills enabled him to value warrants, options, and convertible bonds with unrivaled accuracy. Other key characters in this book, such as Howard Marks and Joel Greenblatt, gained similar advantages by specializing in neglected or detested niches of the financial markets. As we shall see, there are many ways to win, but they all require some form of edge. When I asked Thorp how to tell whether I have one, he offered this disconcerting thought: "Unless you have a rational reason to believe you have an edge, then you probably don't."

When my investment journey began twenty-five years ago, I yearned to be financially free and answerable to nobody. The best investors had cracked the code, which seemed almost magical to me. But what I realize now is that understanding how these individuals think and why they win can help us immeasurably in so *many* ways—financially, professionally, and personally.

For example, when I asked Thorp how to maximize my odds of a happy and successful life, he illustrated his characteristic approach by discussing health and fitness. Thorp, who was eighty-four but looked twenty years younger, observed, "Genetically, you're dealt certain cards. . . . You can think of that as chance. But you have choices about how to play those cards," including the choice to avoid cigarettes, have annual medical checkups, keep your vaccinations up-to-date, and exercise regularly. In his thirties, Thorp was "in terrible shape" and found himself "gasping for breath" after jogging for a quarter of a mile. So he started running one mile every Saturday, improving gradually until he completed twenty-one marathons. He still sees a personal trainer twice a week and walks three miles a day four times a week. But when someone suggested that he take up biking, Thorp scrutinized the number of "deaths per hundred million passenger miles for cycling" and "decided that the risk was too high."

When I spoke with him again, it was June 2020 and the world was gripped by a pandemic that had already killed more than one hundred thousand Americans. Thorp explained how he'd analyzed the mortality data from around the globe, paying particular attention to "unexplained deaths" that were probably caused by the virus; how he'd drawn "inferences" from the 1918 flu pandemic that had killed his grandfather; how he'd produced his own estimate of "the true fatality rate"; and how he'd predicted in early February (before a single death was recorded in the United States) that the country would lose two hundred thousand to five hundred thousand lives to this new coronavirus over the next twelve months.

Thorp's methodical analysis of the data enabled his family to take timely precautions when few Americans—least of all, the nation's leaders—recognized the magnitude of the threat. "We prudently put away supplies of all kinds, including masks," he said. "It was about a month later that people woke up and started cleaning out store shelves." Three weeks before the government declared a national emergency, Thorp placed himself in isolation at his home in Laguna Beach and "stopped seeing everybody" except his wife. "There's no point being scared," he told me. But he understood the risks and acted decisively to augment his odds of survival. Thorp may be the only person I've ever met who actually calculated his own "chance of dying."*

That mental habit of thinking dispassionately about facts and figures, probabilities, trade-offs between risk and reward, and the paramount importance of simply *avoiding catastrophe* does much to explain how the savviest investors live long and prosper. As Thorp sees it, every aspect of our behavior should be guided by an attitude of "generalized rationality." For example, he knows that he's more likely to make bad decisions when he's "in emotional mode." So, if he's "irritated or mad" at somebody, he takes a step back and asks himself, "What do you *really* know? Is your feeling justified or not?" His measured analysis often indicates to him that his adverse reaction was unwarranted. "We jump to conclusions when we shouldn't," he observed. "And so withholding judgment is, I think, a key element of rational behavior."

All of this leads me to believe that the true titans of the investment world can help us to become richer, wiser, and happier. My goal is to show you how they win both in markets and life by finding countless ways to optimize the odds of success.

Playing the odds is an extraordinarily effective way to operate, and it pervades everything they do, including how they manage their time, how they construct a calm environment in which to think, whom they hang out with and steer clear of, how they guard against biases and blind spots, how they learn from mistakes and avoid repeating them, how they handle stress and adversity, how they think about honesty and integrity, how they spend money and give it away, and how they attempt to build lives imbued with a meaning that transcends money.

In writing this book, I've drawn deeply from the most important interviews I conducted in the distant past with many of the world's

* How did Thorp estimate the odds that COVID-19 would kill him? "A random eighty-seven-year-old male has about a twenty percent chance of dying if he gets the virus," he told me. "My risk is lower because a lot of eighty-seven-year-old males have significant other health problems, and I don't. I have no comorbidity. I'm also super-careful. And I'm quite fit for my age. So, I figured my chance of being killed by it is between two and four percent. But that's still plenty high."

best investors. But I've also spent hundreds of hours interviewing more than forty investors specifically for this book, reporting everywhere from Los Angeles to London, Omaha to Mumbai. Between them, the characters you will meet here have overseen trillions of dollars on behalf of millions of people. My hope is that these extraordinary investors will enlighten—and enrich—your life. I would bet on it.

# CHAPTER ONE

# The Man Who Cloned Warren Buffett

## How to succeed by shamelessly borrowing other people's best ideas

---

A wise man ought always to follow the paths beaten by great men, and to imitate those who have been supreme, so that if his ability does not equal theirs, at least it will savor of it.

—Niccolò Machiavelli

I believe in the discipline of mastering the best that other people have ever figured out. I don't believe in just sitting down and trying to dream it all up yourself. Nobody's that smart.

—Charlie Munger

It's 7:00 a.m. on Christmas Day. Mohnish Pabrai steps into a minivan in Mumbai as the sun rises in the smoggy sky. We drive for hours along the western coast of India toward a territory called Dadra and Nagar Haveli. Our driver intermittently executes terrifying maneuvers, swerving wildly between trucks and buses. I close my eyes and grimace in horror as horns blare on all sides. Pabrai, who grew up in India before moving to the United States for college, smiles serenely, always calm in the presence of risk. Still, he concedes, "The accident rate in India is high."

It's a riveting drive, full of mind-bending sights. At one point, we pass a plump man by the side of the road who's stacking bricks on top of a skinny woman's head so she can carry them. As we drive deeper into the countryside, we see squat huts covered with grass—structures that seem to belong to another millennium. Finally, we reach our destination: a rural high school called JNV Silvassa.

Pabrai, one of the preeminent investors of his generation, has traveled here from his home in Irvine, California, to visit forty teenage girls. They are part of a program run by his charitable foundation, Dakshana, which educates gifted children from disadvantaged families across India. Dakshana is providing these girls with two years of free schooling to prepare them for the infamously difficult entrance exam to the Indian Institutes of Technology (IIT), a group of elite engineering colleges whose graduates are coveted by companies such as Microsoft and Google.

More than a million students apply to IIT each year, and less than 2 percent are accepted. But Dakshana has cracked the code. Over twelve years, 2,146 Dakshana scholars have won places at IIT—an acceptance rate of 62 percent. Pabrai views Dakshana (a Sanskrit word meaning "gift") as a means of uplifting the most underprivileged segments of Indian society. Most Dakshana scholars come from rural families that survive on less than $2 a day. Many belong to lower castes, including "untouchables," who have suffered centuries of discrimination.

Whenever Pabrai visits a Dakshana classroom, he breaks the ice by posing the same mathematical problem. Everyone who has solved it has subsequently won a place at IIT, so it's a useful way to gauge the talent in the room. The question is so hard that almost nobody gets it right, and he expects none of the Silvassa students to meet the challenge. Nonetheless, he writes the problem in chalk on the blackboard at the front of the classroom: *n is a prime number* $\geq 5$. *Prove that* $n^2 - 1$ *is always divisible by 24.* Then he leans back in a flimsy plastic chair while the girls attempt to divine the answer.* I wonder what they make of this flamboyant, larger-than-life creature—a tall, burly, balding moneyman with a luxuriant mustache, who's dressed in a Dakshana sweatshirt and pink jeans.

After ten minutes, Pabrai asks, "Is anyone close?" A fifteen-year-old girl named Alisa says, "Sir, it's only a theory." Her tentativeness

---

* What's the answer to Pabrai's question? This is a mystery that will forever elude me.

instills no confidence, but Pabrai invites her to the front of the classroom to show him her solution. She hands him a sheet of white paper and stands meekly before him, head bowed, awaiting judgment. Above her, a sign on the wall says, in charmingly garbled English, SO LONG AS YOU HAVE FAITH IN YOU, NOTHING WILL BE ABLE TO ABSTRACT YOU.

"It's correct," says Pabrai. He shakes Alisa's hand and asks her to explain her answer to the class. He later tells me that she solved the problem so elegantly that she could rank in the top two hundred in the IIT exam. Pabrai tells her that she's "a sure shot" to get in: "All you have to do is keep working hard." I subsequently learn that Alisa is from the Ganjam district in the state of Odisha, one of India's poorest districts, and was born into a caste that the government calls Other Backward Classes. In her previous school, she ranked first out of eighty students.

Pabrai asks Alisa to pose for a photograph with him. "You will forget about me," he jokes, "but then I can tell you, 'We have the picture!'" The girls laugh delightedly, but I find it hard not to cry. We have witnessed something magical: a child plucked from poverty has just proven that she has the mental firepower to propel herself and her family into prosperity. Given the environment in which she was raised and the odds against her, it's a kind of miracle.

Later that morning, the students pepper Pabrai with questions. Finally, one plucks up the courage to ask what everyone must want to know: "Sir, how did you make so much money?"

Pabrai laughs and says, "I *compound* money."

Searching for a way to illustrate the concept, he says, "I have a hero. His name is Warren Buffett. Who here has heard of Warren Buffett?" Not a single hand goes up. The room is a sea of blank faces. So he tells the students about his eighteen-year-old daughter, Momachi, and how she earned $4,800 in a summer job after high school. Pabrai invested that money for her in a retirement account. He asks the students to calculate what would happen if this modest nest egg was to grow by 15 percent a year for the next sixty years. "It's doubling every five years. That's twelve doubles," he says. "Life is all about doubles."

A minute later, the students have figured it out: in six decades, when Momachi is seventy-eight years old, her $4,800 will be worth more than $21 million. There is an air of wonder in the room at the awesome power of this mathematical phenomenon. "Are you going to forget about compounding?" asks Pabrai. And forty impoverished teenagers from rural India cry out in unison, "No, sir!"

## How to Turn $1 Million into $1 Billion

Not so long ago, Mohnish Pabrai hadn't heard of Warren Buffett, either. Raised in modest circumstances in India, he knew nothing about investing, Wall Street, or high finance. Born in 1964, he spent the first ten years of his life in Bombay (now Mumbai), where his parents rented a tiny suburban apartment for $20 a month. They later moved to New Delhi and Dubai.

The family was full of colorful characters. Pabrai's grandfather was a famous magician, Gogia Pasha, who toured the world posing as a mysterious Egyptian. As a boy, Pabrai appeared with him onstage. His role was to hold an egg. Pabrai's father, Om Pabrai, was an entrepreneur with an uncanny knack for founding companies that went bankrupt. Among his many ventures, he owned a jewelry factory, launched a radio station, and sold magic kits by mail. Like his son, he was an incorrigible optimist. But his businesses were fatally undercapitalized and overleveraged.

"I watched my parents losing everything multiple times," says Pabrai. "And when I say losing everything, I mean not having enough money to buy groceries tomorrow, not having money to pay the rent. . . . I never want to go through that again, but what I saw is that it didn't bother them. In fact, the biggest lesson I learned from them is that I didn't see them get rattled by it. My father used to say, 'You could put me naked on a rock and I will start a new business.'"

As a child, Pabrai performed poorly at school, once placing sixty-second in a class of sixty-five, and he suffered from low self-esteem. Then, in ninth grade, he was given an IQ test that changed his life. "I went to the guy who administered the test and said, 'What does the result mean?' He said, 'Your IQ is at least one hundred eighty. You're just not applying yourself.' It was like someone whipping a horse and it starts. That was a big turning point. People have to be told they have something in them."

After high school, he headed to Clemson University, in South Carolina. There he discovered the stock market. He took an investing class and averaged 106 percent going into the final. The professor tried to convince him to switch his major from computer engineering to finance. "I completely ignored his advice," says Pabrai. "My perspective at that time was that all these fuckers in finance are dumbasses. They don't know shit. And this super-easy class I'm taking in investing is one-tenth as hard as my engineering mechanics class. . . . So why would I want to go into a field with these losers?"

After college, Pabrai took a job at Tellabs. Then, in 1990, he launched a technology consulting company, TransTech, bankrolling it with $70,000 in credit card debt and $30,000 from his 401(k). Most people couldn't stomach that level of risk, but he's always had a gambling streak. Indeed, we once spent an entire flight discussing his adventures at the blackjack tables in Las Vegas, where he doggedly applies "an extremely boring" system developed by a card counter with a PhD in finance. Pabrai's game plan is to make $1 million and get banned from the casinos. By 2020, he'd turned $3,000 into $150,000 and been banned for life by "one small, seedy casino."

TransTech thrived, ultimately employing 160 people, and Pabrai set aside $1 million in savings by 1994. For the first time, he had a war chest to invest. That year, he bought *One Up on Wall Street* by Peter Lynch while killing time in Heathrow Airport. It was there that he first read about Buffett. He was astonished to learn that Berkshire Hathaway's chairman and CEO had racked up investment returns of 31 percent annually over forty-four years, starting at the age of twenty. Thanks to the magic of compounding, this meant that an investment of $1 in 1950 would have grown to $144,523 by 1994. Pabrai reached a logical conclusion: Buffett was not a dumbass.

As a boy, Pabrai had heard a tale about an Indian who supposedly invented chess. He presented his game to the king, who offered him a reward. The game inventor requested one grain of rice for the first square of his chess board, two grains for the second square, four for the third, and so on, all the way to the sixty-fourth square. The king, who was arithmetically challenged, granted the request. Pabrai, who is not arithmetically challenged, says the king owed 18,446,744,073,709,551,615

5

grains of rice, now worth around $300 trillion. Remembering this story, Pabrai grasped instantly that Buffett had mastered the game of compounding. In forty-four years, he'd doubled his money eighteen times and was already well on his way to becoming the richest man on earth.

This set Pabrai thinking. What if he could figure out how Buffett picked stocks and could mimic his winning approach? Thus began what Pabrai describes as a "thirty-year game" to turn his $1 million into $1 billion. "The driver for me is not to get wealthy," he says. "The driver is to win the game. It's exactly the same driver for Warren, which is to show through the results that I did the best and I *am* the best because I played the game by the rules, fair and square, and I won."

Pabrai's approach to the challenge of becoming a billionaire holds important lessons for us all, not just as investors but in every area of life. He didn't attempt to reinvent the wheel by, say, devising a new algorithm to exploit subtle pricing anomalies in the markets. Instead, he identified the most skillful player of this particular game, analyzed why he was so successful, then copied his approach with scrupulous attention to detail. Pabrai's term for this process is *cloning*. We could also call it modeling, mimicry, or replication. But the terminology doesn't matter. This is a technique for people who care more about winning than sounding respectable or highbrow.

By cloning Buffett—and later, his polymathic partner, Charlie Munger—Pabrai has become one of the leading investors of our time. From 2000 to 2018, his flagship hedge fund returned a staggering 1,204 percent versus 159 percent for the S&P 500 index. If you had invested $100,000 with him when he started managing money in July 1999, it would have grown to $1,826,500 (after fees and expenses) by March 31, 2018.*

Yet Pabrai's success both as an investor and a philanthropist is

---

* This assumes you invested in his original partnership (Pabrai Investment Fund 1) at its inception in 1999, and held it till March 31, 2018. Pabrai gave his initial investors a guarantee that he'd make them whole if they lost money. Realizing that this was onerously generous, he closed the fund and merged it with Pabrai Investment Fund 2 in 2002. It's worth noting that his returns have been wildly volatile. For example, he suffered a 15.1 percent loss in the first half of 2020, leaving his fund up 671.3 percent since inception, versus 218.4 percent for the S&P 500. One of his advantages is that these gut-wrenching swings don't bother him.

built entirely on smart ideas that he has borrowed from others. "I'm a shameless copycat," he says. "*Everything* in my life is cloned. . . . I have no original ideas." Consciously, systematically, and with irrepressible delight, he has mined the minds of Buffett, Munger, and others not only for investment wisdom but for insights on how to manage his business, avoid mistakes, build his brand, give away money, approach relationships, structure his time, and construct a happy life.

Pabrai's commitment to cloning raises an array of provocative questions. Is originality overrated? Instead of struggling to innovate, should most of us focus our energy on replicating what smarter and wiser people have already figured out? If cloning is such a powerful strategy for success, why don't more people use it? Are there dangers to cloning? And how can we benefit from it while also being true to ourselves?

Over the last seven years, I've spent a great deal of time with Pabrai. I've joined him on multiple trips to Omaha for Berkshire's annual meeting; I've interviewed him at his office in California; we've traveled together for five days in India, even sharing a bunk bed on an all-night train ride from Kota to Mumbai; and we've overeaten together everywhere from his local Korean barbecue restaurant to a roadside shack in Jaipur.

Along the way, I've come to appreciate the tremendous power of his method of reverse engineering, replicating, and often improving on other people's successful strategies. Pabrai, the most relentless cloner I've ever encountered, has taken the art of appropriation to such an extreme that, paradoxically, it seems oddly original. His thinking has had a profound impact on me. In fact, the overarching purpose of this book is to share what I would call "ideas worth cloning."

## The Laws of Investing

When Pabrai discovers a subject that fascinates him, he attacks it with obsessive fervor. In Buffett's case, the available resources seemed limitless, including decades of letters to Berkshire's shareholders and seminal books such as Roger Lowenstein's *Buffett: The Making of an American Capitalist*. Pabrai devoured it all. He also began to make a pilgrimage each year to Omaha for Berkshire's annual meeting, showing up without fail for more than twenty years.

Eventually, Pabrai would develop a personal relationship with Buffett. Through Buffett, he'd also become friends with Munger, who invites him for meals at his home in Los Angeles and games of bridge at his club. But in those early days, Pabrai's knowledge came entirely from reading. And the more he read, the more convinced he became that Buffett, with Munger's help, had laid out "the laws of investing," which are as "fundamental as the laws of physics."

Buffett's style of investing seemed "so simple" and "so powerful" that Pabrai considered it the only way to invest. But when he studied other money managers, he was perplexed to find that almost none lived by Buffett's laws. It was like meeting "an entire set of physicists who don't believe in gravity. . . . Whether you believe in gravity or not, it's fucking gonna pull you down!"

It was clear to Pabrai that most fund managers owned too many stocks, paid too much for them, and traded them too often. "These mutual funds are sitting there with one thousand positions or two hundred positions. How can you find two hundred companies that will all double? Then I look at what they own, and they own things that are trading at thirty times earnings. . . . I saw that they were all hosed."

Pabrai had read a book by the management guru Tom Peters that told a cautionary tale of two self-service gas stations on opposite sides of the street. One prospers by providing high-quality service, such as cleaning windshields for free. The other does the bare minimum. What happens? Its customers inevitably drift to the better gas station. This error amazed Pabrai, since nothing could have been easier than simply to copy the superior strategy sitting in plain view.

"Humans have something weird in their DNA which prohibits them from adopting good ideas easily," says Pabrai. "What I learned a long time back is, keep observing the world inside and outside your industry, and when you see someone doing something smart, *force* yourself to adopt it." This sounds so obvious, even trite. But this one habit has played a decisive role in his success.

So, with the zeal of a true disciple, Pabrai committed to invest "the way Warren said I should." Given that Buffett had averaged 31 percent a year, Pabrai naively assumed that it shouldn't be hard to average 26 percent. At that rate, his $1 million would double every three years and hit $1 billion in thirty years. As a reminder of this compounding target, his license plate reads COMLB 26. Even if he missed by a mile, he expected to do fine; if, say, he averaged 16 percent a year, his $1 million would turn into $85.85 million in thirty years. Such is the glory of compounding.

Of course, he had no MBA from a fancy school such as Wharton or Columbia, no qualification as a certified financial analyst, no experience on Wall Street. But Pabrai, who regards his entire life as a game, expected his rigorous application of Buffett's methodology to give him an edge over all of the fools who failed to follow the Sage of Omaha. "I want to play games that I know I can win," says Pabrai. "So how do you win the game? You've got to play according to the rules. And the good news is, I'm playing against players who don't even fucking *know* the rules."

As Pabrai saw it, Buffett's approach to stock picking grew out of three core concepts that he'd learned from Benjamin Graham, the patron saint of value investing, who taught Buffett at Columbia and later hired him. First, whenever you buy a stock, you're purchasing a portion of an ongoing business with an underlying value, not just a piece of paper for speculators to trade.

Second, Graham viewed the market as a "voting machine," not a "weighing machine," which means that stock prices frequently fail to reflect the true value of these businesses. As Graham wrote in *The Intelligent Investor*,* it's useful to think of the market as a manic-depressive who "often lets his enthusiasm or his fears run away with him."

Third, you should buy a stock only when it's selling for much less than your conservative estimate of its worth. The gap between a company's intrinsic value and its stock price provides what Graham called a "margin of safety."

But what does all of this mean in practical terms? Graham's insight

* Published in 1949, *The Intelligent Investor* has been hailed by Buffett as "by far the best book on investing ever written." We'll meet its remarkable author at greater length in chapter 4.

that Mr. Market is prone to irrational mood swings has profound implications. For master investors such as Buffett and Munger, the essence of the game is to detach themselves from the madness and watch dispassionately until the bipolar market provides them with what Munger calls "a mispriced gamble." **There are no prizes for frenetic activity. Rather, investing is mostly a matter of waiting for these rare moments when the odds of making money vastly outweigh the odds of losing it.** As Buffett has said, "You don't have to swing at everything—you can wait for your pitch. The problem when you're a money manager is that your fans keep yelling, 'Swing, you bum!'"

Sublimely indifferent to the cries of the crowd, Buffett can twiddle his thumbs for years. For example, he bought almost nothing from 1970 to 1972 when euphoric investors drove stocks to crazy valuations. Then, when the market crashed in 1973, he bought a major stake in the Washington Post Company, which he held for four decades. In his classic article "The Superinvestors of Graham-and-Doddsville," Buffett wrote that the market valued the company at $80 million when "you could have sold the assets to any one of ten buyers for not less than $400 million. . . . You don't try and buy businesses worth $83 million for $80 million. You leave yourself an enormous margin. When you build a bridge, you insist it can carry 30,000 pounds, but you only drive 10,000-pound trucks across it. And that same principle works in investing."

In our hyperactive world, few people recognize the superiority of this slow and discerning strategy, which requires infrequent but decisive bursts of activity. Munger, a nonagenarian whom Pabrai considers "the brightest human" he's ever met, embodies this approach. Munger once observed, "You have to be like a man standing with a spear next to a stream. Most of the time he's doing nothing. When a fat juicy salmon swims by, the man spears it. Then he goes back to doing nothing. It may be six months before the next salmon goes by."

Few money managers function this way. Instead, says Pabrai, they "place many bets, small bets, and frequent bets." The trouble is, there aren't enough compelling opportunities to justify all of this activity. So Pabrai, like his two idols, prefers to wait for the most succulent salmon.

During a conversation in his office in Irvine, he says, "The number one skill in investing is patience—*extreme patience.*" When the market crashed in 2008, he made ten investments in two months. In more typical times, he bought just two stocks in 2011, three in 2012, and none in 2013.

In 2018, Pabrai's offshore hedge fund owned no US stocks at all because nothing seemed cheap enough. Just think about that for a moment: out of roughly thirty-seven hundred companies listed on the major US exchanges, Pabrai couldn't find a *single* irresistible bargain. Instead of settling for American stocks that seemed richly valued, he took his fishing spear to better-stocked waters in India, China, and South Korea. As Munger likes to say, there are two rules of fishing. Rule no. 1: "Fish where the fish are." Rule no. 2: "Don't forget rule no. 1."

Then, in the spring of 2020, the US market crashed as the COVID-19 virus spread terror among investors. The retail industry was ravaged, with stores forced to close indefinitely and consumers required to stay home in lockdown mode. One company at the epicenter of uncertainty was Seritage Growth Properties, whose tenants included many retailers that could no longer afford to pay their rent. "The market hates all of this near-term noise and pain," says Pabrai. He exploited the panic to buy a 13 percent stake in Seritage at exceptional prices, figuring that he'll ultimately make ten times his money as fears recede and others recognize the value of its prime assets.*

Buffett, Munger, and Pabrai are not alone in pursuing this strategy of extreme patience and extreme selectivity. Their elite cohort includes great investors such as Francis Chou, one of Canada's most prominent fund managers. When I first interviewed him in 2014, Chou had 30 percent of his assets in cash and hadn't made a significant stock purchase in years. "When there's hardly anything to buy, you have to be very careful," he told me. "You cannot force the issue. You just have to

---

* Pabrai also liked that Buffett, whose investment record in real estate is "almost perfect," owned Seritage in his personal stock portfolio. "Not only are we cloning his approach," Pabrai tells me, "we're directly cloning his position at one-fifth or one-sixth of the price he paid." Disclosure: Cloning the cloner, I also invested in Seritage during the depths of the COVID crisis.

be patient, and the bargains will come to you." He warned, "If you want to participate in the market all the time, then it's a mug's game and you're going to lose."

How long can he go without buying? "Oh, I can wait ten years—even longer," Chou replied. In the meantime, he studies stocks that aren't cheap enough to buy, hits balls at a golf range, and reads two hundred to four hundred pages a day. One technique that he uses to distance himself emotionally from the day-to-day drama of the market is to think of himself in the third person instead of the first person.

Like Chou, Pabrai has constructed a lifestyle that supports this heroically inactive investment strategy. When I visited his office in Irvine, he was dressed in shorts, sneakers, and a short-sleeved shirt. He looked less like an adrenaline-fueled stock jockey than a vacationer contemplating a lazy stroll on the beach. Cloning Buffett, who once showed him the blank pages of his little black diary, Pabrai keeps his calendar virtually empty so he can spend most of his time reading and studying companies. On a typical day at the office, he schedules a grand total of zero meetings and zero phone calls. One of his favorite quotes is from the philosopher Blaise Pascal: "All of humanity's problems stem from man's inability to sit quietly in a room alone."

One challenge, says Pabrai, is that "large motors aren't good at grinding away without resulting actions." He thinks Berkshire Hathaway's shareholders have profited immensely from Buffett's passion for playing online bridge, since this mental distraction counteracts the "natural bias for action." Pabrai plays online bridge, too, and he burns off energy by biking and playing racquetball. When there's nothing to buy and no reason to sell, he can also direct more attention to his charitable foundation. He says it helps that his investment staff consists of a single person: him. "The moment you have people on your team, they're going to want to act and do things, and then you're hosed." In most fields, a hunger for action is a virtue. But as Buffett said at Berkshire's 1998 annual meeting, "We don't get paid for activity, just for being right."

Pabrai, a loner with a misanthropic streak, was purpose-built for the bizarrely lucrative discipline of sitting alone in a room and occasionally buying a mispriced stock. Back when he ran a tech company, he hired two industrial psychologists to profile him. They revealed how comically ill-suited he was to managing a large staff: "I'm not this nurturing leader who can have a bunch of weepies and nurture them and babysit them and all this other shit." Investing felt more like a game of three-dimensional chess in which the outcome, crucially, depended solely on him.

## Say No to Almost Everything

One of Pabrai's first stock picks was a tiny Indian technology company, Satyam Computer Services, which he bought in 1995. He understood the business, since he worked in the same industry, and the stock was "ultracheap." Pabrai watched in wonder as it rose about 140 times in five years. He sold in 2000, when it was outrageously overvalued, and pocketed a $1.5 million profit. The late-nineties tech bubble then burst, and the stock dropped more than 80 percent. Amused by his good fortune, Pabrai cheerfully likens himself to Forrest Gump, who made a killing in "some kind of fruit company"—namely, Apple Computer.

Through a combination of luck and smarts, Pabrai turned his $1 million into $10 million in less than five years. Aware that he had more to learn, he wrote to Buffett offering to work for him for free. Buffett replied, "I've given a lot of thought to the optimal use of my time, and I simply do best operating by myself." So Pabrai pursued Plan B. Several friends had profited from his stock tips, and they wanted him to manage their money. In 1999, he launched an investment partnership with $900,000 from eight people and $100,000 of his own. A year or so later, he sold his technology consulting company, TransTech, for $6 million so that he could focus exclusively on investing.

From 1956 to 1969, Buffett had managed investment partnerships with spectacular success. So Pabrai did what came naturally: he cloned every detail of Buffett's partnership model. For example, Buffett charged no annual management fee but collected a performance fee of 25 percent of any profits over an annual "hurdle" of 6 percent. If he made a return of 6 percent or less, he didn't get paid a dime. But outsize returns would be richly rewarded. Pabrai adopted the same fee structure, reasoning that this alignment of interests made it an "honorable way to do business."*

As it happens, Buffett had borrowed this fee structure from Graham, who used it in the 1920s. No stranger to cloning, Buffett has said, "If you learn, basically, from other people, you don't have to get too many ideas on your own. You can just apply the best of what you see." Part of the challenge is to discern the best and jettison the rest, instead of blindly cloning everything. For example, Graham was a devout believer in diversification, whereas Buffett got rich by focusing his bets on a much smaller number of undervalued stocks. This is an important point. Buffett borrowed liberally, but he adapted and refined Graham's practices to suit his own preferences.

Following Buffett's lead, Pabrai constructed an unusually concentrated portfolio. He figured that ten stocks would give him all the diversification he needed. When you're buying so few stocks, you can afford to be choosy. Pabrai glances at hundreds of stocks and rapidly rejects almost all of them, often in less than a minute.† Buffett is a master of this practice of high-speed sifting. "What he's looking for is a reason to say no, and as soon as he finds that, he's done," says Pabrai. Indeed, Buffett has said, "The difference between successful people and really successful people is that really successful people say no to almost everything."

---

*Most hedge funds charge a 2 percent management fee, plus 20 percent of the profits—a structure that Pabrai describes as "heads I win, tails you lose." If these funds make a 10 percent return, their shareholders' take (after fees) is only 6.4 percent. These high frictional costs doom hedge fund investors as a class to lag the market over the long run. By contrast, if Pabrai makes a 10 percent return, his shareholders receive 9 percent. After the 2008–9 financial crisis, he earned no fees for several years. At the time, he told me, "I've been living on fresh air, water, and peanuts. I'm ready for mutton and curry." The feast arrived in 2017 when his flagship fund returned 92.2 percent and he earned more than $40 million in performance fees.

†Where does Pabrai get his investment ideas? He borrows them by analyzing the portfolios of leading investors such as Buffett, Ted Weschler, Seth Klarman, and David Einhorn. Pabrai glances at their top three or four holdings (which are listed each quarter in an investment manager's 13F filings) and tries to figure out why these are their favorite ideas. He couldn't understand why Weschler and Einhorn liked General Motors, which seemed an obvious dud. After six weeks of intense research, he'd figured it out. That led to an enormously lucrative bet on auto stocks, most notably in Fiat Chrysler.

Buffett provided Pabrai with several simple filters that helped him to streamline the sifting. First, says Pabrai, one of Buffett's "core commandments" is that you can invest in a company only if it falls within your "circle of competence." When Pabrai analyzes a company, he starts by asking, "Is this something I truly understand?" He pushes himself to consider whether he's at the center of his circle of competence, approaching its edge, or outside it.

Second, the company has to trade at a large enough discount to its underlying value to provide a significant margin of safety. Pabrai doesn't bother to construct elaborate Excel spreadsheets that might give him an illusion that he can precisely predict the future. He wants an investment that's so cheap that it's a "no-brainer." That usually means paying less than fifty cents for $1 worth of assets. "I have very simple criteria: if something is not going to be an obvious double in a short period of time—you know, two or three years—I have no interest."

Third, under Munger's influence, Buffett gradually shifted away from stocks that were merely cheap toward an emphasis on buying better businesses. Among other things, this meant that a company should have a durable competitive advantage and should be run by an honest, capable CEO. Munger pointed out to Pabrai that Graham, who was fixated on buying stocks that were quantitatively cheap, scored his best returns by owning GEICO. "It didn't make him money because it was cheap," says Pabrai. "It made him money because it was a great business."

Fourth, the company's financial statements should be clear and simple. As Buffett observed, "The only reason that one may not understand a financial statement is because the writer does not want you to understand it." If it isn't easy to figure out how the business generates cash today and roughly how much it's likely to generate in the years to come, Buffett relegates it to what he calls the "too hard" pile. Pabrai once took a photograph of a box on Buffett's desk that is literally labeled TOO HARD—a visual reminder to resist the lure of complexity. Enron and Valeant Pharmaceuticals, both of which blew up, were easy for Pabrai to reject on that basis alone.

For Pabrai, one of the secrets of successful investing is to avoid *anything* that's too hard. He automatically passes on investments in countries such as Russia and Zimbabwe, given their contempt for shareholder rights. He avoids all start-ups and initial public offerings (IPOs), since he's unlikely to find bargains in arenas dominated by sales hype and inflated expectations. He has never sold a stock short because the maximum upside is 100 percent (if the stock falls to zero), while the downside is unlimited (if the stock soars). "Why bet with those odds?" he asks. He also largely ignores the infinite complexity of macroeconomics, focusing instead on a handful of critical microfactors that are likely to drive a specific business. In short, simplicity rules.

These basic principles that we've just discussed are extraordinarily robust and have served Pabrai well. But what's remarkable is that *none of this is original.* Every major idea on which he has built his investment career has been stolen from Buffett—except for the ones stolen from Munger. Writing about this makes me slightly queasy. How can I hope to say anything new or profound while enumerating ideas that Pabrai has ripped off from other people? But that's precisely the point. His competitive advantage lies in the fact that he doesn't care whether you or I think he's derivative. All he cares about is what works.

One evening, over dinner at a Korean restaurant in Irvine, I ask Pabrai why more people don't clone in his systematic way. Between mouthfuls of a dish called "spicy beef danger," he replies, "They're not as shameless as me. They have more ego. To be a great cloner, you have to check your ego at the door."

## The Guru, His Disciple, and Their $650,100 Lunch

Pabrai's purloined investment approach worked like a dream. When he launched Pabrai Funds in July 1999, the tech bubble was about to burst. It was a perilous time to be an investor. Over the next eight years, the best-performing US index—the Dow Jones Industrial Average—eked out an annualized return of 4.6 percent versus Pabrai's annualized return of 29.4 percent after fees. The media hailed him as "a superstar," "the next Warren Buffett," and "the Oracle of Irvine." His assets under management swelled to $600 million. He recalls, "I could do nothing wrong."

Pabrai's returns were driven by a string of bets on undervalued stocks gripped by uncertainty. For example, he invested in Embraer, a Brazilian producer of jets, shortly after the 9/11 terror attacks, which caused many airlines to cancel aircraft orders. This short-term shock led fearful investors to overlook the longer-term reality that Embraer was still a high-quality business with a superior product, low manufacturing costs, first-rate management, and loads of cash on its balance sheet. Pabrai paid about $12 per share in 2001 and sold his last shares for $30 in 2005.

Similarly, in 2002, he invested in a Scandinavian shipping firm, Frontline Ltd., after the price for leasing oil tankers collapsed. The stock had plunged to $5.90, but he calculated that Frontline's liquidation value was more than $11 per share. Leasing prices would eventually rebound, since supply would become constrained. In the meantime, Frontline could survive a cash crunch by selling ships one by one. As with Embraer, uncertainty scared investors away. But the upside potential easily outweighed the downside risk. Pabrai coined a motto that summed up this type of bet: "Heads, I win. Tails, I don't lose much." In a matter of months, he made a 55 percent return.

In 2005, he bet heavily on another no-brainer: a specialty steel producer called IPSCO Inc. Pabrai paid around $44 per share at a time when the company had about $15 per share of excess cash on its books. He expected IPSCO to generate around $13 per share of excess cash in each of the next two years, giving it a total of $41 per share in cash. With the stock trading at $44, he was effectively buying all of IPSCO's steel plants and other assets for only $3 per share. Pabrai couldn't predict what the company would earn beyond the next two years, but, as he saw it, the stock was so cheap that there was scant risk of losing money. When he sold in 2007, his $24.7 million investment was worth $87.2 million—a 253 percent return in twenty-six months.

In recent years, it's become almost an article of faith that it's impossible to beat the market over the long run. But Pabrai, thanks to Buffett and Munger, had found a formula for outperformance. As we've seen, the key principles were not that difficult to identify and clone. *Be patient and selective, saying no to almost everything. Exploit the market's bipolar mood swings. Buy stocks at a big discount to their underlying value. Stay within your circle of competence. Avoid anything too hard. Make a small number of mispriced bets with minimal downside and significant upside.* Yet Pabrai was almost alone in his fanatical determination to observe these rules. "Nobody else is willing to do this," he marvels. "It might as well be the Indian guy."

Pabrai wanted to express his gratitude in person. So in July 2007, he teamed up with his best friend, Guy Spier, to enter a charity auction for a "power lunch" with Buffett.* Pabrai and Spier, a Zurich-based hedge fund manager who is similarly obsessed with Buffett, won the auction with a bid of $650,100. The money would go to the GLIDE Foundation, a charity that helps the homeless. But Pabrai saw the donation as his version of a "guru dakshana"—a Hindu term for a gift presented to your spiritual teacher when your education is complete.

On June 25, 2008, Pabrai finally met his guru. They spent three hours together at a Manhattan steak house, Smith & Wollensky, ensconced in a wood-paneled alcove at the back of the restaurant. Pabrai brought his wife, Harina, and their two daughters, Monsoon and Momachi, who sat on either side of Buffett.† Spier brought his wife, Lory. Buffett, who was jovial and grandfatherly, brought bags of gifts for the kids, including M&M's with his picture on them. The conversation ranged from his favorite company (GEICO) to the person he'd most like to meet (either Sir Isaac Newton, who was "probably the smartest human in history," or Sophia Loren, for less cerebral reasons).

For Pabrai, the lunch yielded two unforgettable lessons—one about how to invest, one about how to live. The first came when he asked Buffett, "Whatever happened to Rick Guerin?" Buffett had mentioned Guerin's superb investment record in "The Superinvestors of Graham-and-Doddsville." But Buffett told Pabrai and Spier that Guerin used margin loans to leverage his investments because he was "in a hurry to get rich." According to Buffett, Guerin was hit with margin calls after suffer-

---

*In the interests of disclosure, I should mention that Spier is one of my closest friends. I've been an investor in his hedge fund, Aquamarine, for twenty years. I've edited his fund's annual report on several occasions. I'm an adviser to the board of his investment firm. I also helped him to write his memoir, *The Education of a Value Investor*. In other words, I'm an unusually close observer of Spier's but not an impartial one.

† Since then, Pabrai has divorced.

ing disastrous losses in the crash of 1973–74. As a result, he was forced to sell shares (to Buffett) that were later worth an immense fortune.*

By contrast, Buffett said that he and Munger were never in a hurry because they always knew they'd become enormously rich if they kept compounding over decades without too many catastrophic mistakes. Over his meal of steak, hash browns, and a Cherry Coke, Buffett said, "If you're even a *slightly* above average investor who spends less than you earn, over a lifetime you cannot help but get very wealthy." Pabrai says this morality tale about the perils of leverage and impatience has been "seared" into his brain: "Right there, the Buffett lunch was worth it."

But what resonated most profoundly for Pabrai was the sense that Buffett was true to himself—that he lived in extraordinary alignment with his own personality, principles, and preferences. Over lunch, Buffett explained that he and Munger always measure themselves by "an inner scorecard." Instead of worrying how others judge them, they focus on living up to their own exacting standards. One way to tell whether you live by an inner or an outer scorecard, said Buffett, is to ask yourself, "Would I rather be the worst lover in the world and be known publicly as the best, or the best lover in the world and be known publicly as the worst?"

Buffett manages every aspect of his life in ways that mesh with his own nature—from his childish diet (which consists largely of burgers, candy, and Coca-Cola) to how he runs his business. For example, he made it clear that Berkshire's decentralized structure was never designed to maximize profits: it simply suited his character to oversee Berkshire's many businesses in a hands-off manner, trusting his CEOs to use their freedom wisely. Likewise, he pointed out that he handles his own daily schedule and keeps it blissfully uncluttered by rebuffing almost any request that might distract him from reading and contemplation. Similarly, he insists on working solely with people he likes and admires. As a stock picker, too, he has always gone his own way, avoiding whatever overvalued asset class is currently in vogue.

This discussion had an enduring impact on Pabrai and Spier. In May

---

*Guerin gave his shareholders quite a ride, losing 42 percent in 1973 and 34.4 percent in 1974. Even so, his compounded rate of return over nineteen years was 23.6 percent after fees.

2014, I joined them at Berkshire's annual meeting. The next day, we flew from Omaha to New York on a private plane that Spier had chartered from NetJets, a Berkshire subsidiary. He and Pabrai had just come from a breakfast with Buffett and Munger and were giddily happy. During the flight, our main topic of conversation was this notion of living by an inner scorecard. As Pabrai saw it, "Probably ninety-nine percent of people on this planet wonder what the world thinks of them." A tiny minority take the opposite view, which he poetically expressed as follows: "Fuck what the world thinks."

Pabrai and Spier reeled off a random list of inner-scorecard exemplars: Jesus, Mahatma Gandhi, Nelson Mandela, Margaret Thatcher, Steve Jobs, and leading investors such as Buffett, Munger, Ted Weschler, Li Lu, Bill Miller, and Nick Sleep (whom we'll study in depth in chapter 6). Pabrai observed, "All the guys who reached the pinnacle, that's the only way they got there."

Nobody I've ever met lives more determinedly by his own rules than Pabrai. Buffett's example strengthened his commitment to construct a life congruent with his personality. On a typical day, Pabrai sleeps late and arrives at his office after 10:00 a.m. with no agenda. An assistant brings him printouts of his emails around 11:00 a.m., and Pabrai scrawls the briefest of replies directly on the paper—a practice cloned from Munger. Like Buffett and Munger, Pabrai spends most of the day reading. He takes a guiltless nap most afternoons, then resumes reading until late in the evening.

As much as possible, Pabrai remains inside this cocoon. He avoids meeting the CEOs of companies that he's analyzing because he thinks their talent for selling makes them an unreliable source of information—a policy he cloned from Ben Graham.* He avoids speaking with his own shareholders, except at his annual meeting, and he refuses to meet with potential investors: "I genuinely don't enjoy that whole interaction, the mumbo jumbo of all that."

It doesn't bother him if this attitude irritates people or costs him

* Pabrai makes an exception to this policy when investing in a less developed market such as India, where he tries to judge in person whether he can trust the management.

millions of dollars a year in forgone fees. "Munger says he doesn't care about being rich. What he really cares about is having independence. I fully endorse that. What the money gives you is the ability to do what you want to do in the way you want to do it. . . . And that's a tremendous benefit."

Pabrai approaches relationships with the same ruthless clarity about his own priorities. During their lunch, Buffett said, "Hang out with people who are better than you and you cannot help but improve." Pabrai acts on this advice to a degree that would horrify many people. "When I meet someone for the first time, I evaluate them afterwards and say, 'Will it make me better or worse to have a relationship with this person?'" If the answer is worse, he says, "I'll cut him out." Likewise, after a lunch meeting, he asks, "How did I enjoy that?" If he didn't, "There will never be another lunch with the person again." He adds, "Most people don't pass the smell test."

Diplomacy is not his strong point, but Pabrai regards truthfulness as a higher concern. In the late nineties, he read a book titled *Power vs. Force: The Hidden Determinants of Human Behavior* by David Hawkins, which Pabrai describes as "a huge part of what I believe in." Hawkins argues that "true power" stems from traits such as honesty, compassion, and a dedication to enhancing other people's lives. These powerful "attractors" have an unconscious effect on people, making them "go strong," whereas traits such as dishonesty, fear, and shame make them "go weak." Pabrai took one specific lesson from Hawkins and determined to live by it. "You can't get away with lying to other humans," says Pabrai, "and that's a very profound idea."

During the financial crisis of 2008-09, Pabrai's highly concentrated funds fell about 67 percent before staging a rapid recovery. At his 2009 annual meeting, he told his shareholders, "Most of the mistakes in the funds occurred because I was stupid. They didn't happen because of market issues." He highlighted several "dumbass" errors he had made in analyzing stocks such as Delta Financial and Sears Holdings, which were crushed. Almost none of his investors abandoned him. The lesson: "You go as far out as you can on the truth variable and the payback is huge."

Indeed, one of the pleasures of interviewing Pabrai is that he answers every question candidly, with no concern for how he might be judged. As an experiment, I once emailed him some impertinently personal questions, including one about his net worth. He wrote back, "Net worth as of 11/30/17 is $154 million." He then shared additional financial details to clarify what this figure excluded. It was a marvelous display of trust in the power of truthfulness.

To my mind, what's most remarkable is Pabrai's unshakable consistency in sticking to such principles. "When you encounter these truths that other people don't understand, you just have to latch on to them big-time," he says. "Anytime you get a truth that humanity doesn't understand, that's a huge competitive advantage. Humanity doesn't understand *Power vs. Force.*"

Intelligent people are easily seduced by complexity while underestimating the importance of simple ideas that carry tremendous weight. Pabrai, the ultimate pragmatist, doesn't fall into this trap. "Compounding is a very simple idea. Cloning is a very simple idea. Telling the truth is a very simple idea," he says. But when you apply a handful of powerful ideas with obsessive fervor, the cumulative effect "becomes unbeatable."

The trouble is, most people dabble half-heartedly when they find an idea that works. Pabrai cannot conceal his contempt: "These fucking humans listen and say, 'Oh, yeah, that makes sense. Whatever. So what? I'll try to incorporate it.' And you know, that fucking doesn't work. You've got to go ten thousand percent or not at all!"

As he sees it, the attitude we should clone is that of the nineteenth-century Hindu sage Swami Vivekananda, who told his followers, "Take up one idea. Make that one idea your life. Think of it, dream of it, live on that idea. Let the brain, muscles, nerves, every part of your body, be full of that idea and just leave every other idea alone. This is the way to success."*

*As you may have guessed, Swami Vivekananda wasn't discussing the path to investment glory. Rather, he was teaching would-be Yogis how to become "spiritual giants." His advice was to renounce once and for all the habit of "nibbling at things" and focus instead on a single objective: "To succeed, you must have tremendous perseverance, tremendous will. 'I will drink the ocean,' says the persevering soul, 'at my will, mountains will crumble up.' Have that sort of energy, that sort of will, work hard, and you will reach the goal."

## Welcome to the Kidnapping Capital of India

As Pabrai's fortune grew, he faced a pleasurable problem: what to do with all the money. Once again, he turned to Buffett for inspiration. Over the years, Buffett has repeatedly spoken about how little his wealth contributes to his contentment. I remember sitting with Pabrai and Spier at one of Berkshire's annual meetings when Buffett told the audience, "My life would be worse if I had six or eight houses. . . . It just doesn't correlate."

Pabrai is not exactly ascetic. He once spent thousands of dollars on a pair of bespoke shoes, and he drives a blue convertible Ferrari—a fitting reward for a huge home run on Ferrari stock. But he knows that hedonism is an unreliable route to happiness. He's also wary of bequeathing hundreds of millions to his daughters, having internalized Buffett's advice that the ideal amount to give your kids is enough so they can do anything, but not so much that they can do nothing. Buffett had pledged to give the bulk of his billions back to society, so Pabrai decided to "clone the giving."

He began by asking, "If I were to die today, what cause or organization would I want most of my assets to go to?" He wanted a charity managed like a cost-efficient business, with precise metrics tracking how much good it did for every dollar spent. Nothing excited him until, in 2006, he stumbled on an article about a program in rural India run by Anand Kumar, a math teacher who gave free coaching and accommodation to thirty poor high school graduates each year. The Super 30 program had an incredible success rate in preparing them for the IIT entrance exam.

Pabrai grasped at once the strength of this model: it was low cost, offered talented teenagers a life-changing chance to escape from poverty, and provided measurable results. He emailed Kumar, offering him money to enlarge the program. But Kumar didn't want to expand. Undeterred, Pabrai made a fateful decision: "You gotta take a trip and just show up."

Bihar, which was often described as the "kidnapping capital of India," wasn't an alluring destination for a high-flying hedge fund manager. So Pabrai hired two bodyguards from a New Delhi security firm to accompany him on his mission. One was a former Black Cat commando—an Indian counterterrorism specialist "trained to storm hijacked aircraft and take the kidnapper out. . . . From being asleep to killing the guy was less than three seconds!" The commando had to travel separately by train to Bihar because he couldn't carry his gun on the plane. It later turned out that Kumar had also hired four body-guards to ensure Pabrai's safety.

Pabrai found Bihar a desolate and desperate place where thieves would sometimes steal railway tracks and sell them for scrap. His grumpy verdict: "The weather sucks, the infrastructure sucks, the hotel sucks." Pabrai harbors fantasies of becoming so enlightened that he could happily stay in one-star hotels. Alas, he's not there yet. Still, despite the discomfort, he would never forget the day he spent with Kumar, who taught his students in a rented shed without walls. Pabrai was blown away by his intellect, passion, and gift for teaching: "He's one in hundreds of millions."

Unable to convince Kumar to take his money, Pabrai requested per-mission to replicate—and scale up—the Super 30 program. His appro-priation of Buffett's investment strategy had proven to him the power of cloning. So why not apply the same approach to philanthropy? Kumar gave him his blessing, and Pabrai set to work.

Kumar's renown meant that thousands of students applied to his program. He then handpicked the most brilliant. Pabrai solved the problem of sourcing brainiacs by partnering with a government-run network of almost six hundred selective boarding schools, which educate tens of thousands of poor rural children each year. Pabrai's Dakshana Foundation offered scholarships to hundreds of the "most promising brains" from this pool and gave them two years of coaching in math, physics, and chemistry to prepare for the IIT exam. "If they don't bust their asses, they're going back to the villages with nothing," says Pabrai. "This is their one shot."

The strength of this philanthropic model is that it costs so little to change so many lives. In 2008, Dakshana's total cost per scholar was $3,913, and 34 percent of its students won places at IIT. By 2016, Dak-shana had become so efficient that its cost per student had dropped to $2,649, and its success rate hit an astonishing 85 percent. Even bet-ter, the government heavily subsidizes both the boarding schools and

IIT: Pabrai figures that for every dollar Dakshana spends on a student, the government spends more than $1,000. So he's effectively making a leveraged bet with an enormous social return on his invested capital.*

Before meeting Buffett for lunch in 2008, Pabrai sent him Dakshana's first annual report. Buffett was so impressed that he shared it with Munger and Bill Gates. Then, in an interview with Fox TV, Buffett declared that Pabrai "thinks as well about philanthropy as he does about investments. . . . I admire him enormously." The disciple—the shameless copycat—had been blessed by the master. "After that," says Pabrai, "I felt that I could die and go to heaven."

Since then, Dakshana has grown exponentially. By 2018, it was coaching more than one thousand students simultaneously at eight sites across India, including a 109-acre campus called Dakshana Valley, which Pabrai bought at a discount from a distressed seller. Eventually, this site alone could accommodate twenty-six hundred students. Meanwhile, Dakshana has broadened its focus beyond IIT: it now also prepares hundreds of poverty-stricken students for the entrance exam to medical schools. In 2019 alone, 164 Dakshana scholars won places to study medicine—a 64 percent success rate. All of these initiatives are managed by Dakshana's CEO, a retired artillery officer named Colonel Ram Sharma, who charges one rupee per year for his services.†

In other words, what began as a humble replica of Kumar's program has become a behemoth—a testament to the fact that intelligent cloning involves more than crude imitation. In Dakshana's case, Pabrai borrowed a model that worked in miniature and rebuilt it on an industrial scale. "His success is because of his attention to detail," says Colonel Sharma. "I can definitely say that."‡

---

* By the end of 2018, Pabrai's family had given more than $27 million to Dakshana. The biggest outside donors are Prem Watsa (the CEO of Fairfax Financial Holdings and a graduate of IIT) and Radhakishan Damani (who is said to be India's second-richest person). Disclosure: I've given a few thousand dollars to Dakshana.

† The Colonel, who is one of the most admirable people I've ever encountered, has a deep sense of mission that's connected to the loss of his daughter. He once told me that God had taken one child from him and given him a thousand.

‡ After reading a draft of this book, Guy Spier wrote me an email to emphasize that there's nothing "nonchalant" about Pabrai's approach to cloning: "I worry that 'shameless cloner' does not quite capture the remarkable intensity and ferocity with which

When Pabrai and I traveled to Dakshana Valley, we met with Ashok Talapatra, one of the foundation's star alumni. Talapatra told me that he grew up in a $6-per-month shack in a slum in Hyderabad as the son of a tailor who earned $100 a month. Their home was so basic that it had a pink shower curtain instead of a front door and an asbestos roof that failed to keep out the rain. When Pabrai and his daughter, Monsoon, visited Talapatra there, his mother served them chai and snacks on top of a stool because the family didn't own a table.

But Talapatra was a brilliant student. He aced the IIT entrance exam, ranking 63rd out of 471,000 applicants—the highest position that any Dakshana scholar had ever achieved. He went on to study computer science and engineering at IIT Bombay, then landed a six-figure job at Google. After a stint in London, he moved to the company's headquarters in California, where he now works as a software engineer. "He's moving up the ranks," says Pabrai. "He's on a very rapid trajectory." Within a year of joining Google, Talapatra bought his parents a new apartment with two bedrooms, a kitchen, air-conditioning, and an impermeable roof.

Talapatra's remarkable journey hasn't stopped there. Inspired by Pabrai, who has become a friend and mentor, he's increasingly fascinated by investing. Pabrai recommends investment books to him, and Talapatra regularly joins him at Berkshire Hathaway's annual meeting. When I see them together in Omaha and consider the impact that Pabrai has had on Talapatra's life, I'm amazed that one man's knack for betting on mispriced stocks has produced so much good. In sentimental moments, I find myself thinking of the Talmudic saying "Whoever saves one life, it is considered as if he saved the whole world."

But Pabrai, in his brutally honest way, ridicules any notion that he's some sort of righteous savior. While sitting in a taxi in Mumbai, he tells me, "Once you have a sense that life is meaningless, what should you do? Not fuck up life for other people. Leave the planet a better place than you found it. Do a good job with your kids. The rest of it is a game. It doesn't matter."

---

Mohnish has cloned the right things. . . . Indeed, it seems to me that underlying all of the personalities in your book, there is a deep intensity and ferocity of purpose that is obscured by their calm exteriors."

## Lessons from Mohnish

After many conversations with Pabrai, I found myself thinking more and more about the power of cloning and how to use it in my own life. On a plane ride home from Irvine, I even wrote a memo to myself entitled "Lessons from Mohnish." It began with two fundamental questions: "What winning habits are out in the open that I should clone, and who should I clone?" For example, it makes sense for me, as a nonfiction writer, to reverse engineer books by authors I admire, such as Michael Lewis, Malcolm Gladwell, and Oliver Sacks.*

As I considered Pabrai's life and what I should learn from him, several principles particularly resonated with me. In my memo, I wrote:

Rule 1: Clone like crazy.

Rule 2: Hang out with people who are better than you.

Rule 3: Treat life as a game, not as a survival contest or a battle to the death.

Rule 4: Be in alignment with who you are; don't do what you don't want to do or what's not right for you.

Rule 5: Live by an inner scorecard; don't worry about what others think of you; don't be defined by external validation.

Finally, quoting a line of Munger's that Pabrai often cites, I wrote, **"Take a simple idea and take it seriously."** Of all these lessons, that last

---

*While reading Sacks's autobiography *On the Move*, I discovered that his writing was also the product of cloning. Sacks, a neurologist who wrote spellbinding case histories about his patients' disorders, recalled reading *The Mind of a Mnemonist*, a 1968 book by a Soviet neuropsychologist named A.R. Luria. That book, which recounts the history of a patient of Luria's who had a limitless memory, "altered the focus and direction of my life," wrote Sacks, "by serving as an exemplar not only for *Awakenings* but for everything else I was to write." When I read Luria's book, I was thrilled to discover that he, too, was a cloner. In writing his medical case histories, Luria said, "I tried to follow in the steps of Walter Pater in *Imaginary Portraits*, written in 1887." Once I started searching, I found a whole host of cloners in various fields, including business. For example, in explaining Walmart's success, Munger observed, "Sam Walton invented practically nothing. But he copied everything anybody else ever did that was smart—and he did it with more fanaticism. . . . So he just blew right by them all."

one might just be the most important. Too often, we encounter a powerful principle or habit and we contemplate it, take it for a quick spin, and then forget about it. Pabrai becomes consumed by it. He lives by it. That's a habit I *have* to clone.

But the goal here isn't to become a slavish follower of someone else's ideas. It's often smarter to take the spirit of a principle and adapt it to suit our own priorities. For example, I kept thinking about Pabrai's fixation on going "as far out as you can on the truth variable." That led me to wonder, What if you were to focus instead on going as far out as you can on the kindness variable or the compassion variable? Pabrai's habit of focusing single-mindedly and without compromise on a specific virtue has real power, but we don't have to choose the same virtue.

I think it also works best when we clone in ways that match our own talents and temperament. Pabrai and Spier often discuss companies before deciding whether to invest in them—a practice they cloned from Buffett and Munger. As a result, they tend to own many of the same stocks. But Spier's position sizes are significantly smaller because he's more cautious and less self-confident than Pabrai. As he puts it, "I don't have balls of steel like Mohnish."

In 2015, Pabrai had half of his funds' assets in just two investments: Fiat Chrysler and General Motors warrants. Spier, who had about a quarter of his assets in them, found Pabrai's level of concentration "breathtakingly scary" and worried that he'd failed to protect his friend from hubris and overconfidence. Another hedge fund manager warned that Pabrai's overweighting of the auto sector was "batshit crazy." But Pabrai made seven times his money in six years as Fiat's stock surged. Unrepentant, he had 70 percent of his offshore fund's assets in two stocks in 2018—a fearlessly aggressive stance that led to a 42 percent loss that year. As Spier once told me, "The border between brilliance and stupidity is hard to discern."

Pabrai's strategy of "extreme concentration" is influenced by Munger, who has said that "a well-diversified portfolio needs just four stocks." But it would be suicidal for you or me to clone that approach unless we share Pabrai's extreme intestinal fortitude and analytical gifts. When I asked him how he coped with the stress of a 67 percent drawdown during the financial crisis of 2008-09, he said, "I don't have stress. . . .

My wife couldn't even detect that there was an issue." On the contrary, the stocks he bought amid the crash were so cheap that he found the experience "orgasmic."

Psychologically, it also helps that Pabrai doesn't take anything too seriously. He once told me, "On my gravestone, I want them to write, 'He loved to play games, especially games he knew he could win.' Cloning is a game. Blackjack is a game. Bridge is a game. Dakshana is a game. And, of course, the stock market is a game. It's just a bunch of games. It's all about the odds."

What's amazing to Pabrai is how easy it's been to stack those odds in his favor by studying other people's playbooks and consistently borrowing their best moves. "The thing is, none of this stuff is hard," he says, with an exuberant laugh. "Don't spill the beans, man! Don't tell the world!"

# CHAPTER TWO

# The Willingness to Be Lonely

### To beat the market, you must be brave enough, independent enough, and strange enough to stray from the crowd

---

It is impossible to produce superior performance unless
you do something different from the majority.

—Sir John Templeton

Walking along a beach in the Bahamas more than twenty years ago, I stumbled upon a peculiar sight. An old man was immersed up to his neck in the ocean, dressed in a long-sleeved shirt and a ridiculous-looking hat with a visor and earflaps. His face was smothered with thick dollops of sun cream. I ducked behind a palm tree so that he wouldn't catch me spying on him. Then I watched for several minutes while he pumped his arms and legs back and forth, power walking against the resistance of the water. I later discovered that he did this for forty-five minutes each day.

The old man was Sir John Templeton, probably the greatest international investor of the twentieth century. I'd traveled from New York to the Bahamas to interview him in his home at the Lyford Cay Club, a gated idyll whose residents have included Prince Rainier III of Monaco, the Aga Khan, and Sean Connery. But if my memory serves me, we weren't scheduled to meet until the following day. This was the kind of reporting trip that makes a journalist's heart sing—an interview with a fabled icon in an exotic location, with all expenses paid by a rich magazine that hadn't yet been clobbered by the advent of the internet.

Templeton had a spectacular investment record. The Templeton Growth Fund, which he'd founded in 1954, racked up an average annual return of 14.5 percent over thirty-eight years. A $100,000 stake would have grown to more than $17 million in that time. Templeton, who was born in 1912 in a small town in rural Tennessee, had started out with nothing and ended up a billionaire. I wanted to know how he had done it and what the rest of us could learn from this act of alchemy.

He was eighty-five at the time, the grand old man of the investment world, and I'd half expected him to look like a sage. Instead, I found myself spellbound by this unlikely image of him marching through the surf in his comical hat. But as I would eventually realize, my glimpse of his fitness regimen provided an important insight into his greatness. Templeton had figured out an efficient way to exercise for free in a gorgeous setting. It was utterly irrelevant to him that anyone might think he looked strange, and this indifference was essential to his success.

Michael Lipper, the president of an investment firm called Lipper Advisory Services, once remarked to me that Templeton, George Soros, and Warren Buffett shared one invaluable characteristic: "the willingness to be lonely, the willingness to take a position that others don't think is too bright. They have an inner conviction that a lot of people do not have."

That phrase—*the willingness to be lonely*—has stuck in my mind for many years. It eloquently conveys the critical idea that the best investors are not like other people. They are iconoclasts, mavericks, and misfits who see the world differently from the crowd and follow their own peculiar path—not just in the way they invest but in the way they think and live.

François Rochon, a Canadian money manager who has beaten the market by a mile over the last quarter of a century, has an intriguing theory. As we all know, the human genetic code developed over hundreds of thousands of years to support the primary objective of survival. One lesson we learned at least two hundred thousand years ago is that it's safer to belong to a tribe. That unconscious instinct tends to kick in almost irresistibly when we feel under threat, says Rochon. For example, when stocks plummet, the average investor sees others panicking and instinctively follows the tribe by selling stocks and fleeing to the safe haven of cash. What the tribe followers fail to recognize is the counterintuitive truth that this might be the perfect time to *buy* stocks, since they're now on sale.

"But I think some people in the race don't have that tribal gene," says Rochon, "so they don't feel the urge to follow a tribe. And those people can become good investors because they can think for themselves." Rochon, who uses his talent for stock picking to bankroll his passion for collecting art, suspects that many artists, writers, and entrepreneurs also lack the tribal gene.

Rochon's theory is entirely unprovable, but there's plenty of anecdotal evidence that the best investors are wired in unusual ways that may be financially advantageous. One famed investor who asked not to be quoted by name on this subject told me that many of his most successful peers are "kind of Aspergerish" and that almost all are "unemotional." He points out that "it's a help to be unemotional" when making unconventional bets that the crowd would consider foolish. He adds that people with developmental conditions such as Asperger's syndrome "often have something else in compensation, and very often it's numeracy. . . . Being unemotional and [numerate] is a great combination for investing."

I mentioned this idea to another hugely successful fund manager who is mathematically gifted and extremely uncomfortable in social situations. He confided, "When I was a child, my parents were concerned that I was autistic or might have a touch of Asperger's. I think they concluded no. Or, at least, it wasn't damaging enough. So, yeah, it might be that I'm slightly on the spectrum or not." He then recalled a devastating childhood trauma that also led him to "distance" himself from his emotions. "So, if you're thinking I'm a psycho chicken, you may be right."*

One of the most insightful perspectives on this subject comes from Christopher Davis, who oversees about $25 billion in assets at Davis

* It's worth acknowledging that there are intense controversies over diagnostic labels such as Asperger's syndrome, a form of high-functioning autism named for a Nazi pediatrician who advocated child euthanasia. My goal here isn't to make amateur diagnoses of great investors but to suggest that many seem to be wired in ways that give them a temperamental edge.

Advisors, an investment firm founded by his father in 1969. He's unusually well positioned to observe the idiosyncratic personalities of the most successful investors. He's friends with high-profile practitioners such as Buffett, Munger, Mason Hawkins, and Bill Miller. Moreover, his grandfather (Shelby Cullom Davis) and father (Shelby M. C. Davis) were both investment legends who amassed colossal fortunes in the stock market.

"A necessary characteristic of great investors is that they can't be overly influenced by what other people think," says Davis. "The easiest way not to be overly influenced by what other people think is not to be that *aware* of what they think. If you don't really notice that and don't really *care* about what other people think, that will make it easier to be a great investor." It follows, says Davis, that "a prevalent characteristic in great investors would be low emotional intelligence." He observes that many of the best investors struggle when it comes to "bonding with others" and nurturing "warm attachments in their family life."

By contrast, says Davis, you tend to encounter an entirely different psychological profile among CEOs. They require the emotional intelligence to empathize with others, understand their thoughts, and influence them. But for a contrarian investor, it would be "catastrophic if you were constantly burdened by an awareness of what everybody else was thinking about your decision." In their youth, he adds, many CEOs played team sports, captained a team, or led a fraternity. What about the best investors? "By and large," says Davis, they favored individual sports such as "running, tennis, golf, or swimming. You won't get a lot of football, lacrosse, that sort of thing."

His father, now in his eighties, was one of the investment titans of his generation. During Shelby Davis's twenty-eight years as manager of the New York Venture Fund, a $100,000 investment would have grown to about $3.8 million. So how did he fit the psychological profile painted by his son? "My father was very deeply a loner," says Davis. "I can't imagine him playing team sports, being president of a fraternity, or leading a nonprofit. . . . He just was constantly looking for information, grilling people, and reading annual reports. It was a lonely sort of work. I mean, it was him at a telephone or him and a stack of annual reports and quarterly reports."

His description reminds me of Buffett's politely dismissive response to Mohnish Pabrai after the latter offered to work for him for free: "I simply do best operating by myself." Indeed, Buffett famously spends much of his time sitting alone in his office in Omaha with the blinds drawn, enraptured by the solitary joy of reading annual reports.

Beyond these broad patterns, there are plenty of exceptions and nuances. I'm not suggesting that all of the best investors have developmental disorders or lead lonely lives or are destined to divorce (though the list of divorced investment giants is certainly long, including Munger, Miller, Pabrai, Bill Ackman, Carl Icahn, David Einhorn, and countless others). That would be a gross exaggeration. Plus, it's inane to pathologize every quirk or eccentricity.

Still, despite these caveats and disclaimers, I think it's true that all of the investors you'll meet in this book are nontribal freethinkers. They have a rare capacity to defy conventional opinion. They care much more about being right and winning than gaining social acceptance or approval.

Matthew McLennan, who oversees more than $100 billion at First Eagle Investment Management, describes his job this way: "Every day you're trying to understand how the world works—bottom up, top down—and you're trying to synthesize it in a way that's different from the consensus. . . . At the end of the day, we're paid to see the world through a different prism."

The only way to beat the market is to diverge from the market. That's a task best suited to people who are, quite literally, extraordinary—both intellectually and temperamentally. So perhaps it's no surprise that this is a game that favors brilliant oddballs. And in my experience, nobody was more brilliant—or odd—than Sir John Templeton.

A pioneer of global value investing, he figured out entirely for himself a set of principles and practices that can benefit any investor to this day. But looking back now, long after his death in 2008 at the age of ninety-five, I realize that I failed to grasp the most valuable lessons of his life.

## The Making of a Maverick

It was the fall of 1998 when I met Templeton. Even then, a couple of weeks before his eighty-sixth birthday, he still showed up for work each day at his office in the city of Nassau, a short drive from his home. Our day together began in that office, where he greeted me in a genteel manner from a bygone era. "My time is at your discretion," he said, with a soft Southern twang. "I'll stay as long as you need me."

He was dressed in a pale yellow sports jacket, an open-necked shirt, and gray trousers without a belt. Small, lean, and tanned, he looked fifteen years younger than his age. His office was filled with an unusual range of honors. There was an award for best performance by a mutual fund over thirty-five years; a trophy from PBS television to mark his induction in Louis Rukeyser's *Wall $treet Week* Hall of Fame; an entire wall decorated with his honorary degrees; his award for International Churchman of the Year; and his Norman Vincent Peale Award for Positive Thinking.

Templeton had moved to the Bahamas in the 1960s after a stint in New York. Abandoning his tribe, he renounced his US passport, became a British citizen, and built a house in Lyford Cay. He'd grown up in a devoutly Christian home in Winchester, Tennessee, and his deep-seated faith played a part in his decision to settle in the Bahamas. "This nation has more churches per person than anywhere else in the world," he informed me, "which makes it very attractive and harmonious."

There was also the social allure of the exclusive Lyford Cay Club: "In general, the admissions committee has done a good job of keeping the really top people in the club. So this was a chance to spend our lives with really fascinating people." He mentioned Joseph Lewis, a commodities billionaire with "the most magnificent yacht I've ever seen in my life, other than the queen's yacht. It's huge. He's very private—the kind of fella we like to have here. He's not flamboyant. I've met him in parties. He just quietly does investment trading from his yacht or home."

The club boasted its own marina, tennis courts, and beachfront golf course. But Templeton refused to indulge in such decadent frivolities. "My neighbors go out golfing and yachting and so forth. But my own viewpoint is that it's far more important to be useful," he said. "I've never thought it wise to pursue pleasure.... There must have been some deeper reason why God created human beings. And one of the fairly obvious things is that the people who are busy with some really useful work are happier than the ones who are idle."

He was equally adamant about the perils of retirement, which he disdained as "deadly" both for the body and mind. As Templeton saw it, the misguided notion of retiring at sixty-five had created "enormously increased numbers of idle people, *useless* people" who are "a drag on civilization." It was my first view of this aspect of his character—a hard-edged, moralistic side that seemed at odds with his old-world charm and courtly manners.

While others frittered away their lives, Templeton said he was the busiest he'd ever been. He had sold his investment firm for hundreds of millions of dollars a few years earlier. So he now devoted his time to philanthropy, overseeing the money in his charitable foundations, managing his personal fortune, and writing books with titles such as *Worldwide Laws of Life: 200 Eternal Spiritual Principles*. As we'll see, his gift for making immense sums of money never deserted him, but his primary passion had shifted to spreading what he called "spiritual wealth."

It was a characteristically unconventional crusade. For example, among his many philanthropic initiatives, Templeton spent millions funding scientific research at Harvard Medical School and elsewhere on whether prayer works. He excitedly listed for me some of the many questions he hoped to answer: "Do the people who are prayed for get well quicker? Does the prayer work only if the person who is sick does the praying, or can it be done by somebody else? If it's done by somebody else, is it important that the person praying put his hands on the person prayed for? Do you pray for the cancer to disappear, or do you pray that God's will be done?"

Templeton also funded scientific studies that investigated the benefits of virtues such as forgiveness, humility, honesty, and love. He provided financial incentives for university professors to teach courses on "how science reveals more about God." He also funded the Templeton Prize for Progress Toward Research or Discoveries about Spiritual Realities, which rewarded "entrepreneurs of the spirit" for "expanding our vision of human purpose and ultimate reality." Eager to emphasize that these ethereal matters are more important than worldly concerns, he structured the annual award so that it would always be more lucrative than the Nobel Prize. These days, the winner pockets £1.1 million (about $1.4 million).

This was all part of Templeton's grandiose campaign to "multiply spiritual information one-hundred-fold." It was not an endeavor that everyone applauded. At one end of the spectrum, secular scientists were bemused by his interest in measuring experimentally the effects of spiritual principles. At the other extreme, religious conservatives were appalled by his free-spirited readiness to question their beliefs. He recalled a recent encounter with a "nice lady" who asked his opinion about the biblical story of Noah and the flood. He suggested that it was a "useful allegory, but not literal truth." Her outraged response: "Well, you're not a Christian."

When I asked impertinently if many people regarded him as "a kook," Templeton replied, "Yes, sure. But I have more self-confidence than the average person." It struck me that this trait also lay at the heart of his success as an investor. Templeton agreed. "When you're sticking your neck out, you have to be self-confident enough or brave enough to do it. . . . I did that in the investment field, and I'm doing it now in the spiritual area."

He attributed this attitude to his unusual upbringing: "In all of my childhood I can't remember either my mother or my father ever telling me, 'Do this' or 'Don't do that.' They thought it would help me to become self-reliant and self-confident if I had to do everything myself. And, boy, was that a marvelous education. . . . It's the greatest gift, having to rely on yourself."

On one occasion, his parents appointed him navigator on a family road trip. Templeton, still a young boy, misread the map and took them an hour or two in the wrong direction. Nobody corrected him. They simply waited until he figured out for himself that he'd made a mistake. This laissez-faire parenting strategy wasn't without its risks. When Templeton was about eight, his parents granted his request for a shotgun, so he could go out hunting. They also allowed him to buy gunpowder for fireworks and cyanide for his butterfly killing jars.

Templeton took great pride in his self-reliance. After eleven years of scoring straight A's at school, he headed to Yale in 1930. Gutted by the Great Depression, his father—a lawyer and businessman—wrote to Templeton at the end of freshman year to say that he could no longer pay "even $1" for his education. Templeton lined up part-time jobs, received scholarship money from Yale, and supplemented his income with winnings from playing poker. At the same time, he worked so hard that he was the top student in his class by the end of his third year.

It was at Yale that he decided he would make his living as an investor. He loved arithmetic and solving problems methodically. It also seemed like a profession in which he could serve others, helping them to attain the financial security that his own family lacked. The accepted strategy in those days was for Americans to invest exclusively in US assets. But he saw even then that this narrow-mindedness was "contrary to common sense. If a person were going to own stocks and bonds, it would be much wiser to search everywhere, rather than limiting themselves to one nation."

After Yale, Templeton spent two years at Oxford as a Rhodes Scholar. He wanted to study business management, but his professors didn't regard it as a legitimate subject: "They looked at me in a funny way as if I'd told them I wanted to study garbage." He studied law instead. In his spare time, he read about business. At the time, he could find only one book about investing.

In the depths of the Depression, the stock market was a toxic wasteland. From October 1929 to July 1932, the Dow Jones Industrial Average plunged 89 percent. In the wake of that catastrophe, few people had the financial or emotional fortitude to pick through the rubble in search of bargains. But the fact that others were too scared to invest did nothing to diminish Templeton's interest. Against this backdrop of widespread gloom, he asked himself a critical question: How can I buy a stock for a fraction of what it's worth? His answer: "Absolutely nothing will make a stock go down to an extremely low price except for other people urgently trying to sell."

Templeton had witnessed firsthand how financial distress had forced farmers in Tennessee to sell their land for next to nothing. The lesson was etched in his brain: **You have to buy at a time when other people are desperately trying to sell.** He later coined a marvelous phrase to describe these moments when fear and desperation go viral: "the point of maximum pessimism."

In the meantime, Templeton grabbed every opportunity to travel, eager to learn more about foreign markets where he might eventually invest. After graduating from Oxford, he spent seven months visiting twenty-seven countries, carrying a sleeping bag, one change of clothing, four guidebooks, and a Bible. He stayed in Berlin during the 1936 Olympics, which the Nazis used as a propaganda showcase; traveled to Eastern Europe; visited Egypt and Palestine; and even made it to India, Japan, and China. At a time when few Americans ventured overseas, he was already building an informational edge over investors who lacked his insatiable thirst for knowledge.

Returning to America in 1937, Templeton married, spent three months at a Wall Street brokerage firm called Fenner & Beane, then quit to work for an oil exploration company. By 1939, he'd saved about $30,000. The investment environment could hardly have seemed less inviting even for a seasoned stock picker, let alone a novice. The United States was trapped in a vortex of depression, deflation, and mass unemployment. The Dow, which had peaked at 381 in 1929, still languished below 150 in 1939. Worst of all, the world was poised for war.

In short, it was the perfect time for a twentysomething Southerner with almost no experience in the markets to demonstrate that he was the smartest, most coolheaded investor of his generation.

## The Bet of a Century

In September 1939, Germany invaded Poland. Over the next few months, Norway, Holland, and Belgium surrendered to the Nazis. In May 1940, when Germany invaded France, the Dow sank to a new low of 112. The UK stock market crashed about 40 percent in less than four months amid fears of an imminent German invasion of the British Isles. Winston Churchill would later describe 1940 as "the most splendid, most deadly year in our long English and British story."

When the world is teetering over the edge of the abyss, how should a savvy investor respond? Conventional opinion might suggest that this was a prudent time to beat a retreat. With stocks crashing to new lows and panic rampant, surely the appropriate response was to seek safety in more defensive assets such as cash, gold, or land. But Templeton was not conventional.

After Germany's invasion of Poland, he realized that the world was plunging inexorably into war and that the United States would ultimately have to fight, too. But his icily logical response set him apart. Templeton told me, "I thought, if there's any time when every product is in demand, it's during a war. So I said, 'If this is going to develop into a world war, which companies will prosper?'"

He concluded that "maybe ninety percent" of American businesses "would have more demand and less competition during a war." Even the weakest companies were likely to recover as wartime spending surged, reinvigorating the economy and boosting employment. Savaged by the Great Depression, many companies were so close to death that a sudden change in their fortunes would have an outsize impact on their stock price. Reborn, they might well outperform the stocks of healthier companies that weren't so beaten down. You might call it survival of the *unfittest*.

But how best to take advantage of this shrewd insight?

Templeton opened the *Wall Street Journal* and identified 104 American companies that had experienced "such a terrible Depression" that their stocks traded at $1 or less. A couple of days later, he called a stockbroker who'd been his boss at Fenner & Beane and asked to invest $100 in each of those companies. "He called me back and said, 'That's a very unusual order, but we're going ahead with it, except we've eliminated thirty-seven companies that are already in bankruptcy.' And I said, 'Oh, no. Don't eliminate those. They may recover.'"

It was an astonishingly bold bet. But Templeton was so sure of his judgment that he even convinced his ex-boss to lend him $10,000 to fund the investment.* The future had never looked so bleak. Yet so much dire news was already priced into the market that Templeton thought the odds were stacked resoundingly in his favor. He recalled, "It was commonsense arithmetic that attracted me."

---

*This was the equivalent of roughly $183,000 today.

One company that exemplified this arithmetic was Missouri Pacific Railroad, which had been among the world's largest railroads before going bankrupt in the Depression. In its halcyon days, the company had issued preferred stock that was supposed to pay an annual dividend of $7 per share in perpetuity. But shareholders didn't receive their dividends after the firm went bust, and the price of the preferred stock collapsed from $100 to around twelve cents per share.

Psychologically, it's tough to love a money-losing company that has burned all of its investors. But Templeton said he bought eight hundred shares of Missouri Pacific for $100. **Like Buffett and Munger, he had an unemotional appreciation for a mispriced bet that offered an asymmetry between risk and reward.** "The potential on the upside was much greater than on the downside," Templeton explained to me. "Sure, I may lose my hundred dollars. But if I *don't* lose my hundred dollars, I might make a lot."

He was right. Railroads prospered during the war and the stock rebounded from twelve cents to $5 before he cashed out. His only regret was that he sold too soon. "I was so excited about having any stock I bought go up forty times that I thought that was enough," he recalled. "It was foolishness. . . . Within four years thereafter, it went up to $105."

Of course, a bet like this relied on so much more than mere mathematics. Mark Mobius, an eminent investor in emerging markets who worked with Templeton for years, once told me that it required "tremendous willpower and strength of personality" for Templeton to buy at the point of maximum pessimism. As Mobius put it, "Everybody else is running out of the burning building."

What's remarkable to me is not just that Templeton had the courage to invest in 104 reviled stocks as the world went to war. It's that he had the courage to *hold* them for years even as the drumbeat of disastrous news grew more and more deafening. In December 1941, the Japanese attacked Pearl Harbor, spurring the United States to join the war. By 1942, Germany had seized control of most of Europe. Despair about the future ran so deep that the markets took a terrible pounding. In April 1942, the Dow slumped to a generational low of 92.

In his superb book *Wealth, War & Wisdom*, Barton Biggs points out that the State of New York Insurance Commission actually banned stocks from the portfolios of insurance companies in 1942, deeming them an "inappropriate investment." At the time, writes Biggs, "Every right-thinking prognosticator with a head on his shoulders was bearish."

Yet Templeton stood firm. "I had enough self-confidence to think that most of the people called experts were making big mistakes," he told me. He was also sustained by his religious faith, which enabled him to trust that the world would eventually emerge from chaos. Even in the worst of times, he said, "I never was depressed or despairing."

The heavens smiled kindly upon him. In the spring of 1942, the market stopped falling and took flight as the Allies' fortunes improved and the US economy revived. Templeton's stocks, once spurned, now soared. After five tempestuous years, he finally sold. "When I liquidated those holdings, I had a profit on one hundred out of one hundred and four," he said. "I made roughly five times my money."

I've come to regard Templeton's wartime bet as one of the boldest and most prescient investments in history—a triumph of both intellect and character. Despite his inexperience, he understood enough about economic history, financial markets, and human nature to recognize that overwhelming pessimism would eventually give way to unbridled optimism. Even in the darkest of times, he never forgot that the sun also rises.

## Six Guiding Principles for the Nontribal Investor

After we chatted in his office for a couple of hours, Templeton drove me to his home. It was a stately building with white columns designed in the style of an antebellum house in the South. With a view of the ocean and a golf course, it felt quiet and peaceful. He often said that his investment performance improved after moving here because the location strengthened his psychological detachment from the Wall Street herd. In his early years here, the *Wall Street Journal* often arrived days late. For a long-term investor, this could be an unexpected advantage.

The house was furnished with old-fashioned charm. The living room had a wooden rocking chair, silver candlesticks, and leather-bound books such as *The Life of Christ* and the poetry of Henry Wadsworth Longfellow. Upstairs, in his study, Templeton pointed out a painting that depicted him at Buckingham Palace on the day in 1987 when Queen Elizabeth II knighted him for his services to philanthropy. I asked how it felt to receive so many accolades. "It's like winning a game," he replied. "I must admit that I'm human. This year I received my twenty-second honorary doctorate, and that did give me some feeling that maybe I was not too foolish."

We sat down in his living room. Templeton sipped tea out of a mug emblazoned with the FBI's motto: Fidelity, Bravery, Integrity. He then shared with me what he saw as the most important lessons of his investment career. During this conversation and a follow-up phone interview, he mentioned six guiding principles that he believed would help any investor.

This wisdom was the fruit of more than sixty years of practical experience and contemplation by one of the greatest minds of the investment world. It's worth noting that none of these principles was cloned. When I asked Templeton if anyone had influenced him either as an investor or in other areas of life, he replied, "Absolutely no one. . . . I didn't find anyone that I wanted to rely on." What about his parents? "Not that either."

**First of all, said Templeton, beware of emotion: "Most people get led astray by emotions in investing. They get led astray by being excessively careless and optimistic when they have big profits, and by getting excessively pessimistic and too cautious when they have big losses."** One of the primary services he provided as a money manager was to help his clients "get away from that emotionalism. It was a major element in my success."

But he didn't just avoid the pitfalls of emotion. He exploited the wayward emotions of *other* investors, buying from them when they were irrationally bearish and selling to them when they were irrationally bullish. "To buy when others are despondently selling and to sell when others are enthusiastically buying is the most difficult," he said. "But it pays the greatest rewards."

It came naturally for Templeton to approach every decision analytically, whether it was choosing a profession, picking a stock, or deciding where to live. Before moving to Lyford Cay, he took several sheets of paper, wrote a different place name at the top of each sheet, then listed every advantage of that place. Describing this process, he said emphatically, "It was *not* emotional."

**Second, said Templeton, beware of your own ignorance, which is "probably an even bigger problem than emotion. . . . So many people buy something with the tiniest amount of information. They don't really understand what it is that they're buying."** It pays to remember the simple fact that there are two sides in every investment transaction: "The one with the greatest information is likely to come out ahead. It takes a huge amount of work and study and investigation."

Templeton claimed that diligence had played a much greater role in his success than innate talent. He often spoke of his determination to "give the extra ounce"—to make the extra call, to schedule the extra meeting, to take the extra research trip. He was similarly dedicated to his lifelong program of continuous self-education. As a young man, he said, "I searched for anything available in writing on the subject of investing, and I still do." Even in his eighties, he said, "I try to be more knowledgeable each year as an investor."

Templeton argued that amateurs and professionals alike must avoid fooling themselves into believing that it's easy to build a strong investment record: "Even with the professionals, not many of them turn out to produce superior results. So the way to invest is to say to yourself, 'Do I have more experience and wisdom than the professionals?' And if you don't, then *don't* do it. Hire a professional. . . . Don't be so egotistical that you think you'll do better than the experts."

**Third, said Templeton, you should diversify broadly to protect yourself from your own fallibility.** By his calculation, he had made at least half a million investment decisions in his career. For many years, he kept a detailed record of the advice he'd given to clients on which stocks to buy or sell. This revealed an uncomfortable truth: about a third of his advice was "the opposite of wisdom." Investing is so difficult, he concluded, that even the best investors should assume that they'll be right no more than two-thirds of the time, however hard they work.

The moral? Get your ego—and your risk exposure—under control. "Don't put all your money with any one expert. Don't put all your money in any one industry or any one nation. Nobody is that smart. So the wise thing is to diversify." Templeton recommended that the average investor should own a minimum of five mutual funds, each focused on a different area of the financial markets. It's helpful to study a fund manager's long-term record, he added, but this is hardly a guarantee of continued success. Again, we need to be honest about the limits of our knowledge: "Don't be so egotistical that you think you know who is the right expert."

**Fourth, said Templeton, successful investing requires patience.** When he bought US stocks at the outbreak of World War II, he knew how cheap they were, but he couldn't predict how long it would take for the market to agree with him. His edge lay not just in his superior insight, but in his willingness to wait year after painful year for the situation to play out as he'd predicted.

Templeton's affection for math reinforced his conviction that patience pays. To illustrate this, he mentioned the tale of Dutch immigrants buying Manhattan for $24 in 1626.* If the Native American sellers had invested this derisory sum at 8 percent a year, he said, they would have "enormously more than the total value of Manhattan today, including all the buildings." Templeton regarded this as an extreme example of a fundamental financial principle: "In order to have a really good investment result, all you need is patience." He warned that "almost all" investors are "too impatient," adding, "People who change from one fund to another as often as once a year are basing it more on emotion than investigation."

**Fifth, said Templeton, the best way to find bargains is to study whichever assets have performed most dismally in the past five years, then to assess whether the cause of those woes is temporary or permanent.** Most people are naturally drawn to investments that are already successful and popular with the herd, whether it's a high-flying stock or fund or a rapidly growing country. But if a sunny future is already reflected in the price of the asset, then it's probably a bet for suckers.

---

* The actual details of the deal are somewhat murky. Our knowledge of it is based on a 1626 letter from a Dutch merchant who, in those politically incorrect times, wrote, "They have purchased the Island of Manhattes from the savages for the value of 60 guilders."

Templeton, the least tribal of investors, took the opposite approach. He wanted to know "Where is the outlook *worst*?" These pockets of gloom were likely to yield the most enticing bargains, since asset prices would reflect the tribe's pessimism. His contrarian strategy involved scrutinizing stocks in beleaguered industries and markets around the world, constantly asking himself, "Which one is the lowest priced compared to what I believe it's worth?"

At the time of our discussions, the Asian financial crisis of 1997 had left a trail of destruction in countries such as Thailand, Indonesia, and South Korea. If you wanted to identify the most battered investment vehicle on earth, one clear contender was the Matthews Korea Fund, which lost about 65 percent in 1997. The fund had the misfortune of investing solely in a nation traumatized by a lending freeze, a collapsing currency, and deadly levels of corporate leverage.

Templeton decided in late 1997 that South Korean stocks were the cheapest in the world relative to future corporate earnings. The price/earnings ratio of Korean stocks had crashed from more than 20 in June 1997 to 10 in December—a rough but revealing measure of investors' fear and loathing. Still, it was reasonable to assume that the country's history of powerful economic growth would eventually resume, once this vicious liquidity crisis had passed. So Templeton poured $10 million into the Matthews Korea Fund, becoming its single largest shareholder. He told me, "It could hardly get any worse from a psychological and public relations standpoint."

To the typical investor, that might not sound like a rousing endorsement. But just think for a moment about the simple elegance of his logic and the independence of mind required to wade into the South Korean market while everyone else flooded out. Sure enough, the crisis proved to be fleeting, just as he'd surmised. In June 1999, Bloomberg News reported that the Matthews Korea Fund had risen 266 percent in the past year, making it the single best performer in its ranking of 5,307 stock funds. As the Bible says, "The last shall be first, and the first last."

**Sixth, said Templeton, "One of the most important things as an investor is not to chase fads."** In the 1980s, the Templeton Foundation Press republished a timeless book with a magnificent title: *Extraordinary Popular Delusions and the Madness of Crowds*. Written in 1841 by

Charles Mackay, it tells the history of crazes such as tulip mania and the South Sea Bubble. Templeton wrote a foreword that offered a rational antidote to financial insanity: "The best way for an investor to avoid popular delusions is to focus not on outlook but on value."

He suggested that we ground ourselves in reality by investigating an array of specific valuation measures, including a company's market price in relation to its sales volume per share, its net asset value per share, and its average earnings per share for the last five years. This "critical analysis" of an "investment's fundamental value" acts as a safeguard against "crowd madness."

At the time of our meeting, US stocks had enjoyed an eight-year bull run and euphoric investors were betting blindly on technology and internet stocks. It seemed clear to me that we were in the midst of a mania, but I wanted Templeton to confirm what I suspected. He didn't make it easy.

Early in our conversation, he had told me, "The point of maximum optimism is the time to take your profits." But when I asked him repeatedly if we'd reached that point, he evaded the question. Finally, he snapped, "Anybody is *stupid* to ask that question. Is that clear? Nobody ever knows when the point comes. . . . Some experts are right a little more often than *you* might be. But still, it's a human failing to even put your mind on a question of which stock market is going to go up or down. There's never been anybody who knew that."

I felt like I'd been smacked around the head. I understood his broader point that making market predictions is a mug's game. But he knew as well as anyone that many US stocks were poised for pain because their valuations were unsustainable. It was impossible to predict *when* the music would stop, but the outcome was pretty predictable. In retrospect, I suspect he was mad at me for not taking sufficient interest in his philanthropic work, which he insisted was "the real story." Note to self: think twice before asking a revered icon if many people think he's "a kook."

In any case, it later emerged that Templeton hatched an inspired scheme to profit when the dot-com bubble burst. Here's how it worked.

Back then, unscrupulous investment banks were making a killing by taking internet companies public. The Wall Street sales machine moved into overdrive, hyping and hawking any half-credible rubbish that naive, greedy, or reckless investors might be willing to buy. It was a classic outbreak of investment insanity—loads of fun until someone loses an eye. Templeton knew that this tragicomedy would end in tears. After all, he had often cautioned that the four most expensive words in the English language are "This time is different."

His response was to target eighty-four of the most egregiously over-valued internet stocks, all of which had tripled since their initial public offering. After the IPO, a "lockup" period followed in which company employees weren't allowed to sell their shares, typically for six months. Templeton reasoned that these insiders would race to dump their stock at the first opportunity since they'd be anxious to cash out before the euphoria faded. This stampede of insider selling would cause the stocks to crash.

So Templeton "sold short" each of those eighty-four stocks, betting that they'd nose-dive as soon as the lockup period expired. Lauren Templeton, a money manager who is his great-niece, has said that he placed a $2.2 million bet against each stock—a total of about $185 million.

Templeton's short-selling strategy worked like a dream. When the dot-com bubble burst in March 2000, he earned a profit of more than $90 million in months. Years later, when the *Economist* ran an article about the greatest financial trades of all time, it declared that his "ingenious" scheme "wins the 'Wish I'd thought of that' prize by a mile."

It fills me with wonder that a man in his late eighties conjured up this glorious gambit. Best of all, there was an exquisite symmetry at play here. In 1939, he realized that the investment crowd had fallen for the illusion that the future offered nothing but misery and loss. In 1999, he realized that the investment crowd had fallen for the illusion that the future offered nothing but pleasure and profit. On both occasions, he trusted his superior judgment. In 1939, he bought a basket of stocks that the crowd hated. In 1999, he shorted a basket of stocks that the crowd adored. Two masterful investments, the mirror image of each other, separated by six decades.

## Master of His Domain

Before we go any further, let me make a confession. The truth is, I didn't really like Sir John Templeton. Sure, I was excited to meet him, and I was grateful for his time. But I saw in him a cold austerity that I found unnerving.

In his book *Wisdom from World Religions: Pathways Toward Heaven on Earth*, he wrote at length about virtues such as "unlimited love," forgiveness, humility, and compassion. But the warm and generous side of his nature coexisted with a side that could seem stern and severe. He was kind enough to drive me to the airport so that I could continue interviewing him in his car. But after he left, I wrote a note to myself that captured my ambivalence about him: "He's curiously dry, steely, formal. Charming but tough. Incredibly strong-willed. He claims to be open and listening, but he's dogmatic and extreme."

In *The Templeton Touch*, a biography by William Proctor, one of the most perceptive reminiscences comes from Rory Knight, the former dean of Templeton College, Oxford, which Templeton helped to fund. "He was a hard guy," Knight recalls. "He was not a soft man walking around as a seminarian just being nice to people. Now, he was never rude to people and he was an absolute gentleman. . . . I would say, though, that he was demanding of people at all times in the best sense of that word. He brought out the best in people, and set a hard expectation."

To his credit, Templeton was especially demanding of himself. Take his attitude toward saving and spending. "After my education, I had absolutely no money and neither did my bride," he told me. "So we deliberately saved fifty cents out of every dollar we earned." But he had no intention of relaxing his financial discipline even when he was astronomically rich. While many of his peers favored private jets, he always insisted on flying coach. "I've got a lot better ways to spend my money than to waste it by getting a bigger seat," he explained. "I never thought it was wise to waste anything."

When Templeton was a famous fund manager, his employees would chuckle about his habit of writing on scraps of used paper, which he stapled together to create makeshift notepads. Late in life, he relished saving money by driving an inexpensive Kia car from South Korea. Gary Moore, a friend of his who served as an adviser to religious investors, joked to me, "John is what we call a Calvinist. He believes it's okay to make money so long as you don't enjoy it." Given his compulsive cheapness, it's no surprise that Templeton specialized in buying undervalued stocks.

Distrustful of debt, he always paid cash for his cars and homes. He also claimed that his wartime bet was the only time he ever borrowed money to invest. During the Great Depression he'd seen how easy it was for overextended people to come undone, and he regarded fiscal discipline as a moral virtue. As we were leaving his office, a stranger accosted him in the parking lot and asked for money to pay an electricity bill. Templeton handed him $50 in return for a promise that the man would never again ask him for money. In the car, he explained why this was his standard operating procedure: "The type of person who runs out of money will keep on running out of money. And if he got it somewhere, he'll keep on going back there."

Templeton's watchfulness over money also stemmed from his belief that we are merely "temporary stewards" of God's wealth. He liked to begin meetings at his fund company with a prayer, and he saw a strong connection between spirituality and material success. "If you focus on spiritual matters, you will very likely become wealthy," he told me. "I never found a family that tithed ten percent of their income to charity for ten years that didn't become both prosperous and happy. So tithing is the single best investment in the world." He had even developed "a new form" of "super" tithing: "For every dollar I spend on myself, I carefully give away ten dollars."

He was equally exacting in his approach to time management. John Galbraith, who marketed Templeton's funds, recalled, "John won't engage in small talk. The minute you're through with your common business, he's on to something else." Gary Moore added, "The first time I met John, he said, 'Be here at 4:02. I've got another appointment at 4:13.'"

Determined not to squander a minute, Templeton made a habit of doing two things at once. During our meeting in his house, he underlined key passages in a book for me while simultaneously answering my questions. He also liked to multitask by praying as he drove. Obsessed with punctuality, he routinely arrived ten minutes early for meetings. He abhorred procrastination. He disapproved of distractions such as television and movies (especially "unprincipled entertainment"), preferring to read corporate filings or "inspirational" books. He referred to "goofing off" as "a form of theft" and to idleness as "a form of slow suicide."

When I remarked that he seemed hard on himself, he replied, "Let's call it self-control. I do think that I've always worked on having more self-control, and I sure wish other people would."

It wasn't just his money and his time that he managed with fierce self-discipline. He was also fixated on managing his mind. In *Wisdom from World Religions*, he returned over and over to the subject of "thought control." In his daily life, he trained himself to focus on "productive thoughts" and "positive emotions" such as love, thanksgiving, service, and the contemplation of "the infinite good within ourselves and others."

Templeton was equally committed to banishing negative thoughts and emotions such as anger, doubt, worry, guilt, fear, hatred, and envy. One technique that he recommended was to replace any negative thought with the statement "I give thanks for the abundance of good in my life." When faced with difficulties, he suggested uttering a phrase such as "This comes to bless me." He also sought to eradicate any "aimless, undisciplined thinking" that failed to serve the "high aims" of his life. As Templeton put it, we have immense power to shape our lives by choosing "where we wish to place our focus, for *what we focus on expands*."*

Templeton's determination to rule his mind helped him to endure some terrible times. In 1951, he and his first wife, Judith, were on vacation in Bermuda when she died in a motorcycle accident. As a thirty-eight-year-old widower, he suddenly found himself responsible

---

*In *The Templeton Touch*, Lauren Templeton says her great-uncle was "so disciplined that a single unproductive thought was unwelcome in his mind. He once told me that when he detected an unproductive thought, he would seize it 'and banish it to the nothing from which it came.'"

for raising their three children alone. He made it through those years by "crowding out" the wrenching thoughts that might otherwise have overwhelmed his mind. In 1958, he married his second wife, Irene, a Christian Scientist who shared his belief in the power of the mind and prayer.

As a skeptical journalist, my tendency in those days (not now) was to roll my eyes at the mention of "positive thinking" and "thought control." I was so closed-minded that I also gave no serious consideration to Templeton's mission of exploring scientifically whether spiritual practices such as prayer or forgiveness might be beneficial. I'm embarrassed to admit it, but my prejudices made me smug and dismissive. Instead, I should have suspended judgment until I learned more.

What I realize now is that Templeton's habits of positive thinking and prayer must have helped enormously in his battle to gain control over his thoughts and emotions. For an investor who specialized in taking unpopular positions, that mental strength was a powerful advantage.

By contrast, my own mind was hopelessly undirected, and it was easy for me to get swamped by feelings such as fear, doubt, regret, greed, impatience, jealousy, and pessimism—all of which complicate the challenge of making rational investment decisions.

In *Wisdom from World Religions*, Templeton wrote, "To live successfully in the outer world, it is important to live successfully in the inner world. . . . The friends, associates, opportunities, careers, and life experiences of our outer world are reflections of what is happening within us." Templeton took control of his inner world. At the time, he struck me as judgmental and holier-than-thou, which made me less open to learning from him. But twenty years later, I find myself awed by his inner strength and iron will, and I wish that I had half of his self-control.

As I see it now, Templeton didn't just master the markets. *He mastered himself.* He took responsibility for every aspect of his life, including his time, money, health, thoughts, and emotions. This required extraordinary self-discipline. We don't often celebrate self-discipline. It's such an old-fashioned and fusty virtue. But Templeton triumphed by taking self-discipline to an extreme. As Pabrai learned from Munger, "Take a simple idea and take it seriously."

There's so much in investing and life that we *cannot* control. Templeton couldn't be sure that the Allies would prevail in World War II. He could never have predicted that his first wife would die young. But he controlled what he *could* control.

As an investor, that meant focusing with remorseless discipline on valuations, on gathering better information than his rivals possessed, on making fearlessly independent judgments with no concern for the tastes of the tribe. It also meant doing everything in his power to maintain his mental and emotional equilibrium. He couldn't control the outcome, but he could control himself. What I failed to learn from Templeton two decades ago is the supreme importance of this inner game.

CHAPTER THREE

# Everything Changes

How can we make smart decisions
when nothing stays the same and the future
is unknowable? Ask Howard Marks

---

That everything changes is the basic truth for each existence. No one can deny this truth, and all the teaching of
Buddhism is condensed within it.

—Shunryu Suzuki, *Zen Mind,*
*Beginner's Mind*

When Howard Marks was an undergraduate at the University of Pennsylvania, he signed up for a class in studio art. It was an eccentric choice
for a student majoring in finance, but Marks was a talented artist in his
youth. "So I went to the art course, and the teacher walks in and looks
around and says, 'This is too many people. We have to weed out. I'm
going to ask your name and your major.' And so I said, 'I'm Howard
Marks, Wharton School of Finance.' And he says, 'Okay, you're the first
to go. Get out.'"

Evicted from Eden, Marks was forced to find another subject for his
minor. To his surprise, he fell in love with Japanese literature, art, and
civilization. It was in a class on Japanese Buddhism that he encountered the Zen concept of *mujo*, or impermanence.* Sitting in his corner
office on the thirty-fourth floor of a skyscraper in midtown Manhattan, Marks explains how this ancient idea has shaped his philosophy

---

*Shunryu Suzuki Roshi, a famous Zen teacher, used the Japanese phrase shogyō-
mujō, which he translated as "everything is changing."

of investing and life. "Change is inevitable. The only constant is impermanence," he says. "We have to accommodate to the fact that the environment changes. . . . We cannot expect to control our environment. We have to accommodate to our environment. We have to expect and go with change."

Marks acknowledges that everything is in a state of constant flux: nature, economies, markets, industries, companies, and our own lives. This is decidedly awkward for investors, since we're engaged in betting very real money on circumstances that won't last and on a future that's unknowable. How can we make wise decisions in the face of such acute instability and uncertainty? As the famed investor Bill Miller once told me, "The world changes. This is the biggest problem in markets."

Indeed, it's a problem that pervades our lives. The French philosopher Michel de Montaigne wrote, "We, and our judgment, and all mortal things go on flowing and rolling unceasingly. Thus nothing certain can be established about one thing by another, both the judging and the judged being in continual change." A prominent French investor, François-Marie Wojcik, was jubilant when I read him these lines, which Montaigne penned in the 1570s. Wary of overestimating his own (or anybody else's) judgment in a constantly changing world where nothing certain can be established, Wojcik remarks, "I have three principles: doubt, doubt, and doubt."

The problem of transience, which lies at the heart of Buddhist teaching, has long preoccupied the most thoughtful investors. T. Rowe Price,* founder of the Baltimore-based investment firm that bears his name, wrote an essay in 1937 titled "Change—the Investor's Only Certainty." Struggling to assess the geopolitical perils of his time, Price mentioned Hitler's rise to power, then ventured a prediction that "Germany will acquire territory, preferably through peaceful means." Two years later, Hitler invaded Poland, plunging the world into six years of war. Everything changed, but not in ways that Price or anyone else could predict with any precision.

Marks was born in 1946, a few months after the war ended, and grew

---

* Price, who was dubbed "the father of growth investing," founded his eponymous company in 1937. Today, it's a global behemoth with more than $1 trillion in assets.

up in Queens, New York, at a time when the pace of change seemed to him relatively slow and benign. "Comic books cost a dime for my entire youth," he recalls. "We all thought that the world was a stable place and that events played out against an unchanging backdrop. . . . Now it's clear that the world is changing all the time, unpredictably, at incredible speed. Nothing is the same anymore, and for people whose approach to life is based on sameness, that must be very upsetting."

In the world of business, sameness and stability are not an option. Companies rise and fall, locked in a Darwinian struggle for supremacy and survival, and industry after industry is disrupted by technological innovation. Time Inc., where I spent much of my career as a journalist, recently ceased to exist after decades as the world's dominant magazine publisher. When I joined in the 1990s, the firm was known as the "velvet coffin," a resting place so rich and plush that we might never get out alive. In 2018, Time Inc. became a feeble unit within the Meredith Corporation, which made its hay with magazines such as *Successful Farming* and *Fruit, Garden and Home.* Meredith broke up the company like a junkyard car and sold the parts for scrap.

As investors, we long for definitive answers to complex questions about the future. *Will the stock market rise or fall? Will the economy thrive or flounder?* Marks points out that investing consists entirely of "divining the future." In analyzing any asset, we must figure out what price to pay today, given our expectations of future profits and valuations. Likewise, in other areas of life "we have to deal with the future. We have to make decisions on where to live, what job to take, who to marry, and how many kids to have." But if everything is changing faster than ever and tomorrow may look nothing like today, how can we position ourselves adroitly for what lies ahead?

Most people make their investment decisions (and life decisions) on the basis of an unreliable hodgepodge of half-baked logic, biases, hunches, emotion, and vague fantasies or fears about the future. I've moved countries several times without truly thinking it through, largely driven by whims or frustration.

By contrast, Marks is a master of disciplined and dispassionate thinking—a skill that has made him one of the undisputed giants of the investment world. As cochairman of Oaktree Capital Management, he oversees about $120 billion in assets. A pioneer in the field of alternative investing, Oaktree specializes in areas such as distressed debt, junk bonds, convertible securities, commercial real estate, and "control" investments in businesses with "untapped potential." The firm's clients include about seventy of the largest US pension funds, hundreds of endowments and foundations, and many of the world's biggest sovereign wealth funds.

Oaktree's stellar returns and reputation have made Marks rich. *Forbes* estimates his net worth at $2.2 billion. He used to own a $75 million estate in Malibu, and he later bought a $52.5 million pad in Manhattan. But ideas, not money, are his drug of choice. Above all, Marks is an original thinker—a man captivated by subjects such as risk, randomness, cyclicality, the psychology of investing, and the threat of what he calls "improbable disasters."

Marks oversees Oaktree's investment strategy, but he's structured his job so that none of the firm's 950 or so employees report to him. He has also handed off all day-to-day responsibilities for selecting individual investments, leaving himself free to read, think, and write. His memos, which he has penned for more than a quarter of a century, provide a priceless trove of financial wisdom. Warren Buffett once wrote, "When I see memos from Howard Marks in my mail, they are the first thing I open and read. I always learn something." Marks turned his memos into an indispensable book, *The Most Important Thing: Uncommon Sense for the Thoughtful Investor.*

In person, he has the air of an unusually brilliant professor, peppering his speech with phrases such as "the rebuttable presumption has to be" and "in my myth of myself." During our conversations, he naturally assumes the role of a teacher, pausing to draw a graph or to read from his well-thumbed copies of esoteric books such as C. Jackson Grayson's *Decisions Under Uncertainty: Drilling Decisions by Oil and Gas Operators.* One of his greatest pleasures, says Marks, is sharing ideas and having people respond, "That was helpful. I never thought of that."

To my mind, nobody in the investment world has thought more helpfully about what we can and cannot know, and how to *prepare* for the future instead of fooling ourselves into believing we can predict it. Faced with the challenge of making rational decisions, I'm sometimes tempted to throw up my hands in dismay. How can I possibly figure out a smart course of action, given the overwhelming complexity of the forces at play and how little control I have over the outcome? But Marks, whom I regard as a philosopher-king of finance, provides a set of profound insights and practical strategies that can help us immeasurably to navigate through the fog.

### First, Be Lucky. Second, Be Humble

**In a world where nothing is stable or dependable and almost anything can happen, the first rule of the road is to be honest with ourselves about our limitations and vulnerabilities.** As the Athenian playwright Euripides warned nearly twenty-five hundred years ago, "How can you think yourself a great man when the first accident that comes along can wipe you out completely?" Montaigne, one of the wisest of men, had this sentence inscribed on a beam in the library of his château.

Marks, who is keenly aware of the dangers of pride and arrogance, has decorated one wall of his office with a centuries-old painting of wooden sailing ships tossed around by terrifying waves. He bought it in 2001, at a time when foolhardy speculators had been dashed mercilessly against the rocks by the dot-com crash. The painting offers a disconcerting reminder that none of us is immune to the destructive power of forces that are bigger than us and beyond our control—a lesson we learned again in 2020 when, out of nowhere, a virus cast the whole world into chaos.

"Absolutely nobody had a pandemic on their radar screen, and then it turns out to be the defining event of our lives," says Marks. "That in itself should convince us that we don't know what's going to happen.... Sometimes, we don't even know what *could* happen."

In the 1987 novel *The Bonfire of the Vanities*, Tom Wolfe coined the phrase *Masters of the Universe* to describe the hotshot investment bankers pulling down millions of dollars a year in bonuses. But as Marks sees it, "The screwiest thing you can do is to think you're a Master of the Universe. We're all just little cogs, and the universe will go on without us. We have to fit into it and adapt to it."

When I ask him about a fellow billionaire who often makes bold predictions about the economy and the markets, Marks concedes that he's "extremely smart," but adds, "At the end of the day, the world will see if he's as smart as he thought he was. Because if you think you're smarter than you are, you get into trouble. . . . Sometimes I wish he didn't think he's as good as he is."

One way that Marks keeps his own ego in check is by reminding himself of the starring role that luck has played in his life. After reading Malcolm Gladwell's book *Outliers*, which explores various causes of success, Marks compiled a list of lucky breaks that have helped to propel him to where he is today.

His streak began with the "demographic luck" of being born to white, middle-class parents in the United States at the start of a golden era of postwar growth.* Nobody in his family had a college degree, but he was fortunate that his parents valued learning, bought an encyclopedia, and encouraged him to go to college. His high school grades were nothing special, so he thinks he was also lucky that Wharton accepted him. And it was Wharton that exposed him to finance, leading him to jettison his earlier ambition of a career in accounting. His second choice, a large state university, would certainly have lacked Wharton's cachet among Wall Street recruiters.

I once gave an interview in which I mentioned that Marks has a high IQ, which has no doubt contributed significantly to his success. In response, he sent me a charmingly modest email, remarking, "People who don't fully acknowledge their luck miss the fact that being intelligent is nothing but luck. No one does anything to 'deserve' a high IQ."

After Wharton, Marks applied to the MBA program at Harvard, but (like Buffett) was rejected. Bad luck? Hardly. Instead, he ended up at the University of Chicago's business school in 1967, when it was

---

* Similarly, Warren Buffett has often said that he won the "ovarian lottery" when he was born in the United States in 1930. Over lunch with Mohnish Pabrai and Guy Spier, he mentioned traveling with Bill Gates to China and watching a young Chinese man dragging boats to the shore. Buffett was struck by the realization that many opportunities were closed to this man solely because of accidents of birth that were beyond his control. Buffett added that his own investment career would never have been possible if he'd been born in China because he couldn't have read Benjamin Graham's books, which hadn't been translated into Chinese.

leading a revolution in financial theory. The "Chicago School" of academics had recently developed the efficient-market hypothesis, which contends that assets are correctly priced to reflect all of the relevant information available to investors. This theory gave rise to the belief that it's impossible to beat the market consistently, which suggests that investors should settle for owning low-cost index funds that mirror the market's returns. Indexing, as we'll later discuss, is undeniably a smart option, given how difficult it is to outperform the market after expenses. As Marks puts it, "Most people should index most of their money."

When he heard his professors' explanations of market efficiency, Marks says he experienced the financial equivalent of satori, "the moment of enlightenment in Zen Buddhism." It made sense to him that millions of investors hustling to earn a profit would "find the bargains and buy them up." This is "not universally true," he says, "but it makes a hell of a lot more sense than to think that something could be an obvious bargain and nobody else will tumble to it."

Marks regards the efficient-market hypothesis as a "very powerful concept." Still, there's a big enough difference between academic theory and real-world practice for him to have earned billions for himself and his clients. There's an old joke he tells, which goes like this: A professor of finance and a student are strolling across the Chicago campus. The student stops and exclaims, "Look! There's a five-dollar bill on the ground!" The professor replies, "It *can't* be a five-dollar bill or someone else would have picked it up already." The professor walks away, so the student picks up the money and buys himself a beer. Appropriately, Marks keeps in his wallet a folded $5 bill that he once found in the Harvard Business School library—a reminder of the limitations of theory.

**Marks drew a simple but life-changing lesson from these academic debates: if he wanted to add value as an investor, he should avoid the most efficient markets and focus exclusively on less efficient ones.** "The more a market is studied and followed and embraced and popularized, the less there should be bargains around for the asking," he says. For example, it's hard to find outlandish bargains among large US companies, a mainstream market where swarms of intelligent, highly motivated money managers tend to "drive out mispricings." If you want to invest in large-cap stocks, it makes sense to buy and hold an index fund that tracks the S&P 500, accepting that your odds of gaining a long-term edge in this efficient market are poor.

Marks would gain an edge by fishing in less popular ponds, such as the debt of distressed companies—an area that most investors avoid because it seems scary and opaque. He compares investing in inefficient markets to playing poker only against weak and error-prone opponents.

On graduating from Chicago, Marks applied for several jobs, including one at Lehman Brothers. "The one thing I was sure of was that I wanted that Lehman job." To his dismay, the offer never came. So he took a position at First National City Bank, which later became Citibank. He spent the next decade there as a stock analyst and then as the director of research. Many years later, he learned from a campus recruiter that Lehman *had* decided to hire him, but the partner in charge of phoning him had a hangover and failed to deliver the good news. Marks often wonders what would have become of him if he'd received that call and built his career at Lehman. In 2008, the firm went bankrupt, losing all of its partners' money and crashing the global economy.

After ten years in equity research, Marks was informed that Citibank was replacing him as head of the department, so he had to find a new role. He didn't want to waste his time in a well-covered niche such as health-care stocks, where it would be hard to know more than other investors. "So I said, 'I'll do anything except spend the rest of my life choosing between Merck and Eli Lilly.' Nobody is going to get *that* right more than fifty percent of the time."

In the end, his boss told him to run two new funds in a realm where he had no experience: convertible securities and high-yield bonds. This may have been the luckiest break of all. Unwittingly, he was now positioned to ride a multidecade boom in new and exotic forms of credit, far beyond the dull, respectable domain of low-risk bonds with triple-A ratings.

We often assume that skill, not luck, is the most vital ingredient of success. Maybe. But it's hard to beat the good fortune of starting at the ideal time to catch a monster wave. Michael Price, a legendary stock picker, once told me how his career took flight when he was hired at age twenty-four by a veteran value investor named Max Heine, whose lone mutual fund then had assets of just $5 million. "For two hundred dollars a week, I started on January second or third of 1975, which was the low point of the equity market for the century, except for the Great Depression," Price told me. "No one in the US wanted to buy stocks. So I was lucky enough to get with a terrific value investor who'd been in the business for forty years at the low point of the modern bull market, when they were giving away stocks in America. So there was almost no way I could fail." Over the next two decades, assets in the company's mutual funds grew to around $18 billion. In 1996, Price sold the firm for more than $600 million.

It also helps if, like Marks and Price, you stumble into an opportunity that happens to suit your talents and temperament. "Debt fits my personality," says Marks, "because you have a promise of repayment" when the bond matures, plus a promise of annual interest payments. If the debt is repaid, you know in advance what your return will be because it's spelled out contractually.

The key is to avoid getting saddled with bad loans, so the first question to ask is whether the borrower is creditworthy. The second question is whether the borrower's assets are sufficiently valuable, since the creditor will have a senior claim against those assets if the debt isn't repaid. "I think these questions are answerable," says Marks. In an uncertain world where so many questions are *unanswerable*, bonds offer a comforting measure of predictability and control. Bonds are also less risky than stocks, which is reassuring for a natural-born "worrier."

What would have happened if his boss had given him a less appropriate assignment, such as running a venture capital fund? "That would have been terrible for me," says Marks. "In venture capital, you've got to be a dreamer and a futurist."

Still, when he started out in high-yield bonds in 1978, it wasn't exactly a glamorous gig. Known colloquially as junk bonds, they were widely reviled as disreputable assets that posed an unacceptable risk of default. Marks says most investment organizations had a rule against buying them, and Moody's declared that the entire category of B-rated bonds "fails to possess the characteristics of a desirable investment." Ironically, this dogmatic belief that junk bonds *must* be a bad investment was what made them alluring to Marks: "When there's a really powerful bias against an asset class, that's a way to get a bargain. And that's what I did."

What the naysayers failed to grasp is a fundamental truth that enabled Marks, like Sir John Templeton before him, to make a fortune: **Any asset, however ugly, can be worth buying if the price is low enough. Indeed, Marks believes that "buying cheap" is the single most reliable route to investment riches—and that overpaying is the greatest risk. Thus, the essential question to ask about any potential investment should be "Is it cheap?"**

Paradoxically, the prejudice against junk bonds made these supposedly risky assets so cheap that they became relatively unrisky. For Marks, much of the fascination of investing lies in such subtleties. In one of multiple memos that he's written about risk, he muses, "I'm convinced that everything that's important in investing is counterintuitive, and everything that's obvious is wrong."

Marks left Citibank in 1985 to work at a Los Angeles–based investment firm, TCW Group. One of his colleagues there, Bruce Karsh, came up with the idea for a distressed-debt fund, which would invest in the bonds of companies that were either in bankruptcy or veering toward it. Once again, Marks was quick to recognize the strange beauty of a poorly understood market that others found repellent. "If junk bonds are suspect," he says, "what could be more disreputable than investing in the debt of companies that are bankrupt?" He and Karsh forged an enduring partnership. In 1995, they quit TCW and cofounded Oaktree. It would grow into a colossus, built largely on an unseemly foundation of junk and distressed debt.

Without luck, Marks would never have landed in these inefficient, bargain-rich markets. Without intellectual horsepower and independence of mind, he could never have exploited the opportunities he found there. "Look, luck is not enough," he says. "But equally, intelligence is not enough, hard work is not enough, and even perseverance is not necessarily enough. You need some combination of all four. We all know people who were intelligent and worked hard but *didn't* get lucky. It breaks my heart. People come to me all the time looking for jobs. They're fifty years old, they lost their job, and they're no less deserving."

By reminding himself repeatedly of his good fortune, Marks protects himself from what I would call Master of the Universe Syndrome. His humility boosts his immunity against overconfidence, which is a persistent threat to the smartest (or luckiest) investors.

But there's one other great benefit to acknowledging his luck: it makes him happy. "I walk around with this incredible feeling that I'm a lucky guy," Marks confides. "If you're a negative person, you might say, 'Well, I've been lucky in my life and that really sucks because it means that my success is undeserved and may not continue.' But I say, 'Gee, what a great thing to be lucky. And, you know, I really owe it to somebody, whether it's God or chance or whatever.'"

Templeton seemed to have little doubt that his success was divinely ordained. But what about Marks? He's Jewish by birth but was raised as a Christian Scientist and went to church every Sunday as a child. These days, he considers himself Jewish, but not religious. "I'm a big believer in randomness," he says, "and I just believe I've been lucky."


## Know What You Don't Know

Marks maintains a "huge compendium" of useful quotes that he's amassed over decades, and he cites them frequently in explaining his investment credo. One of his favorite insights is from the economist John Kenneth Galbraith, an intellectual hero of his, who said, "We have two classes of forecasters: Those who don't know—and those who don't know they don't know."

The investment world is filled with people who believe (or pretend) that they can see what the future holds. They include smooth-talking "market strategists" from Wall Street brokerage firms who confidently predict the precise percentage rise of the stock market in the coming year, instead of acknowledging that they have no idea whether the market will go up or down; equity analysts who provide quarterly earnings estimates for the companies they cover, thereby feeding the illusion that profits are consistent and predictable, not lumpy and erratic; managers of macro hedge funds who place aggressive wagers on swings in currencies, interest rates, and anything else that moves; TV pundits and financial journalists who claim with a straight face to know what the latest (and mostly inexplicable) market fluctuations portend for investors.

But how much substance lies behind the bluster? Marks often quotes an observation by Amos Tversky, an Israeli psychologist who studied cognitive biases alongside Daniel Kahneman: "It's frightening to think that you might not know something, but more frightening to think that, by and large, the world is run by people who have faith that they know exactly what's going on."

It's worth pausing for a moment to let that unsettling idea lodge forever in your brain.

Occasionally, the forecasters get it right, but Marks regards these successes as proof of the adage that even a blind squirrel sometimes finds an acorn. That said, he acknowledges a small number of legitimate exceptions—investors such as George Soros and Stanley Druckenmiller who have repeatedly defied the odds by betting successfully on their macroeconomic predictions. "There are all these ways that I think you can't be a good investor," such as "forecasting the future" and "making huge bets" on the basis of those forecasts, says Marks. But certain individuals have proved him wrong "because what you mustn't overlook is the human ingredient."

Nonetheless, Marks himself is a staunch member of what he calls the "I Don't Know" school of thought. **As he sees it, the future is influenced by an almost infinite number of factors, and so much randomness is involved that it's impossible to predict future events with any consistency.** Recognizing that we can't forecast the future might sound like a disheartening admission of weakness. In reality, it's a tremendous advantage to acknowledge our limitations and operate within the boundaries of what's possible. Out of weakness comes strength.

How does this awareness of his limitations liberate Marks from useless—or harmful—activities? For a start, he doesn't squander any time attempting to forecast interest rates, inflation, or the pace of economic growth. Following his example, neither should we. If Marks can't forecast such things, I'm fairly confident that I can't do it, either. Unlike many of its rivals, Oaktree doesn't even have an in-house economist, and the firm doesn't invite outside "experts" to read the macroeconomic tea leaves.

Marks also eschews the idea of timing the market, given the impossibility of repeatedly predicting the right moments to jump in and out. He noted in one of his earliest memos that the average annual return for stocks from 1926 to 1987 was 9.44 percent, but "if you had gone to cash and missed the best 50 of those 744 months, you have would have missed all of the return. This tells me that attempts at market timing are a source of risk, not protection."*

Oaktree also tries to avoid what Marks describes as "future-oriented investments," which rules out seductive assets such as tech stocks, purveyors of fashion items, and anything that reeks of faddishness. Early in his career, his department at Citibank was an exuberant cheerleader for one of the most infamous of fads, the Nifty Fifty—a group of high-octane growth stocks such as Xerox Corp., Avon Products, and Polaroid Corp., which reached head-spinning valuations before collapsing in 1973–74.† That experience left him with a permanent distrust for fantasies of never-ending growth projected into a distant, joyous future.

One of our conversations took place in 2017, during a heady period when Marks saw a similar outbreak of investment euphoria over the FANGs—Facebook, Amazon, Netflix, and Alphabet (formerly Google). "People are acting like there's no limit to their success and no price is too high," he warned. "Historically, that's been dangerous in most cases. . . . Trees have never grown to the sky. They may someday. I'm not going to bet on it."

If his habitual skepticism means missing out on an occasional exception to the laws of gravity, that's fine by him. Marks prefers to remain tethered to the ground by focusing on "reasonable propositions" where the price of a specific security is low relative to its intrinsic value. "It's easy to invest in dreams," he says. "The challenge is to discern value in what's tangible today."

Any investor who hopes to achieve enduring success should inter-

---

*More recent studies have highlighted the same risk. A report by Calamos Investments showed that the S&P 500 returned 7.2 percent annually from 1998 through 2017. If you missed the twenty best days in the market over those twenty years, your annual return sagged to just 1.1 percent.

  † Polaroid sported a price/earnings ratio of 94.8 when the Nifty Fifty mania peaked in 1972. By the time the market bottomed in 1974, Polaroid's stock had fallen 91 percent. Avon fell 86 percent, while Xerox dropped 71 percent.

nalize this fundamental idea of buying assets below their value. As we've seen, this is a common thread that unites everyone from Buffett to Pabrai, Templeton to Marks.

**When analyzing any asset, what Marks wants to know, above all, is "the amount of optimism that's in the price."** With the FANGs, "there's a lot of optimism. Too much? Who knows? Will one of them become the world's first perpetual motion machine, the first company that (a) doesn't stumble and (b) is not subject to disruption? I don't know." This combustible mixture of unknowability and rampant optimism is enough to scare him off—not because he knows precisely what will happen but because the probability of disappointment is too high.

In the months after our discussion, the FANGs continued to soar. But Marks is able to watch without regret when others hit the jackpot with what he regards as ill-advised bets. An incorrigible hoarder of wisdom, he has kept an old fortune cookie that says, "The cautious seldom err or write great poetry." He's comfortable with a prosaic approach that reduces the likelihood of catastrophic error: "You have to do what's appropriate for your makeup. That's very important." When I ask about his most damaging investment mistakes, he replies, "I don't remember ever making a big mistake of commission—just omission."

In retrospect, Marks concedes that not owning Amazon was a mistake of omission. "But it was *not* a mistake to take a generally cautious approach" at a time when there was "too much confidence, too little risk aversion, too much capital trying to find a home, and too much use of leverage." Those signs of excess led Oaktree to invest with heightened caution for several years.

Finally, in March 2020, the eleven-year bull market ended when mounting terror over COVID-19 led the S&P 500 to plunge by 33.9 percent in less than a month. Nobody could have predicted that a virus believed to have jumped from bats to humans in Wuhan would catalyze the quickest market meltdown in US history. "But if the market is precarious, you don't *have* to know what the catalyst will be," says Marks. "You only have to know that there's a vulnerability."

As the virus spread, the mood among investors flipped from "I can't imagine what can go wrong" to "I can't imagine what can go right." Their pessimism wasn't unfounded. As Marks told me in 2020, "This is a time when people are afraid of dying, they're afraid of going out of their houses, and they're afraid of a depression." But their readiness to sell assets "at very low prices with urgency" provided him with a long-awaited opportunity. Amid the panic, Oaktree invested "a couple of billion dollars," snapping up high-yield bonds that offered "a vast reward."

The future had seldom seemed more unknowable or less inviting. Yet the investment risks had actually diminished. As Marks saw it, "The odds switched from precarious to propitious" for the simple reason that "things got cheap enough."

The market then confounded expectations once more by staging the fastest rebound since the 1930s. So Marks "recalibrated" again, returning to a defensive posture as surging optimism caused the supply of bargains to dry up. His detached and unemotional behavior reflected perfectly the fundamental investment lesson he had drawn from Buddhism. Remember: **"We have to accommodate to the fact that the environment changes."**

## Find Order within Chaos

When I was in high school, I took an English literature exam that posed an unusually profound question: *The novelist Henry James wrote that life is "all inclusion and confusion," while art is "all discrimination and selection." Discuss.* As a writer, I love this idea that the artist's mission is to find order within the all-inclusive confusion and muddle of life. James likened this search for hidden structure to a suspicious dog's efforts to sniff out "some buried bone."

The investor faces a similar challenge: life is endlessly confusing and complicated. But what if we could detect some underlying patterns within that infinitely complex web? Then, we might have more success in figuring out what the future has in store for us. Marks has a rare gift for identifying cyclical patterns that have occurred again and again in financial markets. Once we understand these patterns, we can avoid being blindsided by them and can even profit from them.

"It's very helpful," Marks tells me, "to view the world as behaving cyclically and oscillating, rather than going in some straight line." He believes that almost everything is cyclical. For example, the economy expands and contracts; consumer spending waxes and wanes; corporate profitability rises and falls; the availability of credit eases and tightens; asset valuations soar and sink. Instead of continuing unabated in one direction, all of these phenomena eventually reverse course. He compares these patterns to the swinging of a pendulum from one extreme to the other.

The financial markets are the perfect laboratory for the study of cyclicality because they're driven by investor psychology, which veers perennially between euphoria and despondency, greed and fear, credulousness and skepticism, complacency and terror. Humans get carried away, so the trend always overshoots in one direction or the other.

But Marks operates on the assumption that the cycle will eventually self-correct and the pendulum will swing back in the opposite direction. **The future may be unpredictable, but this recurring process of boom and bust is *remarkably predictable*. Once we recognize this underlying pattern, we're no longer flying blind.**

The problem is, most investors act as if the latest market trend will continue indefinitely. Behavioral economists use the term *recency bias* to describe the cognitive glitch that leads us to overweight the importance of our recent experiences. Marks notes that the human mind also has a treacherous tendency to suppress painful memories. If this weren't the case, I'm guessing that my wife wouldn't have been willing to endure more than one pregnancy, and I'm not sure how many writers could muster the strength to keep returning to the blank screen. In our financial lives, this life-enhancing ability to forget unpleasant experiences is less helpful because the woes and mishaps of the past tend to provide the most valuable lessons.

One way to combat this costly tendency to forget is through intensive study of market history. **"You can't know the future," says Marks, but "it helps to know the past."**

He pulls from a bookshelf his inscribed copy of Galbraith's book *A Short History of Financial Euphoria* and reads me his single favorite piece of financial writing, which explores the causes of market euphoria: "The first [cause] is the extreme brevity of the financial memory.

In consequence, financial disaster is quickly forgotten. In further consequence, when the same or closely similar circumstances arise again, sometimes in only a few years, they are hailed by a new, often youthful, and always supremely self-confident generation as a brilliantly innovative discovery in the financial and larger economic world. There can be few fields of human endeavor in which history counts for so little as in the world of finance. Past experience, to the extent that it is part of memory at all, is dismissed as the primitive refuge of those who do not have the insight to appreciate the incredible wonders of the present."

Watching the meteoric rise in the price of Bitcoin in 2017, Marks wondered if this was just the latest in a long history of incredible wonders that would prove less than wondrous. Likewise, he could never bring himself to bet that thrilling stocks such as Tesla and Netflix would continue to soar to infinity and beyond: "When things or people are successful, it usually brings in hubris, overexpansion, a belief that we can't miss, which is very dangerous." He always assumes that the pendulum will eventually swing in the opposite direction, just as it did for the "superstocks" that dominated previous bull markets. It's easier to detect such excesses when you've seen a similar movie many times before, he says, "so you should try to get old."

You should also try to read widely. François-Marie Wojcik, the doubt-filled French investor I mentioned earlier, showed me an 1891 novel by Émile Zola, L'Argent (Money), which depicts a speculative frenzy on the Paris stock exchange in the 1860s. Zola provides an oddly familiar account of a disastrous bubble that ends in a banking collapse, even detailing how "popular infatuation" drives a stock beyond its "maximum value" to a point where it will inevitably fall.

For Wojcik, a passionate student of history, Zola's novel provides an early example of these "permanent" patterns of wayward crowd behavior. "Individually we're smart," says Wojcik. "Collectively, we're stupid." As a precaution, he stress tests his opinions constantly in order to reaffirm (or dismantle) his convictions: "I need to say, 'François, are you *sure* about this investment this morning? Let me check again.'" He has a wonderful French phrase to describe his neurotically watchful mindset: *toujours rester en éveil.* "Always stay awake."

Marks, too, never lets down his guard. Most investors grow complacent when times are good. If anything, his vigilance intensifies because he knows that everything changes, that the pendulum will not stop at one end of its arc, that "cycles eventually prevail." As Marks explains, the risk is highest when risk tolerance is most extreme—a paradox that he calls "the perversity of risk."

Marks spends much of his time analyzing the mood and behavior of other financial players, looking to deduce where the markets stand in their cycle. He's particularly proud of a memo he wrote in 2007, a year before the financial crisis, that identified a slew of danger signs. These included idiotically loose lending standards for mortgages in the United States and the UK, a carefree willingness to finance undeserving companies, and a readiness to invest in risky bonds without covenant protections. Writing for emphasis in bold letters, he cautioned that **"times of laxness have always been followed eventually by corrections in which penalties are imposed."**

One way that Marks gauges the current investment environment is by gathering "vignettes" about "stupid deals" that are getting done. For example, in 2017, Argentina issued a hundred-year bond with an annual yield of 9 percent. It was vastly oversubscribed, even though Argentina had defaulted on its debt *eight* times in two hundred years, most recently in 2014. It seemed a fine example of what Samuel Johnson called "the triumph of hope over experience." Sure enough, when I interviewed Marks in 2020, he noted that Argentina had just defaulted for the *ninth* time.

The symptoms of stupidity, overconfidence, greed, and low standards were particularly glaring in the run-up to the global financial crisis. Marks and his partner, Karsh, would compare notes and exclaim, "Look at this piece of crap! A deal like this shouldn't be able to get done—and the fact that it *can* get done means there's something wrong in the market."

Such observations give Marks an impressionistic view of the market, not a numerical one. "All my processes are intuitive, instinctual, gut," he says. "I just try to develop a sense. What's really going on in the world? And what are the important inferences from what you can observe?"

To arrive at a conclusion, he asks himself questions such as *Are investors appropriately skeptical and risk averse or are they ignoring risks and happily paying up? Are valuations reasonable relative to historical standards? Are deal structures fair to investors? Is there too much faith in the future?*

In a sense, says Marks, he's trying to "predict the present"—because, unlike the future, the present is knowable. What *isn't* knowable is when the cycle will turn. "I don't even think about the timing," he says. "In the investment business, it's very hard to do the right thing, and it's impossible to do the right thing at the right time."

The benefit of recognizing where we stand in the cycle is that it enables him to chart an appropriate course based on prevailing conditions, much as he'd drive more carefully on an icy road at night than on a sunny afternoon. "We have to recognize the market for what it is, accept it, and act accordingly," says Marks. For example, when rich returns have made investors less afraid of losing money than missing out on lush gains, that's a signal to lower our expectations and proceed with caution. What does that entail in practical terms? It might involve shifting some assets from stocks to bonds, buying less aggressive stocks, or making sure that you won't need liquidity in the event that it suddenly disappears. "I'm not saying go to cash," says Marks. "All I'm saying is, if the value proposition in the market changes, your portfolio should change."

To my mind, there's profound wisdom in this approach of seeing reality as it is, accepting it, and adapting to it. **As Marks often says, "The environment is what it is." We can't *demand* a more favorable set of market conditions. But we *can* control our response, turning more defensive or aggressive depending on the climate.**

This go-with-the-flow attitude grows directly out of the teachings on impermanence that Marks had studied at college. "You know change is going to occur despite your attempts to resist it," he says. "I think it should make you ease up and say, 'I'm not going to try to control the future. I'm not going to know the future. I'm going to try to prepare for an uncertain future.'" Investors often land themselves in trouble when there's a disconnect between their environment and their behavior— when they ignore or reject reality.

In a 2006 memo, Marks quoted the ancient Taoist philosopher Lao-tzu: "To be strong, you have to be like water: if there are no obstacles, it flows; if there is an obstacle, it stops; if a dam is broken, then it flows further; if a vessel is square, then it has a square form; if a vessel is round, then it has a round form. Because it is so soft and flexible, it is the most necessary and the strongest thing." For an investor, too, it's a strength to be like water, adjusting to whatever we encounter. It sounds so simple, but human nature conspires to make it difficult. Almost all of us are swayed by the mood of the crowd, and we struggle most to act rationally in extreme situations when the stakes are highest.

When markets crashed in 2008, the investment herd panicked, as it always does. Celebration turned to horror as cyclicality reasserted itself with a vengeance. How did Marks respond? He provided a master class in assessing and reacting to his environment with clear-eyed logic— and he led his company to pull off the investment coup of a lifetime.

## "Most of the Time, the End of the World Doesn't Happen"

Months before the credit crisis arrived, Oaktree was already prepared for chaos. In early 2008, when most of the world was bullish and complacent, the firm completed the raising of $10.9 billion in assets to create the biggest distressed debt fund in history.

Of all the cycles Marks has studied, none seems to him more predictable than the credit cycle. As he explains in *The Most Important Thing*, "Prosperity brings expanded lending, which leads to unwise lending, which produces large losses, which makes lenders stop lending, which ends prosperity, and on and on." He'd witnessed years of foolish lending from 2003 to 2007. When the inevitable losses piled up and lending screeched to a halt, he intended to profit from the distress. There's nothing quite like having cash when others are gasping for it.

The credit crisis began with the sick joke of subprime mortgages and then metastasized. Mortgage lending froze. House prices tumbled. Commercial property prices tanked. Bear Stearns collapsed. Improbable disasters became a daily occurrence.

Writing to Oaktree's shareholders on July 31, 2008, Marks reported that he still saw a shortage of beaten-down assets and suggested "going slow" until better bargains came along. Within weeks, the financial system began to disintegrate. In September, the US government seized control of Fannie Mae and Freddie Mac; Merrill Lynch was forced to sell itself to Bank of America; Lehman announced the largest bankruptcy filing in US history; AIG had to be rescued with an $85 billion government loan; even Goldman Sachs was hanging over the abyss.

It was the greatest panic Marks had ever seen. But as the markets plunged and pessimism exploded, he turned bullish for the first time in years. On September 15, the day Lehman died, Oaktree began to amass an immense hoard of busted assets that nobody else would touch. Over the next fifteen weeks, the firm—led by Marks and Karsh—invested an astounding $500 million to $600 million per week.

This was the bet of Marks's career, the making or unmaking of his reputation. So you might imagine that he was certain of what he was doing. But when Lehman went under, it struck him that *nobody* knew what would happen.

On September 19, he wrote a memo to Oaktree's clients that posed an unanswerable question, which somehow *had* to be answered: "Will the financial system melt down or is this merely the greatest down cycle we've ever seen? My answer is simple: we have no choice but to assume that this isn't the end, but just another cycle to take advantage of." With characteristic dry humor, he added, "Most of the time, the end of the world doesn't happen."

When I ask what made him shift his stance from defensive to aggressive in mid-September, Marks replies, "The world went to hell. Assets were being given away. Nobody had any faith that the world would even exist tomorrow, and there were no buyers for any assets. . . . It was a perfect storm of circumstances for disaster."

Marks never thinks of the future as a single predetermined scenario that's bound to occur. He views it instead as a "distribution of different possibilities." His standard approach is to assign probabilities to each of these "alternative futures." But in this case, the uncertainty was so extreme that there was no point even trying to assign probabilities for the array of possible outcomes. He found it more helpful to simplify his decision-making by thinking of the situation in binary terms: "I think you can reduce it to, either the world ends or it doesn't. . . . And if it doesn't end and we didn't buy, then we didn't do our job. That made it awfully straightforward."

But as the markets continued to crash and financial pillars crumbled, few people agreed with him. Some of the best investors he knows were "just shell-shocked. They were saying, 'It's going to melt down.'" Marks knew how close we were to the edge. He could envision outcomes in which dominoes kept falling and we ended up with mass unemployment and societal disaster. "How bad is bad? You can't say what the worst case could be. Anarchy, riots, starvation?"

Then, in mid-October, he had an unforgettable experience that strengthened his contrarian conviction. One of Oaktree's funds made leveraged investments in high-yield debt, borrowing so that it could bet $5 for every dollar it held in equity capital. The fund owned senior loans that were relatively low risk: over the previous thirty years, Oaktree's average default rate for debt of this type had been just 1 percent a year. But prices fell so far below historical norms that Oaktree now faced the threat of a margin call. Marks contacted clients and asked them to put up more equity, which enabled the fund to halve its leverage and avert the margin call. But prices kept plunging, so he had to ask them to contribute *more* money.

It should have been a no-brainer. If they didn't step up, they'd lock in their losses at these catastrophic prices. But Marks met with a pension fund manager who kept asking what would happen to Oaktree's bonds under more and more extreme circumstances. Each time Marks answered with a reassuring fact, he was met with the same panic-stricken response: "What if it's worse than that?"

Marks raced back to his office and dashed off a memo titled "The Limits of Negativism." As he contemplated that meeting, he had a revelation. For decades, he'd warned investors to maintain their skepticism when optimism was so abundant that no story was too good to be true. But pessimism had reached such dire levels that investors now acted as if "no story was too bad to be true." For a rational skeptic, the point is not to be permanently pessimistic; it's to question what "everyone" believes to be true, whether it's too positive *or* too negative. Explaining his epiphany, he wrote: **"Skepticism calls for pessimism when optimism is excessive. But it also calls for optimism when pessimism is excessive."**

Thus Howard Marks, the eternal worrier, became virtually the only optimist on Wall Street.

Going against the crowd in the midst of "total panic" when "everyone's convinced that things can only get worse" requires an uncommon level of intellectual clarity and imperturbability. But when I ask if he found the crisis painful, Marks replies flatly, "I don't remember it being difficult." Was he always unemotional? "Yeah." Knowing that he's been married twice, I wonder if this aspect of his character drives his wife crazy. "Yeah, especially my first wife," he says. "I think I've done a better job with it more recently."

It also helped that he and his Oaktree partner, Karsh, talked constantly, supporting each other and making sure they were moving at the right speed. While Marks provided guidance on the big picture, Karsh and his team did the nitty-gritty work of valuing assets. Two or three years earlier, private equity firms had used massive leverage to buy high-quality businesses at exorbitant valuations. Oaktree now bought the senior debt of these companies for a pittance. In some cases, Oaktree would break even if these businesses proved to be worth *one-fifth* of what the buyout firms had paid. "I always look at things in terms of 'Where's the mistake? Is the mistake in buying or not buying?'" says Marks. "It didn't take an enormous leap of faith to conclude that these were good buys."

The most spectacular score came from Oaktree's $100 million investment in Pierre Foods, which it bought out of bankruptcy in 2008. Reborn as AdvancePierre Foods, it became a nationwide leader in packaged sandwiches and was acquired by Tyson Foods in 2017. Oaktree made about $2.2 billion over eight years—a twenty-three-fold gain on its invested capital.

In all, Oaktree wagered about $10 billion in the depths of the crisis. Marks estimates the gains from those investments at $9 billion—the biggest windfall in the company's history. As its largest shareholders, nobody profited more than Marks and Karsh. But there was also the sheer pleasure of outthinking others and being right. As Marks says, "We have bet and we have won."

"The Question Is, Do You Push the Limits?"

In our conversations and in his writings, Marks returns repeatedly to a handful of themes that have obsessed him for decades. As I see it, five critical ideas come up again and again:

**The importance of admitting that we can't predict or control the future.**

**The benefits of studying the patterns of the past and using them as a rough guide to what could happen next.**

**The inevitability that cycles will reverse and reckless excess will be punished.**

**The possibility of turning cyclicality to our advantage by behaving countercyclically.**

**The need for humility, skepticism, and prudence in order to achieve long-term financial success in an uncertain world.**

Life is so complex that it's useful to internalize a small core of simple and robust insights that can lend order to our diffuse thinking. All five of these ideas have tremendous utility for any investor looking to navigate the unknowable future.

But in synthesizing what I've learned from Marks, I can't help thinking that one lesson in particular has such far-reaching implications that I need to make it central to my view of the world. For me, that tenet is the one he learned at college more than fifty years ago: everything is impermanent.

The financial markets provide us with many examples of this Buddhist teaching. The Asian "economic miracle" was followed by the Asian financial crisis of 1997; the dot-com mania of the late 1990s was followed by the crash of 2000; the housing bubble was followed by the credit crisis, which was followed by an epic bull market that began in 2009; then, in 2020, the market dropped 34 percent in twenty-three days before surging almost 40 percent in the weeks that followed.

If the Buddha had been a hedge fund manager, he might have pointed out that change itself is not ultimately the problem. Rather, we doom ourselves to suffer—both in investing and life—when we expect or yearn for things to stay the same. The real problem is this habit of clinging to or relying on what cannot last.

**As Buddhism teaches, we need to acknowledge the transience of all worldly phenomena so we won't be surprised or dismayed when change occurs.** Shunryu Suzuki said, "If we cannot accept this teaching that everything changes, we cannot be in composure."

Financially, the inevitability of change has important implications. For a start, we need to acknowledge that the current economic climate and market trajectory are temporary phenomena, just like everything else. So we should avoid positioning ourselves in such a way that we're dependent on their continuing along the same path. As Marks notes, investors repeatedly make the mistake of overestimating the longevity of the market's upswings and downturns; they forget that nothing lasts forever. Likewise, many home buyers ruined themselves during the financial crisis by taking on too much debt in the belief that house prices would continue to rise from here to eternity. The moral? **Never bet the farm against the inexorable forces of change.**

The recognition that all things are transient can fill you with a destabilizing sense that your life (and everything you cherish) is hopelessly precarious. It's tempting to live in denial. But it's prudent to acknowledge that we're skating on thin ice and can never be sure when it might crack. This awareness doesn't mean that we should hide at home forever—or that we should sit permanently on cash, refusing to take any risk. **Both in markets and life, the goal isn't to embrace risk *or* eschew it, but to bear it intelligently while never forgetting the possibility of an unpleasant outcome.**

It's not an easy balance to achieve. In the darkest days of 2008, Marks had to keep reminding himself to resist his tendency to worry: "If I overdo it, then I'm not doing my job for my clients because they didn't hire me to be a chicken. They want me to be a safe investor, but not a chicken." When taken too far, he adds, "risk avoidance" condemns you to "return avoidance."

Fortunately, we're not powerless in the face of change. There are many ways to make ourselves less vulnerable. Instead of trying to predict the unpredictable, Marks suggests that we focus on building "unfragile portfolios and unfragile lives" that are unlikely to collapse even in dire conditions.* What does that mean for regular investors? "Avoid a lot of debt and leverage," and don't let your dreams of a "bonanza" lead you to "expose yourself to the possibility of a catastrophe," he says. **"Not trying to maximize is an important component in preparing for what life may throw at you, and that's true in investing and living. So the question is, do you push the limits?"**

That question applies not just to investing, but to spending. "Financial independence doesn't come from making or having a lot of money," says Marks. "You know what it comes from? Spending less than you make. Living within your means. It's important to know that your antifragility comes from the extent to which you are not at the limit."

The trouble is, we tend to forget this when we're thriving—or when we're watching others thrive while we lag behind. So we edge closer to our limits and eventually stray beyond them.

Marks adds that we also need to recognize our financial and psychological fragility. "You *better* be scared—scared in the sense of acknowledging the possibility of bad things happening and being realistic about your own ability to withstand bad outcomes." He warns against "macho" claims that we won't mind if the stock market plunges: "What normally happens when it goes down a third is that people panic and they sell and they turn that downward fluctuation into a permanent loss, which is the worst thing you can do."

It's vital, then, to be honest with ourselves about how much risk we can handle: "If you take on too much, it will overwhelm your emotional resilience and you will be forced to do the wrong thing even if nothing else transpires against you—like a margin call or a need to buy bread."

There's a Buddhist quality to this habit of seeing reality as it is, without aversion or self-delusion. One of the greatest texts of Buddhism is the *Satipatthana Sutta*, the Buddha's discourse on mindfulness as a means to nirvana. He explains that the path to awakening requires us to become "ever mindful" of whatever presents itself to us—to observe with detachment as all things (including our thoughts, feelings, and

---

* In speaking about fragility, Marks is borrowing terminology used by Nassim Nicholas Taleb in *Antifragile: Things That Gain from Disorder*. But another of Taleb's books had a more profound influence on him: *Fooled by Randomness: The Hidden Role of Chance in Life and in the Markets*.

sensory perceptions) arise and pass away. Freedom comes from "clearly knowing" that everything is ephemeral and training ourselves to stop grasping at what is inherently unstable. The Buddha repeats the same refrain thirteen times: "And one abides independent, not clinging to anything in the world."

This idea of nonattachment can sound cold or unnatural. But a recognition of impermanence has its benefits. For one, it's not just the good stuff (our youthful beauty, our loved ones, economic booms, and bull markets) that will fade away. The bad stuff (emotional and physical pain, lousy political leaders, recessions, and pandemics) will also pass. Given that everything changes, we shouldn't get too carried away when times are good or too despondent when they're bad.

A sense of impermanence can also inspire us to value and nurture our relationships (since we don't know how long any of us will be here) and to live more fully now. In his book *The Science of Enlightenment*, Shinzen Young writes of learning to experience the world with "radical fullness" by focusing on every moment with "extraordinary concentration, sensory clarity, and equanimity. . . . You can dramatically extend life—not by multiplying the number of your years, but by expanding the fullness of your moments."*

Now in his seventies, Marks has a keen sense of his own impermanence. His father lived to 101, so he may have inherited a genetic edge. Even so, he knows that the odds are against his being immortal. At this stage of life, he reflects increasingly on whether he's conducted himself admirably—not least, in the way he's treated colleagues and clients. "What you accomplish in life is not the only important thing. It's also important *how* you do it," he says. "Maybe I'm insecure. But to me, it's very important that I'm acknowledged to have led a good life." He delights in Oaktree's returns, but he's also proud of its reputation for integrity and of his relationship with his cofounder, Karsh. Marks says they've never argued in three decades of working together.

---

* Shinzen Young describes equanimity as a "detached, gentle matter-of-factness within which pleasure and pain are allowed to expand and contract without self-interference." It's not dissimilar to the way Marks views the markets, recognizing and accepting that "it is what it is" and, in that nonreactive state, having the clarity to respond logically and without emotion.

What does he hope to achieve in the years to come? "I don't have any grand ambitions," says Marks. "My life is terrific. I want to be a good husband, father, grandfather. And I want to keep seeing things in the investment world that other people don't see and describing them clearly for my clients."

He plans to work indefinitely because he finds it intellectually rewarding, not because he has an "unquenchable" thirst for money or status. He recalls his Japanese studies professor explaining a Buddhist teaching that "you have to break the chain of getting and wanting"—an aimless cycle of craving that leads inevitably to suffering. Perhaps. But Marks acknowledges that amassing wealth has given him freedom and security and made him "less afraid." So far, at least, becoming a billionaire doesn't seem to have caused him a whole lot of suffering.

Looking back on his "lucky life," he has the humility to recognize that his talent alone was never enough—that so much had to break in his favor for him to achieve this level of success. That knowledge helps to protect him from the pride that goeth before a fall. For now, Marks is about as close as anyone gets to being a Master of the Universe. But if there's one thing he knows for sure, it's that change will come—and all of us will need to adapt.

CHAPTER FOUR

# The Resilient Investor

## How to build enduring wealth and
## survive the wildness that lies in wait

———————————

The real trouble with this world of ours is not that it is an
unreasonable world, nor even that it is a reasonable one.
The commonest kind of trouble is that it is nearly reasonable, but not quite. Life is not an illogicality; yet it is a trap
for logicians. It looks just a little more mathematical and
regular than it is: its exactitude is obvious, but its inexacti-
tude is hidden; its wildness lies in wait.

—G. K. Chesterton

As a young investment analyst at Société Générale in Paris in the 1960s,
Jean-Marie Eveillard had no idea what he was doing. His bosses indoc-
trinated him in the conventional stock-picking strategy of their era.
"Basically, their game was to trade actively the big stocks in the index,
and that was all," he says. Like everyone around him, he obediently
followed this respectable path to mediocre returns. As he would later
observe, "It's much warmer inside the herd."

Eveillard began to stray in 1968 after the bank posted him to New
York. That summer, he was biking in Central Park with two French students from Columbia Business School. They told him about Benjamin
Graham, who'd developed the discipline of value investing while teaching there in the 1920s.* Eveillard read his books *Security Analysis* and

———

* Graham's relationship with Columbia made it the intellectual hub of value investing—a status that it retains to this day. He won a scholarship to Columbia and proved

*The Intelligent Investor* and instantly saw the light. He compares his discovery of Graham to the religious conversion of Paul Claudel, a French writer who found God spontaneously while standing in Notre-Dame cathedral in 1886: "I was illuminated by Ben Graham's approach. I had found what I was looking for." Eveillard tried to convince his bosses to let him invest according to his new beliefs, but they hadn't heard of Graham and couldn't see the attraction of his alien philosophy. So Eveillard kept playing the game the old way. In all, he says, "I wasted fifteen years of my professional life."

Finally, at the age of thirty-nine, he was set free. The bank made him the manager of SoGen International, a mutual fund so small and obscure that nobody cared what he did with it. When Eveillard took charge in 1979, the fund had only $15 million in assets. Based in Manhattan, he worked alone for years, relishing the lack of interference from his corporate overlords back in France.

His new investment strategy was built on one all-important insight that he drew from *The Intelligent Investor*. **"Because the future is uncertain, you want to minimize your risk,"** says Eveillard. Like most great truths, it is so simple that it's easy to miss its significance, to gloss over its surface without internalizing its far-reaching implications.

It was a lesson that Graham had learned from harrowing experience. Born in London in 1894, he grew up in a prosperous household in New York, supported by a family business that imported porcelain from Europe. But Graham's father died at thirty-five, leaving his widow to raise three sons on her own. The business collapsed, so she converted their home into a boardinghouse, which also failed. To make matters worse, she borrowed money to buy shares and was cleaned out in the Panic of 1907, when the stock market lost nearly half its value within weeks. Graham, who had grown up with a cook, a maid, and a governess, later recalled the "shame at our disgrace" when the family was forced to sell its possessions in a public auction.

---

so polymathically brilliant that, before graduating in 1914, he was invited to teach in three different departments: English, mathematics, and philosophy. He became an investor instead. But he returned to Columbia as an evening lecturer in 1928 and taught there for the next twenty-eight years, grooming a generation of investors that included Warren Buffett, Irving Kahn, and Bill Ruane.

These childhood memories alone could have explained Graham's fixation on how to achieve resilience in the face of uncertainty. But in the years that followed, he confronted a series of calamities: World War I, the Crash of 1929, and the Great Depression. After making a fortune as a money manager in the 1920s bull market, he lost 70 percent from 1929 to 1932. These experiences led him to a disturbing realization: **"The future of security prices is never predictable."**

Forged in fire, Graham constructed an investment credo that prioritized survival. He summed it up in the final chapter of *The Intelligent Investor*, which was written in the wake of the Holocaust: "In the old legend the wise men finally boiled down the history of mortal affairs into the single phrase, 'This too will pass.' Confronted with a like challenge to distill the secret of sound investment into three words, we venture the motto, MARGIN OF SAFETY."*

Graham explained that a margin of safety could be attained by buying stocks and bonds at a "favorable" discount to their "appraised value." That gap between price and value would provide a cushion to absorb the impact of an investor's own "miscalculations," "worse than average luck," and "the unknown conditions of the future." It was a worldly-wise strategy, built on a recognition of human frailty and the hazards of history. *We make mistakes. We have bad luck. The future is unknown.*

Graham concluded that buying undervalued assets would give investors "a better chance for profit than for loss," but he warned that this was *still* no guarantee that a specific investment wouldn't go horribly wrong. The solution? Diversification.

Eveillard, like Graham, was a child of uncertainty. He was born in the French city of Poitiers in 1940, just months before Germany invaded the country. His wary, fretful, slightly mournful view of life was influenced by sermons he heard as a child while visiting his grandmother's Roman Catholic church in the French countryside. Speaking to a community that had suffered the recent trauma of defeat, blood-

---

* Graham, who was originally named Benjamin Grossbaum, came from a family of Orthodox Jewish immigrants from Poland. As someone who shares that background, I think it's not unreasonable to draw a connection between his family history (which was fraught with the persecution and danger faced by Eastern European Jews) and his investment philosophy (which centered on mitigating risk and seeking safety).

shed, and bombing, the priest would say, "Don't count on being happy on this earth. This is a valley of tears. You can only be happy in the afterworld."* Thus Eveillard was primed to accept Graham's warnings that investors must expect and withstand adversity.

In Graham's heyday, there were so many distressed assets in the United States that he didn't need to look for bargains overseas. But Eveillard cloned and then modified the strategy for another era, scavenging globally for stocks that cost at least 30–40 percent less than his estimate of their value. He based his appraisals on a conservative view of what a reasonable acquirer might pay in cash for the entire company. To borrow Graham's phrase, this was an approach based "not on optimism, but on arithmetic." For good measure, Eveillard routinely owned more than one hundred stocks. Buffett and Munger had the stomach to hold a more concentrated portfolio, but Eveillard couldn't bring himself to do it. "I'm too skeptical about my own skills," he admits, "and too worried that it could just blow up."

His strategy worked, and he earned a reputation for high returns with low risks. *Business Week* and Morningstar feted him. Financial planners and brokers flooded him with their clients' assets. He hired a team of analysts and launched two new funds. Still, he never lost his sense of trepidation. As his funds grew, Eveillard felt the burden of managing money for hundreds of thousands of investors saving for retirement or their children's education. "It's money they cannot afford to lose," he says. "If I screwed up, I was very aware of the fact that I was making daily life more difficult for the investors in my funds. . . . That pushed me to try to be cautious."

Eveillard's rigorous focus on valuation kept his shareholders safe. For example, in the late 1980s, investors were so infatuated with Japan that asset prices ceased to reflect economic reality. By 1989, Japan accounted for 45 percent of the world's stock market capitalization— more than the United States and the UK combined—and most of the world's largest companies were Japanese. Eveillard exited Japan entirely

---

* When I ask Eveillard if he remains a practicing Catholic, he replies, "I do believe. But the Church annoys me." He's a nontribal outsider not only as an investor but even in his religious life.

in 1988, unable to find a single Japanese stock that met his valuation requirements. The bubble burst in late 1989, and Japanese stocks fell into a decades-long death spiral. At its low in 2009, the Nikkei 225 stock index had lost more than 80 percent in twenty years. During one of our conversations, Eveillard marveled that, in 2020, the Japanese market was "*still* 30 percent below where it was thirty years ago."

In a preface to *The Intelligent Investor*, Buffett wrote, "To invest successfully over a lifetime does not require a stratospheric IQ, unusual business insights, or inside information. What's needed is a sound intellectual framework for making decisions and the ability to keep emotions from corroding that framework." How did Eveillard measure up? His intellectual framework, with its time-tested emphasis on the margin of safety, was sound. He also had the emotional strength to distance himself from the crowd, resisting any temptation to relax his standards when others were gunning the engine. For a while, he enjoyed one other critical advantage: he had the institutional latitude to go his own way, partly because he worked nearly four thousand miles from his firm's headquarters and partly because his returns gave nobody cause to complain or meddle.

These were prerequisites for outperformance. But as Eveillard would soon discover, there are forces that conspire almost irresistibly to produce fragility and humdrum returns. We need to understand those forces because they are remorseless enemies of resilience. In this chapter, we'll see what it took for Eveillard and his brilliant successor, Matthew McLennan, to navigate that minefield, producing an outstanding record over more than four decades. Their thinking offers many lessons on how to build—and *keep*—a fortune over your investment lifetime.

### "To Lag Is to Suffer"

Eveillard's troubles began in 1997. By then, he had an eighteen-year record of avoiding mishap and beating the market. In his worst year—1990—SoGen International had lost a paltry 1.3 percent. Along the way, his assets under management had soared to $6 billion. Unexpectedly, the threat to his financial fortress came not from a market meltdown but a frenzy of speculation.

From January 1997 to March 2000, the tech-heavy Nasdaq index rose 290 percent, fueled by a mania for internet and telecom stocks. To appreciate the thrilling absurdity of those times, consider the rise and fall of theGlobe.com: the social media site went public in 1998, saw its stock price surge 606 percent on its first day of trading, and was delisted by Nasdaq in 2001 when the stock was languishing below $1. Or consider the fate of eToys: the online retailer went public in May 1999 at $20 per share, peaked at $84 that October, and went bankrupt eighteen months later. Or consider Cisco Systems: the networking firm's market value rocketed from $100 billion to $500 billion in less than five hundred days, making it (briefly) the world's biggest company; then the bubble burst and the stock plunged 86 percent.

Eveillard, a man who fretted for a living, refused to board the roller coaster. Analytically, it wasn't a hard decision, given the ludicrous valuations and the notorious difficulty of predicting which tech companies will endure and which will flame out. But he took the extreme position of owning no tech at all. It requires real bravery for fund managers to diverge radically from the market indexes because, if they're wrong, they can jeopardize their entire career. That's particularly unappealing if you're married, have kids, or just fancy the idea of preserving your luxurious lifestyle. An easier option is to "underweight" certain stocks or sectors, instead of avoiding them entirely. The specter of "career risk" helps to explain why many funds "hug" the index, condemning themselves to unexceptional returns but sparing themselves exceptional grief.

Eveillard, who has a streak of indomitable obstinacy, did not take the easy option. As a result, he lagged the market by miles for three long years while tech stocks went nuts. In 1998 alone, the Nasdaq gained 39.6 percent and the MSCI World Index gained 24.3 percent, while SoGen International *lost* 0.3 percent. The following year, SoGen International roared back, returning 19.6 percent. Pretty good, right? Wrong. That year, the Nasdaq shot up 85.6 percent. Eveillard's relative returns looked pitiful in an era when any buffoon could hit the jackpot, and his shareholders weren't inclined to thank him for acting responsibly. On the contrary, his prudence started to seem like slow professional suicide.

"To lag is to suffer," says Eveillard. "It becomes psychologically pain-ful, but also financially painful. . . . After one year, your shareholders are upset. After two years, they're furious. After three years, they're gone." Indeed, SoGen lost 70 percent of its shareholders in less than three years, and its assets under management dwindled from more than $6 billion to barely $2 billion.

Understandably, his bosses were not amused. His employer, Société Générale, seldom fired anyone. "If they thought you couldn't do the job anymore, they put you in a small office with nothing to do." Still, in 1999, he began to think the unthinkable: "Maybe they'll kick me out."

The mutual fund business can be marvelously profitable. It's not cap-ital intensive, and it boasts unusually high operating margins. The late Marty Whitman, a renowned investor with a gift for tactless truth-telling, once told me that fund managers are competitive in every way—except when it comes to lowering their fees. The executives who run mutual fund companies have strong incentives to keep gathering assets. They're not fools or villains. They're pragmatic businesspeople who focus heavily on sales and marketing. An outperformer such as Eveillard was a prized asset in good times. But in bad times, it was easy to cast him as a zealot whose extremism placed everyone's bonuses at risk. If credulous investors wanted to buy dot-com stocks, why not give them what they wanted? Why not feed the ducks while they were quacking?

The pressure was palpable. Eveillard heard that one senior execu-tive had grumbled behind his back that he was "half-senile." Eveillard, who was only fifty-nine, reported the incident to his wife, Elizabeth, a battle-hardened investment banker. "My wife did not even lift her eyes from the magazine she was reading. She said, 'Only half?'" Another executive analyzed the alarming rate of redemptions from SoGen's funds and claimed to have "figured out the exact date, which was not very distant, at which we would be left with zero to manage."

Eveillard felt under siege. "Even the board of the fund went against me. They said, 'How come you don't see what everybody else is seeing, which is that you have to be in the tech, media, and telecom stocks?" He tried to explain that his investment style was ill-suited to fast-changing sectors filled with racy companies trading at irrational valuations. But he sounded out of touch—a relic who didn't understand the wondrous innovations of the New Economy.

He'd always expected to suffer bouts of underperformance. In the past, he'd trailed the market for several months at a time. *But three years?* "It had gone on for so long that there were days when I thought I was an idiot," he confesses. "You do, in truth, start doubting yourself. . . . Everybody seems to see the light. How come *I* don't see it?"

Was it possible that the markets had changed beyond recognition and his investing style was no longer applicable? Julian Robertson, a hedge fund legend who'd generated stunning returns for two decades by betting on undervalued stocks and shorting overvalued stocks, closed his funds in early 2000. "In a rational environment, this strategy functions well," Robertson grumbled. "But in an irrational market, where earnings and price considerations take a back seat to mouse clicks and momentum, such logic, as we have learned, does not count for much."

Still, Eveillard struggled on, refusing to abandon logic or retire. His mother once told him that he'd found the only occupation in which he could be reasonably successful: "I think she may be right. On top of that, I only know how to do value investing. . . . I could not operate differently."

In the end, Société Générale found a tactful way to get rid of him. It sold his fund group to a small investment bank, Arnhold & S. Bleichroeder. Eveillard, who owned a 19.9 percent stake in the fund business, had worked at the same firm since 1962. Now, after three years of dismal underperformance, he was traded to another team like some washed-out athlete.

The sale was almost comically mistimed. It was announced in October 1999 and the deal closed in January 2000. Two months later, on March 10, the tech bubble burst.

Eveillard's portfolio of bargain-priced stocks performed superbly as rationality reasserted itself. His flagship investment vehicle, now renamed the First Eagle Global Fund, trounced the Nasdaq by 49 percentage points in 2000, 31 percentage points in 2001, and 42 percentage points in 2002. Morningstar anointed Eveillard the International Stock Fund Manager of the Year for 2001. In 2003, he received Morningstar's inaugural Lifetime Achievement Award in recognition of his "outstanding long-term performance," alignment with his shareholders' best interests, and "courage to differ from consensus."

Investors are a fickle bunch. One year, Eveillard was a fossil and a fool. The next, he was a sage, revered by all. So much money poured in that his assets under management eventually rose to about $100 billion. His former bosses had sold the business at the bottom for "five percent of its worth today," he says, with a mixture of resentment, sorrow, and satisfaction. "Somebody told me that shortly afterwards they were eating their balls."

Graham, who had also suffered on the road to glory, wouldn't have been surprised by the tale of Eveillard's rise and fall and rise. Graham opened *Security Analysis* with a quote from the Roman poet Horace: "Many shall be restored that now are fallen and many shall fall that now are in honor."

## The Unkindness of Strangers

Eveillard had done everything right, yet his career was almost destroyed. So what's the lesson of his story? Above all, it highlights just how difficult it is to build sustainable investment success over decades, given the multitude of destabilizing forces and unpredictable hazards we encounter along the way.

Unlike many of his peers, Eveillard had some powerful advantages. He had the good fortune to stumble upon Graham's value-oriented principles, which gave him an analytical edge. He had the discipline to adhere to those principles through thick and thin, resisting the allure of overvalued stocks. And he had the emotional fortitude to endure his colleagues' contempt and override his own doubts. In short, he belonged to a small minority that's equipped intellectually and temperamentally to outperform over the long haul. Even so, these formidable strengths weren't sufficient to make him a truly resilient investor. How come?

The trouble was, Eveillard operated from a position that was *structurally* unsound. First, he was at the mercy of his investors, since they could redeem their shares daily, forcing him to sell stocks when they were cheapest, instead of buying them. Their wayward emotions and erratic judgment posed an external threat over which he had no control. Second, he was acutely vulnerable to pressures from inside his own firm, including his colleagues' concern that he threatened their financial interests by refusing to invest in tech. Even worse, he served at the pleasure (or displeasure) of his corporate masters. He wasn't in charge.

It's hard enough to make rational decisions in a crazy market that has renounced traditional valuation measures. It's infinitely harder if you're also barraged by external pressures from shareholders jumping ship, colleagues with their own commercial agenda, and bosses who lose faith in you at precisely the wrong moment. As you can see from Eveillard's travails, fragility comes in many forms. So it follows that *financial resilience must also be multifaceted.*

It's revealing that Buffett and Munger have structured Berkshire Hathaway to be resilient in every way. For example, they've vowed never to keep less than $20 billion in cash, so they'll never be caught out by a shortage of liquidity. When COVID-19 caused a market crash in 2020, Berkshire had $137 billion in cash, making it indestructible even in the face of unprecedented uncertainty. Buffett and Munger also buy high-quality businesses that should prosper for decades, even in times of turmoil or inflation. And their insurance operations are vastly overcapitalized, so they can withstand catastrophes that would bury weaker firms.

Berkshire also has the structural advantage of being a public company, not a fund, so they're investing permanent capital that can never be yanked away by panicked shareholders. "If you run a mutual fund, you're always worried that the shareholder will abandon you if you're temporarily not doing well," says Eveillard. "To some extent, what Buffett has with Berkshire Hathaway is a closed-end fund. He *can't* suffer from redemptions."

During the financial crisis, Berkshire's stock took a hit, plunging 50.7 percent from September 2008 to March 2009. But this short-term market volatility had zero impact on the long-term value of the business. On the contrary, Buffett used the crisis to boost Berkshire's value by injecting billions of dollars on preferential terms into wounded giants such as Goldman Sachs, General Electric, and Bank of America. Guy Spier, whose hedge fund has owned Berkshire for more than twenty years, says Buffett has systematically set himself up to be "the last man standing."

In *A Streetcar Named Desire*, Blanche DuBois says, "I have always depended on the kindness of strangers." It's a sweet sentiment, except that she's gone mad and is speaking to a doctor who has come to lock her away. In his 2018 letter to shareholders, Buffett added his own twist, pledging, "Charlie and I *never* will operate Berkshire in a manner that depends on the kindness of strangers—or even that of friends who may be facing liquidity problems of their own. . . . We have intentionally constructed Berkshire in a manner that will allow it to comfortably withstand economic discontinuities, including such extremes as extended market closures."

If our goal is financial resilience, it's probably best to clone Buffett, not Blanche. So we need to make sure that we, too, will get along just fine without the kindness of strangers. As a fund manager, Eveillard couldn't escape from his dependence on others. But individual investors have one significant advantage: they're not answerable to trigger-happy shareholders or any other disgruntled critics (except, perhaps, their own family members).

How, then, can individuals reduce their vulnerability and bolster their resilience? **Following Buffett's lead, we should always keep enough cash in reserve so we'll never be forced to sell stocks (or any other beleaguered asset) in a downturn. We should never borrow to excess because, as Eveillard warns, debt erodes our "staying power." Like him, we should avoid the temptation to speculate on hot stocks with supposedly glorious growth prospects but no margin of safety. And we should bypass businesses with weak balance sheets or a looming need for external funding, which is liable to disappear in times of distress.**

None of this is brain surgery. But it requires us to take seriously that oft-forgotten commandment *Thou shalt not depend on the kindness of strangers*.

## The Long Game

It also helps if we're not in an excessive rush to get rich. In 2014, I asked Irving Kahn to share the most important lessons of his extraordinarily long career. By then, he was 108 years old and had worked on Wall Street since 1928. Nobody in the investment business had survived more turmoil, so I regarded him as the living embodiment of financial (and biological) resilience.* Kahn was too frail to see me in person. But his grandson Andrew—an analyst at the family's investment firm, Kahn Brothers—read him my questions and wrote down his answers. It turned out that this was Kahn's final interview as he died just three months later at the age of 109.

Kahn became Graham's teaching assistant at Columbia in the 1920s, and they remained friends for decades. I wanted to know what he'd learned from Graham that had helped him to prosper during his eighty-six years in the financial markets. Kahn's answer: "Investing is about *preserving* more than anything. That must be your first thought, not looking for large gains. If you achieve only reasonable returns and suffer minimal losses, you will become a wealthy man and will surpass any gambler friends you may have. This is also a good way to cure your sleeping problems."

As Kahn put it, the secret of investing could be expressed in one word: "safety." And the key to making intelligent investment decisions was always to begin by asking, "How much can I lose?" He explained, "Considering the downside is the single most important thing an investor must do. This task must be dealt with before any consideration can be made for gains. The problem is that people nowadays think they're pretty smart because they can do something quite rapidly. You can make the horse gallop. But are you on the right path? Can you see where you're going?"

---

* Biologically, Kahn was a magnificent specimen. He seldom exercised, had an insatiable appetite for red meat, and smoked until he was about 50—yet still made it to the age of 109. It makes you wonder how long he would have lived if he'd taken better care of himself. His son Thomas says Irving's inquisitive mind helped to keep him young. But he also had spectacular genes: he was one of four siblings who lived beyond 100.

Kahn's defensive mindset reminds me of the warning that's pounded into the heads of medical students: "First, do no harm." For investors, that instruction requires a minor tweak: *First, do no self-harm.* When we try to explain investment success, we're naturally drawn to racier aspects of the game. It's more fun to tell tales of bold bets that earned billions than to drone on about all of the accidents that never happened. But accident avoidance matters because it's so hard to recover from disaster. Consider the brutal mathematics of financial loss: if you lose 50 percent on an ill-considered bet, you'll need a 100 percent gain just to get back to where you started.

What made Eveillard an enduring giant of global investing was that he avoided losses by repeatedly escaping the deadliest dangers in his path. It was a triumph of omission, not commission. Looking back on his career at SoGen and First Eagle, he says, "To the extent that we've been successful over the decades, it's due mostly to what we did *not* own. We owned no Japanese stocks in the late eighties. We owned no tech in the late nineties. And we didn't own any financial stocks to speak of between 2000 and 2008." His ability to sidestep those three disasters over three decades made all the difference between failure and success.

### Everything Fades

Eveillard retired as a fund manager in 2008 and moved to a senior adviser role at First Eagle. He passed the torch to Matthew McLennan, a thirty-nine-year-old Australian, who started in the job one week before Lehman Brothers went up in smoke and the global financial system began to fall apart. Today, with more than $100 billion in assets and millions of shareholders in his funds, McLennan is one of the world's most influential investors—and one of the most thoughtful.

At first glance, he could hardly be more different from his predecessor. Eveillard, with his hangdog facial expression and somber worldview, reminds me of Eeyore in *Winnie-the-Pooh*—a melancholy figure who lives in a spot that's marked on the map as "Eeyore's Gloomy Place: Rather Boggy and Sad." McLennan, almost three decades younger, exudes bright-eyed enthusiasm and easygoing charm. Almost every sentence he utters is accompanied by a smile.

But as investors, Eveillard and McLennan have much in common. When they first met in 2008, they shared war stories about the tech bubble. McLennan, who had been running a value-oriented global investment portfolio at Goldman Sachs, recounted his own experience of refusing to buy into a mania that offered no margin of safety. Eveillard approved. "He took comfort in the fact that I was willing to be 'short' social acceptance and stand apart from the herd," says McLennan. "It's lonely sometimes if you're not part of the fad of the moment. . . . And so we struck a bond."

McLennan's unconventional background helps to explain his readiness to take the road less traveled. Born in 1969, he spent the first six years of his life in Papua New Guinea, where his father (a surveyor) and mother (a physiotherapist and artist) moved in search of adventure. When I joke that he is Papua's most famous investor, he replies, "Sample size of one." His parents, whom he describes as "freethinkers" who "felt no need for conventional signs of accumulation," later bought an idyllic piece of land in Australia that was bordered on one side by rain forest. They couldn't obtain permits to connect to the electricity grid, so McLennan spent much of his youth without creature comforts, detached from the "normal, literal buzz of existence."

The house was full of books, but it didn't have hot running water. So he showered under a tree, using water from a black plastic bag that had been left to warm up in the afternoon sun. They had no refrigerator. Their heating came from a cast-iron stove, which routinely woke him up by smoking him out of the house. "We didn't have a television for a long time," he recalls. "But then we got one that my father was able to hook up to the car battery. That didn't last very long because, relatively soon after getting it, he reversed out of the driveway with the television still attached to the car battery, dragging it through the front door."

McLennan spent much of his time reading, often by the light of a gas lamp. He also hung out with his grandfather, "a real thinker" who bought stocks, collected wine, cultivated roses, and reminisced about living in Antarctica as a doctor on a geophysical expedition. McLennan inherited his family's passion for intellectual exploration. His conversation is filled with references to great thinkers—from Heraclitus to Thucydides, Montesquieu to Schrödinger. Nothing gives him greater pleasure than the life of the mind: "When I have a thought or I'm developing a way of looking at things that rings true, it's the same joy as catching a wave."

McLennan's voracious reading led him to the same wary conclusion that Graham and Eveillard had reached: **The future is so "intrinsically uncertain" that investors should focus heavily on avoiding permanent losses and building "a portfolio that can endure various states of the world."** As McLennan sees it, we should start by defining our overarching goal, which ought to guide all of our investment choices. He makes the point by quoting the Roman philosopher Seneca: "If one does not know to which port one is sailing, no wind is favorable." For McLennan, the destination is clear: "Our goal is not to try to become rich quickly. It's resilient wealth creation." For almost all of us, this is a much wiser goal than trying to trounce the market.

McLennan's "respect for uncertainty" stems in part from his study of history. He's particularly fascinated by the relative calm of the early 1900s. He points out that an investor surveying the world in, say, 1908–11, had every reason to feel confident about the future. The global economy had enjoyed a long period of unprecedented growth. Asset values seemed reasonable. And it was widely believed that inflation had been vanquished. Why worry? Then all hell broke loose.

The unsinkable *Titanic* sank on its maiden voyage in 1912—a reminder that man cannot tame nature. An assassination by a Bosnian revolutionary triggered a chain reaction that precipitated the outbreak of World War I in 1914. The New York Stock Exchange closed for four months during the war, and every major European exchange shut down. The flu pandemic of 1918–19 killed as many as 50 million people. Hyperinflation gripped Germany in 1922, setting the stage for Hitler's rise to power, which began in 1923. The Crash of 1929 was followed by the Great Depression. Then World War II struck from 1939 to 1945. Thus, a period of calm prosperity gave way to *three decades* of disaster. Whipsawed by world events, the stock market was ferociously volatile from 1926 to 1945, leaving a generation of investors with a lingering dread of risk.*

A dangerous blunder that investors repeatedly make is to assume that the period ahead will resemble the period they most recently experienced. "But the future can be *incredibly* different," says McLennan. "That *next* generation had a very different life experience from the *prior* generation."† Buffett made a similar point after 9/11, which cost Berkshire billions of dollars in insurance losses. Writing to shareholders in 2002, he admitted, "We had either overlooked or dismissed the possibility of large-scale terrorism losses. . . . In short, all of us in the industry made a fundamental underwriting mistake by focusing on experience, rather than exposure." **With that lesson in mind, McLennan focuses considerable attention on his *exposure*—and on preparing for a future that may look nothing like his recent experience.**

When we first spoke in his sleek Manhattan offices in the summer of 2017, he listed a litany of threats to which investors were exposed. For example, he pointed out that the United States had even more debt relative to GDP than before the 2008 financial crisis. Interest rates were so low that savers were being penalized for prudence. The rise of automation was fomenting social and political upheaval. The geopolitical backdrop was fraught with the risk of conflict, not least from China's emergence as a rival to the US. And a low cost of capital had driven asset prices to exuberant levels, making it hard to find stocks that offered a wide margin of safety. He described these phenomena

---

* In *Against the Gods: The Remarkable Story of Risk*, Peter Bernstein writes that total returns averaged only 7 percent a year from 1926 to 1945. Meanwhile, the standard deviation of annual returns (a measure of their variation from the mean) was 37 percent a year. It was an awful combination: lackluster returns and sickening volatility.

†Indeed, the decades *after* 1945 proved to be a glorious era for investors. Those who learned from 1926 to 1945 that stocks were too treacherous to touch would have missed out as the Dow Jones Industrial Average rocketed from about 150 in 1945 to almost 1,000 in 1966. Bernstein notes that the standard deviation of total returns from 1945 to 1966 fell to *one-third* of what it had been from 1926 to 1945. It was an awesome combination: lavish returns and gentle volatility. The lesson for investors is extraordinarily important. If you ever expect the world to remain stable or financial markets to continue along one consistent path (either good or bad), just remind yourself of the differences between those three periods: 1908–11, 1912–45, and 1945–66. Change is the norm. Complacency is the enemy.

as "forms of fragility and frailty that history shows it's dangerous to ignore."

McLennan, who views market predictions as "a fool's errand," didn't pretend to know what would come next. However, like Howard Marks, he thinks it's vital to recognize that "the pricing of risk goes through enormous cycles. . . . You want to be more willing to commit capital to investments when risk is obviously being well priced, such as late 2008 or 2009. And you want to be more cautious when risk is *not* being as well priced, like 1999 or 2007 or perhaps today."

He likened the situation to living on a fault line in San Francisco. "Maybe we have ten great years ahead of us [and] the earthquake doesn't surface." But it would be foolhardy to act as if the threat doesn't exist. "We just want to acknowledge that there are things that may not play out so well in the future," he told me. **"You want to be structured to participate in the march of mankind, but to survive the dips along the way."** That's a useful maxim for investing and life.

When the threat finally surfaced, it was an epidemic, not an earthquake, that triggered a market collapse in early 2020. Speaking that June from a house in Greenwich, Connecticut, that he'd rented to escape from Manhattan during the pandemic, McLennan remarked that the crash—which struck at a time of "complacency" after a decade of almost "uninterrupted growth"—highlighted his belief that "the markets are part of a complex ecosystem that is *inherently unpredictable*. You know, there was no economist in December of 2019 calling for a COVID disruption to the business cycle." One key to resilience, then, is to ensure that you're "prudently positioned" when "things feel good," since "the future is uncertain and can hold events like this."

How does McLennan construct a portfolio to achieve his goal of resilient wealth creation? He starts by envisioning the global markets as one giant block of marble. He then begins "chipping away" every piece that he *doesn't* want to own, removing whatever promotes fragility, in order to "sculpt a better outcome." The guiding principle behind this process is one of "error elimination." As McLennan explains, there's a "fundamental insecurity" to this way of thinking. It reflects his recognition that "there are lots of things that can harm us" and that resilience requires him to "eschew them."

McLennan has the flexibility to search anywhere in the world for opportunities, since he manages a global fund and an international fund. Most investors would approach the task by seeking out what he calls "heated pockets" of "thematic growth"—fashionable bets such as Brazilian stocks in 2010, social media companies in 2017, or electric cars in 2020. Influenced by their recent experience, investors often load up on whatever has been performing best. But widespread expectations of continued success lead to inflated prices. What's more, areas of high growth ultimately attract fierce competition. As Marks puts it, "Success carries within it the seeds of failure."

**If your goal is resilient wealth creation, you can't operate like a heat-seeking missile.** The risks are too extreme because the most popular assets provide no margin of safety. So McLennan begins by chiseling away anything that looks faddish, including countries and sectors that have attracted "indiscriminate" flows of capital. That habit protected his shareholders when the beloved BRICs (Brazil, Russia, India, and China) stumbled and Brazil blew up. He also avoids countries with political systems that don't respect property rights. That's you, Russia.

Likewise, McLennan chips away any company that he believes would add fragility to his portfolio. For example, he avoids business models that are particularly vulnerable to technological change. He's equally averse to companies with opaque balance sheets, too much leverage, or imprudent management that is "too expeditionary." That protected him from time bombs such as Enron, Fannie Mae, and all of the banks that imploded during the financial crisis.

Instead of assuming that successful businesses will grow in perpetuity, McLennan views them through a darker lens, which he has borrowed from science. "I happen to believe that *everything* is on a path to fade," he says. "If you think of evolution, ninety-nine percent of species that have ever existed are extinct. And businesses are no exception."

He regards the economy as an ecology in which the current lords of the jungle will eventually be defeated by disruptive technology and new competitors. "Businesses that were robust today won't be robust in the future," says McLennan. "Uncertainty is intrinsic to the system. It's entropy—the second law of thermodynamics. Basically, things tend toward disorder over time, and it takes a lot of energy to keep structure and quality in place. So, philosophically, we have great respect for the fact that things are not structurally permanent in nature, that things fade."

This realization has profound implications when it comes to picking stocks. Most investors want to own glamorous companies with heady growth prospects. McLennan focuses instead on a more negative mission of "avoiding fade." How? By identifying "persistent businesses" that are less vulnerable to "complex competitive forces." Think of it as an anti-entropy strategy.

One example of a business that he expects to "persist" is FANUC Corp., a Japanese firm that has maintained a remarkably stable position as the world's leading seller of robotics products such as servomotors. Whatever car you buy in the United States, says McLennan, it's likely that it was painted by a FANUC robot. The company has an entrenched customer base that's used to its products. It gathers real-time data from those clients and harnesses this superior knowledge of the market to keep expanding its lead over competitors. FANUC also benefits from the trend of automation within manufacturing, instead of being a victim of technological change. Its finances are strong, with net cash on the balance sheet, and it's run by a farsighted management team that speaks explicitly about the priority of positioning the company to "survive forever." None of this guarantees that FANUC is immune to entropy, but McLennan believes it's "difficult to displace."

Another example of a dominant business that he regards as "built for resilience" is the consumer goods firm Colgate-Palmolive. The company has been selling toothpaste since the 1870s and controls more than 40 percent of the worldwide market. It's an inexpensive and habitual product that's resistant to disruption—except in the unlikely event that, say, an active ingredient turns out to be carcinogenic. Even in times of economic mayhem, such as 2008 or 2020, it's a business that "just tends to grind on," says McLennan. And, as with FANUC, "that combination of scale and customer captivity tends to produce better margins and therefore more cash flow."

This is a company with no novelty or sex appeal. Yet its business model would be so hard to replicate that it possesses what McLennan calls "mundane scarcity." There's a counterintuitive elegance to this idea that, when it comes to investing, *beauty often lies in mundanity, not glamour*. Over the years, he's detected the hidden allure of countless ugly ducklings—from a timberland company acquired during a cyclical downturn to a firm that rents uniforms. Not exactly Tesla.

Similarly, as stocks tumbled in March 2020, McLennan added to his stake in a Japanese firm, Hoshizaki—another exquisitely mundane and persistent business that he describes as "the world leader in ice machines for restaurants." He explains, "Restaurants always come and go, but they need the same equipment. So the equipment maker is a far safer bet than betting on a restaurant."

McLennan also insists that any stock he buys should be "priced for fade." In other words, the valuation must be low enough to compensate for his assumption that the company, like every business, is ultimately on "a path to irrelevance." He typically seeks to invest at a 30 percent discount to his estimate of the company's intrinsic value. If the business *doesn't* fade but instead continues to grow, "then we get the growth for free."

What remains after McLennan's painstaking process of elimination? A "resilient core" of unusually persistent, conservatively managed, well-capitalized, undervalued businesses that are likely to thrive even in a Darwinian ecosystem where nothing lives forever.

On average, he holds these positions for the best part of a decade, trimming or adding to them as their valuations fluctuate. McLennan recognizes that all of these businesses are imperfect and some will disappoint. So he adds another layer of resilience by owning about 140 of them. Like Graham and Eveillard, he sees diversification as a vital component of an "error-tolerant" strategy that can survive his own mistakes, bad luck, and inability to see the future.*

Opportunities to buy "good businesses at good prices" tend to arise

---

* It's also worth acknowledging that a fund manager with $100 billion in assets *can't* run a concentrated portfolio. Mohnish Pabrai, who has most of his money in a handful of stocks, views diversification as a recipe for mediocre returns. But there's a tension between outperformance and survival. Pabrai is more likely than McLennan to produce dazzling returns, but he's also more likely to fly his fund into the side of a mountain. McLennan adds that, since 1926, "the vast majority of the market's performance came from about four percent of the stocks. . . . If you try to be too concentrated, your chances of being in that right four percent are probabilistically quite low."

erratically, often amid outbreaks of volatility. But McLennan is perfectly happy to wait five or ten years for a desirable company on his watch list to meet his valuation hurdles. In the meantime, he has the discipline to let cash pile up, instead of feeling obliged to invest when prices are too high for comfort. Indeed, the most critical idea he tries to instill in his analysts is the importance of saying no.

When markets are ebullient and bargains elude him, McLennan's capacity for saying no becomes positively Eveillardian. On February 19, 2020, the day before the COVID crash began, First Eagle Global had only 71 percent of its assets in stocks, with 15 percent stashed securely in cash and sovereign debt—a reflection of his concern about high valuations and the brewing risks he'd described back in 2017. He observes, "It's the fact that we didn't *force* capital to work at a time when prices weren't conducive to investing that helps us to be resilient in the downdraft."

McLennan also held 14 percent of the fund's assets in gold, which he views as a long-term hedge against market meltdowns, geopolitical chaos, or a loss of confidence in paper money systems. "Gold has a negative correlation to stocks in really bad extreme states," he says. It's also "one of the scarcest and most resilient elements on the periodic table. . . . It doesn't rust, it doesn't rot, and it doesn't fade like a business or a regime." In a world of man-made instability, he argues (unfashionably) that gold adds "natural" resilience to his all-weather portfolio, helping to ensure that he can survive those unexpected dips. After all, companies may die, but gold endures.

True to form, the Global Fund held up well amid the tumult of 2020, steadied by its "ballast" of cash and gold. "It's a classic example of the fact that you need to buy the umbrella *before* it rains," says McLennan. "By the time you're hunting around for an umbrella in the middle of a storm, it's pretty difficult to find one. So having the right mindset in advance was critical here." While others panicked, he was also able to invest in battered stocks "at prices that were now much more sane." He observes, "It's not enough just to be conservative. You need to be willing to put cash to work when others feel least comfortable doing it."

McLennan's resilient approach provides a stark contrast to the behavior of most investors. His systematic focus on removing fragility requires him to avoid all of the "obvious behavioral defects" they exhibit. For example, they're too impatient to wait for the right purchase price. They "rent" stocks, instead of owning them for years. They succumb to the egotistical delusion that they can predict the future, instead of recognizing the limits of their knowledge. And they leap blindly into manias, their judgment fogged by "return envy" and the fear of missing out.

One book that has influenced his ideas about why people make such self-destructive decisions is the *History of the Peloponnesian War*, written by the Athenian general Thucydides some twenty-four hundred years ago. McLennan says Athens and Sparta ended up at war because both sides made "hasty" and "hubristic" decisions "in the passion of the moment." He reasons that the opposite traits—*patience* and *humility*—offer a temperamental edge whether we're defusing a conflict or building wealth. Once again, success stems from consciously resisting everything that promotes fragility.

As McLennan describes the process of building a portfolio that can flourish over time, he's reminded of watching his mother gardening while he was growing up in Australia. There was always a problem. Dry weather. Wilting vines. Bug infestations. He often wondered why she bothered to keep going. It would have been so much easier to let the forest grow or just settle for a lawn that needed mowing once a week. But her care yielded remarkable results over three decades. "What I saw play out over time was the gradual emergence of this beautiful, beautiful garden that took time. It took selectivity. And I think it's a good metaphor for investing."

The First Eagle Global Fund is much like that garden. So much has happened since Eveillard took charge of the fund in 1979—bull markets, bubbles, inflation, wars, crashes, crises, and a pandemic. Yet the same disciplined, risk-averse strategy has remained in place throughout. The result? Since 1979, the fund has averaged 12.46 percent a year, versus 9.35 percent for the MSCI World Index.* If you'd invested $100,000 in the Global Fund in 1979, it would have grown to $12.94

---

* That figure, which excludes a sales charge for buying the First Eagle Global Fund, covers the period from January 1979 through May 2020. The fund's cumulative return over those four decades (or so) was 12,845 percent, versus 3,945 percent for the MSCI World Index. The lesson? Steady Compounding – Disaster = Spectacular Success.

million in 2020, versus $4.05 million if you'd invested in the index—a difference of almost $9 million. That's the beauty of compounding. Small advantages build over decades into an overwhelming margin of victory.

The paradox is that Eveillard and McLennan hit the ball out of the park without ever swinging for the fences. McLennan attributes their success to a consistent focus on "risk mitigation," "error elimination," and "prudent acts of omission." In essence, "it's winning by not losing."

## "Life Is Not Simple"

Still, the path to prosperity has not been painless. Eveillard, now retired, makes no secret of the emotional scars that he carries from the time when his career almost ran off the rails. Looking back on his life, he also regrets that he struggled to balance work and family. His job was so "absorbing" and "sometimes psychologically painful" that he "neglected" his two daughters. Would he have been a less successful stock picker if he'd given them more attention? "I don't know, and I'll never know," he says. "The Catholic priest was right. Life is not simple."

Nonetheless, he feels a deep sense of pride in what he's achieved. "What gave me pleasure was not that I did better than others, but that I delivered returns over a long period of time that were vastly in excess of an index fund," he says. "It's a game where the numbers don't lie."

McLennan, like the rest of us, has also had his share of ups and downs. When I ask how the forces of entropy and impermanence have affected his life, he replies, "Oh, I've experienced it personally. You know, I had a wife." They split up after many years, having had three children together. Since then, he's fallen in love again, remarried, and had a fourth child—a daughter named Tennyson, "like the poet."

Both professionally and personally, says McLennan, he has often found that "moments of extreme pain" were followed by "new beginnings" and "extremely propitious opportunities." For example, the late nineties were a brutal time for value investors such as him and Eveillard, "but the early 2000s were a golden age. So, if you were able to endure it, the upside was enormous."

**In markets, as in life, so much hinges on our ability to survive the dips.**

McLennan spent fourteen years at Goldman Sachs, working with some of the top performers on Wall Street. He initially wondered if the senior brass had some unique talent that set them apart. "What I learned over time is that often it was just the people who didn't give up, who just kept learning, kept evolving, stuck to it, and were willing to live through adversity." He sees the same trait among the best investors: "They just haven't given up. They're constantly captivated by cracking the code" and have the strength "to endure the inevitable periods of disappointment."

McLennan knows that the future will bring more trouble, more instability, more decay. After all, "entropy is the ironclad rule of the universe." But he thinks of himself as an "informed realist," not a pessimist. "I'm a believer in human potential, but I think the path is not linear," he says. "It's punctured by episodic disruption. So, if you structure your portfolio and your way of thinking to *endure* those pockets of disruption, you're more likely to be able to benefit from the march of humankind over time than if you depend on it going well."

## Five Rules for Resilience

Let's step back for a moment and try to distill a few practical lessons from Graham, Kahn, Buffett, Eveillard, and McLennan on how to strengthen our resilience as investors. For me, there are five fundamental ideas that I can't afford to forget.

**First, we need to respect uncertainty.** Just think of all the turmoil that Graham and Kahn witnessed over the last century or so and you begin to realize that disorder, chaos, volatility, and surprise are not bugs in the system, but features. We can't predict the timing, triggers, or precise nature of these disruptions. But we need to expect them and prepare for them, so we can soften their sting. How? By identifying and consciously removing (or reducing) our vulnerabilities. As Nassim Nicholas Taleb writes in *Antifragile: Things That Gain from Disorder*, "It is far easier to figure out if something is fragile than to predict the occurrence of an event that may harm it."

**Second, to achieve resilience, it's imperative to reduce or eliminate debt, avoid leverage, and beware of excessive expenses, all of which can make us dependent on the kindness of strangers.** There are two critical questions to ask: "Where am I fragile? And how can I reduce my fragility?" If, say, all of your money is in one bank, one brokerage, one country, one currency, one asset class, or one fund, you may be playing with a loaded gun. With luck, you can get away with anything in the short term. With time, the odds rise that your vulnerability will be exposed by unforeseen events.

**Third, instead of fixating on short-term gains or beating benchmarks, we should place greater emphasis on becoming shock resistant, avoiding ruin, and staying in the game.** To some degree, the upside will take care of itself as economies grow, productivity improves, populations expand, and compounding works its magic. But as Kahn warned, we can't afford to ignore the downside.

**Fourth, beware of overconfidence and complacency.** Aristotle observed, "The character which results from wealth is that of a prosperous fool." Personally, if there's anything I'm sure of, it's that I'm irrational, ignorant, self-deluding, and prone to all of the behavioral mistakes I laugh at in others—including the perilous habit of trusting that the future will resemble the recent past.

**Fifth, as informed realists, we should be keenly aware of our exposure to risk and should always require a margin of safety.** But there's an important caveat. We cannot allow our awareness of risk to make us fearful, pessimistic, or paranoid. Nietzsche warned, "Stare too long into the abyss and you become the abyss." As McLennan demonstrated during the pandemic, the resilient investor has the strength, confidence, and faith in the future to seize opportunities when unresilient investors are reeling. Defense suddenly turns into offense. Disruption brings profit.

CHAPTER FIVE

# Simplicity Is the Ultimate Sophistication

## A long and winding search for the simplest path to stellar returns

---

Our life is frittered away by detail. . . . Simplify, simplify.
—Henry David Thoreau

The great paradox of this remarkable age is that the more complex the world around us becomes, the more simplicity we must seek in order to realize our financial goals. . . . Simplicity, indeed, is the master key to financial success.
—Jack Bogle

The humidity is stifling. On summer days like this, even the hardiest New Yorkers fantasize about escaping from the heat trapped between the city's skyscrapers. Down on Wall Street, the aspiring plutocrats buttoned up in their formal business suits must be gasping for air.

One hundred miles away, Joel Greenblatt has taken refuge from the city and is working at his beach house in the Hamptons today. We're seated in the shade of his elegantly furnished patio, savoring the cool breeze and his magnificent view of the Atlantic. The house has a swimming pool with a basketball hoop and a lawn with soccer goalposts. A couple of surfboards lean against a wall behind us. Sunlight shimmers on the ocean's surface.

Suntanned and relaxed, Greenblatt is dressed in jeans and black leather loafers without socks. His sleeves are rolled up. A keen tennis player, he looks trim and fit on the brink of his sixtieth birthday. The giants of investing are not always endowed with an abundance of social skills. But Greenblatt, a giant among giants, has a beguiling manner and a warm smile. Above all, there's a quiet confidence and poise about him—a sense that he is beyond the usual craving for approval. He's comfortable with who he is, secure in the knowledge of all that he's achieved.

Perhaps that's not surprising, given the extent of his accomplishments. Greenblatt's investment returns are the stuff of legend. In 1985, at the tender age of twenty-seven, he founded Gotham Capital and launched a hedge fund with assets of about $7 million. In 1989, he was joined by Robert Goldstein, who remains his partner three decades later. In its first ten years, the fund scored returns of 50 percent a year (after expenses but before fees). Over twenty years, it averaged an astonishing 40 percent a year. At that rate, $1 million grows to $836 million—a nifty trick.

After five years, Gotham returned half of its investors' money. After ten, it returned the rest, so that Greenblatt and Goldstein could concentrate on managing their own fortunes. Most fund managers are vulnerable to their shareholders' whims. But they had the ultimate luxury of being answerable to nobody.

Free to pursue his curiosity wherever it took him, Greenblatt forged an unpredictable path. Many of the best investors have narrow interests, since excellence demands focus. But Greenblatt has led a rich and varied life. For a start, he's an enthusiastic family man with a wife, five kids, and two dogs. He's also an annoyingly talented writer. He's published three investment books, which are filled with his unique blend of granular advice, irreverent wisecracks ("*Note*: There are three kinds of people—those who can count and those who can't"), exuberant wordplay (*ipso facto* is spelled *ipso fatso*), and amusing tales of his youthful misadventures involving imitation dog vomit and underage bets at the greyhound racetrack.*

---

\* Part of the pleasure of Greenblatt's wisecracks is that they are entirely gratuitous. For example, he includes the following definition in the glossary section of *You Can Be a Stock Market Genius*: "VILLAGE IDIOT: Someone who spends $24 on an investment book and thinks he can beat the market. (Just kidding.)"

His first book, *You Can Be a Stock Market Genius (Even If You're Not Too Smart!)* was intended for a general audience, but became a bible for hedge fund managers in search of an edge. His second, *The Little Book That Beats the Market*, was designed to demystify investing for his children, but sold more than three hundred thousand copies and was hailed by Michael Price as "one of the most important investment books of the last fifty years." His third book, *The Big Secret for the Small Investor*, fared less well. Greenblatt jokes that "it's still a secret" because "no one read it."

Since 1996, he has also taught the course "Value and Special Situation Investment" at Columbia Business School. So far, he's instructed an elite cohort of around eight hundred MBA students, sharing with them the intellectual framework that enabled him to beat the market. Greenblatt begins the course by informing them that the skills he's about to teach can make them extremely rich, but he warns that this pursuit has about as much social value as a knack for handicapping horses. With that caveat in mind, he asks them to "find some way to give back."

Writing and teaching have provided Greenblatt with two rewarding ways of giving back. In a field that's rife with self-serving and misguided advice that may be hazardous to your financial health, he has followed in the grand tradition of Ben Graham, Warren Buffett, and Howard Marks by sharing investment wisdom that has demonstrably worked. Meanwhile, as a philanthropist, Greenblatt has also played an instrumental role in creating a network of forty-five free, public charter schools that serve eighteen thousand students across New York City. Most come from low-income and minority households in areas such as the Bronx and Harlem.

In recent years, Greenblatt has also returned to managing outside money. He and Goldstein have created a family of long/short mutual funds, which represent an intriguing and unexpected departure from the strategy that propelled them to stardom. Greenblatt, who has a strong entrepreneurial streak, loves starting new ventures. But his underlying ambition isn't to maximize his own wealth by building a financial empire. "I have nothing against making money," he says. "But it's not really what drives me. I have enough."

Rather, he's motivated primarily by a game player's delight in devising ingenious ways to win. "It's the fun of the challenge of figuring things out that I'm most attracted to," he says. "And since everyone else in the world is trying to figure it out, it's a nice feeling to solve the puzzle." Indeed, I see Greenblatt as a kind of code breaker who is drawn inexorably to the intellectual challenge of beating the system.

I wanted to understand what he had discovered in more than three decades of attempting to decrypt the market and outwit the competition. As I would soon learn, the principles underpinning his strategies are surprisingly simple. In fact, what makes Greenblatt such an illuminating guide to investing is his gift for reducing this complex game to its purest essence. For example, during a conversation at his office in midtown Manhattan, he tells me that the entire secret of successful stock picking comes down to this: "Figure out what something is worth and pay a lot less."

Is it really that straightforward? Well, we shall see.

But first, let's take a brief detour to explain why it's so important to identify a few fundamental principles that are, at least, approximately true. Then, with help from Greenblatt and some other financial titans, we'll narrow everything down to a handful of specific investment principles that should help us to stay on track for decades to come. The goal? In this overcomplicated world of ours, we are searching for a simple, logical, and dependable path to superior returns.

### The Simplicity That Lies on the Other Side of Complexity

Growing up in London in the 1970s, I could choose from a grand total of three television channels. I still remember the magical evening in 1982 when my motherland was blessed by the miraculous arrival of Channel 4, which promised to deliver a limitless feast of televisual wonders. Nowadays, in twenty-first-century New York, I have at least one hundred channels. Yet I can seldom be bothered to switch on my TV, except for the reliable disappointment of watching England's soccer team getting knocked out of the World Cup every four years.

We often assume that additional choices will make us happier. Up to a point, it may even be true. But I'm hardly alone in finding all of this added complexity overwhelming. The psychologist Barry Schwartz argues in *The Paradox of Choice: Why More Is Less* that many shoppers become paralyzed by the first world problem of supermarket shelves heaving under the weight of twenty-four types of gourmet jam.

When it comes to investing, the proliferation of choices can make your head spin. Should you buy individual stocks, ETFs, hedge funds, or mutual funds? Actively managed funds or index funds? Should you favor one investment style or mix and match among such categories as growth, value, growth at a reasonable price, deep value, momentum, macro, or market neutral? And how should you divide your money between domestic and foreign stocks, bonds, cash, and "alternatives" such as private equity, venture capital, REITs, gold, and pork-belly futures?

In practical terms, the ability to reduce complexity is immensely valuable. Just think for a moment about the Old Testament, which contains no fewer than 613 commandments. Who can remember so many rules, let alone obey them all? Maybe that's why we needed a top ten list. But when I tried to jot down the Ten Commandments just now, I got only six of them right—and that was with the assistance of some dishonest grading.

Still, I *do* remember this: About two thousand years ago, a sage named Hillel was asked to teach the entire Old Testament while standing on one leg. He replied, "What is hateful to you, do not do to your neighbor. All the rest is commentary." The Old Testament requires just three words to convey this overriding rule: *Veahavta lereacha kamocha*, which is translated from the Hebrew as "And you shall love your neighbor as yourself."

Likewise, when Jesus was asked about the most important of all the commandments, he opted for deep simplicity, declaring, "Thou shalt love the Lord thy God with all thy heart, and with all thy soul, and with all thy strength, and with all thy mind; and thy neighbor as thyself."

I'm also partial to this wonderfully concise exhortation from the Buddha: "Refrain from what is unwholesome. Do good. Purify the mind." As an instruction manual for life, how much more do we need than those ten words? Like Hillel and Jesus, the Buddha presumably recognized that we lesser mortals are acutely vulnerable to confusion in the face of complexity—and that a minimal number of simple, memorable guideposts can steer us pretty effectively in the general direction of nirvana.

Simplification is an equally important strategy in more worldly realms such as science and business. For example, scientists often invoke the Occam's razor principle, which is attributed to a fourteenth-century English friar and philosopher named William of Occam. His principle holds that "all things being equal, the simplest solution tends to be the best one."

Occam's image of a razor captures the critical notion that we're more likely to find the right answer by shaving away all unnecessary details. Albert Einstein agreed, observing, "All physical theories, their mathematical expressions apart, ought to lend themselves to so simple a description that even a child could understand them." Lord Ernest Rutherford, the father of nuclear physics, reached a similar conclusion, reputedly remarking, "If a piece of physics cannot be explained to a barmaid, then it is not a good piece of physics."*

Simplicity also plays an important role in many of the most successful businesses. Take the Google home page, which consists primarily of a logo and a pill-shaped space in which to type your search words. Or consider the sleek, uncluttered elegance that Steve Jobs—inspired by the minimalist esthetic of Zen Buddhism—brought to Apple's products. As Jobs often explained, his devotion to simplicity went far beyond design: "The way we're running the company, the product design, the advertising, it all comes down to this: 'Let's make it simple. Really simple.'" As far back as 1977, the company's first marketing brochure featured a photograph of a shiny red apple under the tagline "Simplicity is the ultimate sophistication."†

---

* Another of my favorite examples of simplicity in science comes from Dr. Dean Ornish, the father of lifestyle medicine, who synthesized in eight syllables everything that he's learned from his four decades of trailblazing research on health and nutrition: "Eat well, move more, stress less, love more." Ornish recently told me, "When you really understand something deeply, spend your whole life doing something, then you can make it simple. . . . You can reduce it down to its essence. And that *is* the essence." I'd strongly recommend his remarkable book *Undo It! How Simple Lifestyle Changes Can Reverse Most Chronic Diseases*, which might just save your life.

† This phrase is often attributed to Leonardo da Vinci, but it's not clear that he actually said it.

The financial services industry tends *not* to favor simplicity—hence the rise of mind-boggling "innovations" such as collateralized debt obligations, structured investment vehicles, and credit default swaps, which came close to destroying the global economy in 2008. The late Jack Bogle, who founded the Vanguard Group in 1975 and created the first index fund a year later, observed in a book titled *Enough*, "Financial institutions operate by a kind of *reverse* Occam's razor. They have a large incentive to favor the complex and costly over the simple and cheap, quite the opposite of what most investors need and ought to want."*

When I interviewed Bogle in 2001, he pointed out that nothing could have been simpler than his theory that low-cost index funds would beat actively managed funds as a group, since the latter would be burdened by higher operating expenses and transaction costs. "When there's a financial intermediary—a croupier—it takes a lot out of the market return," he told me. "So index funds *have* to win. It was not complicated." That elementary insight into the mathematical advantages of index funds proved so powerful that Vanguard's assets have since grown to $6.2 trillion.†

One of the most thoughtful proponents of simplicity is Josh Waitzkin, an expert on peak performance in fields as diverse as chess, martial arts, and investing. As a child prodigy, he was a national chess

---

* In his 2016 letter to Berkshire Hathaway's shareholders, Buffett wrote, "If a statue is ever erected to honor the person who has done the most for American investors, the hands-down choice should be Jack Bogle. . . . In his early years, Jack was frequently mocked by the investment-management industry. Today, however, he has the satisfaction of knowing that he helped millions of investors realize far better returns on their savings than they otherwise would have earned. He is a hero to them and to me." Bogle died in 2019.

† When Bogle launched the first index fund in 1976, it attracted a grand total of $11.4 million. His ambition of merely matching the market's return was dismissed as an exercise in mediocrity. But Bogle understood a profound truth: over time, the lavish fees and expenses levied by active managers can have a devastating impact on investors' net returns. To market the novel concept of indexing, Bogle presented a table showing that $1 million invested at 10 percent a year would grow to $17.5 million in thirty years. By contrast, an active investor who blew 1.5 percent a year in expenses (thereby reducing that 10 percent return to 8.5 percent) would turn $1 million into $11.5 million in thirty years. In other words, by saving 1.5 percent a year in expenses, the cost-conscious investor ended up with an extra $6 million. As Bogle told me, "I just knew that the math of investing was eternal."

champion and the subject of the movie *Searching for Bobby Fischer*. As an adult, he became a world champion in tai chi chuan push hands, a coach to hedge fund managers, and the author of a fascinating book, *The Art of Learning: An Inner Journey to Optimal Performance*.

Based on his own experience as a world-class performer, Waitzkin stresses the importance of breaking down complicated challenges into simple components. When teaching chess, he would remove all but three pieces (two kings and one pawn) as a way of exploring the game's essential principles in a context of reduced complexity. Similarly, he mastered tai chi by "incrementally refining the simplest of movements—for example pushing your hands six inches through the air." By obsessively practicing such "simplified motions," he gradually internalized the underlying principles of the entire martial art, such as "the coordination of mind, breath, and body." He concludes, "It is rarely a mysterious technique that drives us to the top, but rather a profound mastery of what may well be a basic skill set."

This is a crucial insight that can benefit even the smartest investors. After all, complexity can be a particularly seductive trap for clever people. They were rewarded at school for solving complex problems, so it's no surprise if they are drawn to complicated solutions when confronted by the puzzle of investing. But in financial markets, as in martial arts, victory doesn't depend on dazzling displays of esoteric techniques. It depends on a firm grasp of the principles of the game and a deep mastery of basic skills. As Buffett has said, "Business schools reward difficult, complex behavior more than simple behavior. But simple behavior is more effective."

Buffett himself is a grand master of simplification. Writing to his shareholders in 1977, he laid out his four criteria for selecting any stock: "We want the business to be (1) one that we can understand, (2) with favorable long-term prospects, (3) operated by honest and competent people, and (4) available at a very attractive price." These may not strike you as earth-shattering secrets. But it's hard to beat this distillation of eternal truths about what makes a stock desirable. More than forty years have passed, yet Buffett's four filters remain as relevant and useful as ever.

I've been struck again and again by the ability of the best investors to condense many years of learning into a few key principles. This isn't a matter of dumbing things down or pretending that complications and contradictions don't exist. It's about synthesizing the details of an endlessly rich and nuanced subject, then crunching it down into an irreducible essence. This reminds me of a remark that's often attributed to the Supreme Court justice Oliver Wendell Holmes: "For the simplicity that lies this side of complexity, I would not give a fig, but for the simplicity that lies on the other side of complexity, I would give my life."*

Why is it so valuable to reduce investing to a few core principles? For a start, it forces us to think through what we truly believe. These convictions are especially useful in tempestuous times when we're barraged by uncertainty, doubt, and fear. Just think how disoriented we felt in the early months of 2020 when COVID-19 killed more than one hundred thousand people in the United States alone, threw tens of million into unemployment, and drove the market down by a third in a matter of weeks.

But it's almost as easy to get knocked off course in the best of times. There's so much anxiety-inducing noise in the news; so many competing sales pitches from hawkers of awful investment products and dubious expertise; so many temptations to switch to whatever fashionable strategy or overheated asset class seems to be making everyone else ludicrously rich.

The best investors have the discipline not to be swayed by such distractions. As Greenblatt says, "I have a simple way of looking at things that makes sense to me and that I'm going to stick with through thick and thin. That's it."

## Will Danoff's Secret Sauce

The virtues of a simple, deeply held investment credo struck me with particular force when I interviewed Will Danoff at the Boston head-

* Inconveniently, I suspect that Holmes never uttered these exact words. But he came close in a 1902 letter that he wrote to Lady Georgina Pollock: "The only simplicity for which I would give a straw is that which is on the other side of the complex—not that which never has divined it. With which remark I shut up."

quarters of Fidelity Investments. There's nothing slick or showy about Danoff, a genial workaholic with a gap-toothed grin and a wry sense of humor. He looks more like a rumpled, sleep-deprived middle manager than a Master of the Universe. Still, since taking charge of the Fidelity Contrafund in 1990, he has built it into a colossus with about $118 billion in assets, making it America's largest actively managed fund run by a single person. In all, he manages more than $200 billion.

It's notoriously difficult to outperform the market with a huge fund. But when we met in 2017, Danoff had the remarkable distinction of having whipped the S&P 500 over one, three, five, ten, and twenty-seven years. I was eager to uncover the subtle ingredients of his secret sauce. But he managed to sum up his entire investment philosophy in three words: "Stocks follow earnings."

With that principle in mind, he searches with relentless drive for "best-of-breed businesses" that he thinks will "grow to be bigger in five years." Why? Because if a company doubles its earnings per share in the next five years, he believes the stock price is also likely to double (more or less). This generalization is easy to dismiss because it sounds suspiciously simplistic. But remember: investing isn't like Olympic diving, where the judges award extra points for difficulty.

Danoff is unapologetic about his single-minded focus on predicting earnings growth. Unlike most of the investors in this book, he doesn't even worry that much about valuation levels, except when they get "ridiculous." He asks, "Do you want to win the game for shareholders and own great companies? Sometimes, to own a great company, you've got to pay a fair price."

This mindset has led him to amass enormous, long-held positions in dominant, well-managed businesses such as Berkshire Hathaway (a major holding since 1996), Microsoft, Alphabet (he was one of the largest investors in Google's 2004 IPO and has held it ever since), Amazon (his biggest position), and Facebook (he was among the biggest buyers in the IPO). "This is pretty basic stuff," he says. "My attitude with investing is, Why not invest with the best?"

To explain his way of thinking, Danoff shows me a stack of tattered and coffee-stained notes that provide a partial record of his meetings with tens of thousands of companies over the past three decades. He pulls out one of his favorite mementos: two pages of his messy, handwritten scribblings from a meeting with Howard Schultz, the visionary who transformed Starbucks into a global brand. They met in June 1992—exactly one week before the company went public with a market value of $250 million. These days, Starbucks is valued at about $120 billion.

Looking over his notes from that meeting, Danoff tells me, "Everything you needed to know was laid out here. There was a huge opportunity." For example, Schultz pointed out that Italy alone had at least 200,000 coffee bars. By comparison, Starbucks had 139. But the Seattle-based company was aggressively expanding into other cities, opening new cafés at a modest cost of about $250,000 apiece. In its third year, a café could generate $150,000 in profits—a 60 percent return on the initial investment. "The key," says Danoff, "is that the return on each store was quite high," so the company "could grow at a fast pace without needing external financing."

Danoff says he didn't appreciate Schultz when they first met. But Starbucks would ultimately become one of the Contrafund's largest holdings. Along the way, the company would provide the perfect illustration of why it's so valuable to invest for the long run in great businesses that sustain an unusually high growth rate. Danoff points to a chart that tracks the company's stupendous performance over two decades: its earnings per share grew by 27.45 percent annually for twenty years, while the stock soared by 21.32 percent a year. Over the same period, the S&P 500's earnings grew by 8.4 percent a year, while the index rose just 7.9 percent a year.

Danoff runs a finger along the fever lines on his chart and asks me what lesson they demonstrate. I reply, "The stock price is eventually going to follow the earnings." His eyes open wide and he flashes me a joyous smile: "Exactly! Bingo! *That's* what I've learned. *Stocks follow earnings!*"

His mantra doesn't sound particularly profound. But Danoff's edge lies partly in his consistent refusal to overcomplicate. His friend Bill Miller, one of the most insightful thinkers in investing, says Danoff consciously focuses on the questions that matter most, instead of getting tangled up in distracting details: "Will once said to me, falsely, 'Look, I'm not that smart and there's a lot of information out there. So when I look at a company, I just ask myself: "Are things getting better or are they getting worse?" If they're getting better, then I want to understand what's going on.'"

Miller, too, has learned to simplify his investment process. "I'm trying to get rid of the unnecessary parts of what I used to do," he says. For example, he used to build elaborate financial models in an attempt to grasp the complexities of each company he was analyzing. "I don't build models anymore. It's just stupid. It doesn't make any sense." Instead, he concentrates on three or four critical issues that he believes will drive the business. "For every company, there are a few key investment variables," he says, "and the rest of the stuff is noise."

The pattern is clear. In their own ways, Greenblatt, Buffett, Bogle, Danoff, and Miller have all been seekers of simplicity. The rest of us should follow suit. **We each need a simple and consistent investment strategy that works well over time—one that we understand and believe in strongly enough that we'll adhere to it faithfully through good times and bad.** We'll return to this idea later because it's so important. But for now, let's delve deeper into Greenblatt's mind and find out what he figured out about how to solve the puzzle of investing.

### Efficient Markets, Crazy People, and Dynamite

When Greenblatt was an undergraduate at Wharton in the late 1970s, his professors insisted that there was no point even *trying* to beat the market. As proponents of the efficient-market theory, they claimed that stock prices incorporate all of the information that's publicly available. As they saw it, the interaction between knowledgeable buyers and sellers results in stocks being priced efficiently at their fair value, which means that it's futile to hunt for bargains.

Intellectually, it's an elegant theory—a testament to the collective wisdom of crowds. What's more, it's had the positive effect of drawing many regular investors into index funds. They are built upon the disheartening but realistic notion that, if you can't *beat* the market, you should focus on matching its returns at the lowest possible cost. For the vast majority of investors, indexing is the most rational—and simplest—strategy of all.

But Greenblatt didn't buy what he was being taught. "I had a visceral response to what I was learning about efficient markets," he says. "It didn't seem to make sense to me just on a basic level of looking at the newspaper and seeing what was happening."

For a start, he could see that stocks routinely experience wild swings between their fifty-two-week highs and lows. If a stock trades at $50 in February and shoots up to $90 in November, how could it be correctly priced at both extremes? And what about hot stocks, such as the Nifty Fifty, that suddenly burst into flames? For example, did the purportedly all-knowing crowd price Polaroid fairly at $150 in 1972 *and* at $14 in 1974? It seemed highly unlikely.

Greenblatt saw that the overall market also lurches erratically from one extreme to another. The euphoric boom and sickening bust of 1972–74 established a pattern of head-wrenching volatility that he would observe throughout his career. He points out that the S&P 500 doubled from 1996 to 2000, halved from 2000 to 2002, doubled from 2002 to 2007, halved from 2007 to 2009, and tripled from 2009 to 2017. Were investors logically and efficiently setting stock prices as the market soared, stumbled, and swooned? Or were they much less rational than the academic theorists wanted to believe?

Greenblatt graduated summa cum laude in 1979 and enrolled in Wharton's MBA program. But his formal education did little to resolve these market mysteries. He took a class on investment management, but failed to find enlightenment in abstruse topics such as quadratic parametric programming. He did achieve one distinction: "I was able to get the lowest grade in the class."

Greenblatt was saved by *Forbes*. In his junior year at Wharton, he had chanced upon a short article about Ben Graham's strategy for identifying bargain stocks. That led him to read *Security Analysis* and *The Intelligent Investor*, which he describes as "the antithesis of what I was learning at school." Graham's perspective on how the market works "was so simple and clear," says Greenblatt, "that it got me very excited."

Above all, Graham taught him one life-changing lesson. As Greenblatt puts it, "Stocks are ownership shares of businesses," which "you're valuing and trying to buy at a discount." The key, then, is to identify situations in which there's a particularly large spread between the *price* and the *value* of the business. That spread gives you a margin of safety, which Greenblatt (like Graham and Buffett) regards as the single most important concept in investing.

**Once you realize that your entire mission is to value businesses and pay much less for them than they're worth, it's incredibly liberating.** "If you see it that simply and can keep that simplicity in your mind, it's very compelling and almost makes a lot of what *else* you see look silly," says Greenblatt. "It kind of gets rid of ninety-nine percent of everything else that anyone had ever told me about how to look at the world and the market."

Many investors get rattled when they read the latest news about, say, a Greek debt crisis that threatens the European economy. But Greenblatt says, "The way I look at it is, if I own a chain store in the Midwest, am I all of a sudden going to sell it for half of what it's worth because something bad happened in Greece? I don't think so! But that's what you read in the newspaper, and that's what everyone is looking at. If you have a context to say, 'Well, does it matter or doesn't it matter?'— it's just very helpful."

Indeed, you start to realize that much of the investment world is engaged in fruitless nonsense. Wall Street economists and market strategists pontificate about macroeconomic headwinds and tailwinds that nobody can reliably or consistently predict. Media pundits muse about the significance of short-term price fluctuations that are random and meaningless. Highly intelligent analysts at brokerage firms squander their time calculating next quarter's corporate earnings to the exact penny—an absurd guessing game that's irrelevant to successful, long-term investors.

Not to be outdone, academics teach complicated mathematical formulas and speak in a private code about Sharpe ratios, Sortino ratios, alpha, beta, the Modigliani-Modigliani measure, and other arcane concepts that lend an air of scientific exactitude to the messiness of the markets. Meanwhile, investment consultants harness these highfalutin notions to convince clients that their portfolios need frequent, subtle fine-tuning. Buffett has derided these high-priced peddlers of complexity as "hyper-helpers" whose "advice is often delivered in esoteric gibberish."

By contrast, Graham wrote simply and clearly about "Mr. Market." He encapsulated the entire game of investing in one brief parable about this muddle-headed character. In *The Intelligent Investor*, Graham suggests imagining that you own a $1,000 stake in a private business. Every day, your partner—the obliging but irrational Mr. Market—provides you with a valuation of that stake. His price quote changes based on how enthusiastic or fearful he feels that day: "You may be happy to sell out to him when he quotes you a ridiculously high price and equally happy to buy from him when his price is low." The rest of the time, you can sit on your hands, waiting for Mr. Market to lose his mind once more and offer you another deal that you can't refuse.

In other words, the market isn't an efficient machine that reliably and consistently sets fair prices. It's a comedy of errors, a festival of folly. "People are crazy and emotional," says Greenblatt. "They buy and sell things in an emotional way, not in a logical way, and that's the only reason why we have any opportunity. . . . So if you have a way to value businesses that's disciplined and makes sense, you should be able to take advantage of other people's emotions."

This raises an obvious but crucial question: *Do you know how to value a business?*

There's nothing admirable or shameful about your response. But you and I need to answer this question honestly, since self-delusion is a costly habit in extreme sports such as skydiving and stock picking. "It's a very small fraction of people that can value businesses—and if you can't do that, I don't think you should be investing on your own," says Greenblatt. "How can you invest intelligently if you can't figure out what something is worth?"* He adds that "most people should just index" because "they don't understand what they're doing."

I don't have the technical skills, patience, or interest to value businesses. So it makes sense for me to outsource the job to professionals who are better equipped for the task. This self-restraint should save me a lot of pain. As Greenblatt observes in *The Little Book That Beats the*

---

* If you want to improve your ability to read balance sheets and income statements, Greenblatt recommends books such as Benjamin Graham's *Interpretation of Financial Statements*, James Bandler's *How to Use Financial Statements*, and John Tracy's *How to Read a Financial Report*.

*Market,* "Choosing individual stocks without any idea of what you're looking for is like running through a dynamite factory with a burning match. You may live, but you're still an idiot."

Every few years, I ignore this warning and buy an individual stock, despite my better judgment. I currently own three stocks. One is Berkshire Hathaway, which I expect to hold for many years. I'd like to think that I understand the business well enough to justify this long-term investment. Less defensibly, I also own a tiny stake in a mining-and-property company recommended to me by a well-known investor who shall remain nameless. How has it done? So far, it's down 87 percent. For now, I'm keeping it as a painful reminder to be more careful around lit matches and dynamite. Stock number three is Seritage Growth Properties, a contrarian investment that I cloned from Mohnish Pabrai when the retail real estate sector crashed in 2020.

Depending on the business, Greenblatt uses some combination of four standard valuation techniques. Method 1: he performs a *discounted cash flow analysis*, calculating the net present value of the company's estimated future earnings. Method 2: he assesses the company's *relative value*, comparing it to the price of similar businesses. Method 3: he estimates the company's *acquisition value*, figuring out what an informed buyer might pay for it. Method 4: he calculates the company's *liquidation value*, analyzing what it would be worth if it closed and sold its assets.

None of these methods is precise, and each has its limitations. But Greenblatt works on the basis that, if a stock is sufficiently cheap, the upside potential significantly outweighs the downside. The underlying concept of buying bargains is simplicity itself. But the execution process *isn't* that simple because it involves such complexities as (roughly) predicting a company's future earnings and cash flows. This reminds me of an acerbic comment about investing that Charlie Munger once made at the end of a lunch with Howard Marks: "It's not supposed to be easy. Anyone who thinks it's easy is stupid."

Greenblatt insists that his own valuation skills are merely "average." Rather, his advantage stems chiefly from his ability to "contextualize" everything he sees in the market, fitting it all into a coherent framework. His faith in this framework is so strong that he issues a guarantee to his Columbia students: if they do a decent job of valuing businesses, buy them at a steep discount to their intrinsic value, and wait patiently for the gap to close between the current price and their appraisal of the value, the market will eventually reward them.*

The hitch is that you can never tell how long the process of convergence between price and value will take. Still, he says, "I'm a firm believer that, in 90 percent of the cases, the market will recognize that value within two or three years."

This points to a fundamental truth that is one of the most dependable laws of the financial universe. In the short term, the market is irrational and frequently misprices stocks—but in the long term, it's surprisingly rational. "Eventually," says Greenblatt, "Mr. Market gets it right."

## Unfair Bets and Ugly Ducklings

After leaving Wharton, Greenblatt headed to Stanford Law School, mostly to avoid getting an actual job. He dropped out after a year. Many of his peers followed well-trodden paths to become corporate lawyers or investment bankers. But he didn't fancy toiling for a hundred hours a week at a vast, faceless corporation in the pursuit of a conventional career. Ultimately, he wanted to find an enjoyable way to "get paid for smart ideas, rather than punching a clock."

In the meantime, he took a summer job at Bear Stearns, where he fell into a relatively new field: options trading. He recalls, "I was executing riskless arbitrage trades by literally running across the trading floor, getting a printout from the one printer, running back to my desk," and scouring the printout to "look for anomalies that I could trade." By using put and call options, he could lock in "automatic profits" with no risk of loss. "It opened me up to what was possible on Wall Street."

---

* In the "Owner's Manual" for Berkshire Hathaway's shareholders, Buffett explains, "Intrinsic value is an all-important concept that offers the only logical approach to evaluating the relative attractiveness of investments and businesses. Intrinsic value can be defined simply: It is the discounted value of the cash that can be taken out of a business during its remaining life. . . . Over time, stock prices gravitate toward intrinsic value."

Greenblatt had always been fascinated by gambling. At fifteen, he'd discovered the furtive joy of sneaking into a dog track and wagering a couple of bucks on a greyhound. His brain was built for betting. "I like calculating the odds," he says. "Consciously or unconsciously, I'm calculating the odds on every investment. What's the upside? What's the downside?" When I mention that all of the best investors seem to think probabilistically, carefully weighing the odds of different outcomes, he replies, "I don't think you can be a good investor *without* thinking in that way."

Greenblatt spent the next three years as an analyst at a start-up investment firm, making "risk arbitrage" bets on companies involved in mergers. It didn't take him long to realize that this was a game with odious odds. If a merger went ahead as planned, "you could make a dollar or two," he says. But if the deal unexpectedly fell apart, "you could lose ten or twenty." This was "the exact opposite" of Graham's strategy of buying dirt cheap stocks, "where you can lose a dollar or two and *make* ten or twenty. *That's* a good risk/reward."

In 1985, Greenblatt launched Gotham Capital with the intention of applying the principles he had learned from Graham. Greenblatt started with $7 million in capital, most of it supplied by Michael Milken, the king of junk bonds, whom he'd met through a classmate from Wharton. Milken reputedly earned more than $1 billion in four years at Drexel Burnham Lambert, so a little side bet on a promising but unproven twenty-seven-year-old wasn't much of a risk.*

Greenblatt says his investment strategy at Gotham involved "making money not from taking risk but from making unfair bets." That's to say, he invested only when the odds seemed to favor him overwhelmingly. The details changed from one investment to the next, but he always sought "asymmetric" propositions where "I can't lose much and maybe I'll make a lot." He quips, "If you don't lose money, most of the other alternatives are good."

---

* Unbeknownst to Greenblatt, Milken was flying too close to the sun. In 1990, Milken pled guilty to six counts of securities and tax violations, and he ultimately paid more than $1 billion in legal settlements and fines. He spent twenty-two months in the jailhouse, but avoided the poorhouse: according to *Forbes*, he's now worth about $3.7 billion. In 2020, Milken controversially received a presidential pardon.

Unfair bets are rare, but Greenblatt didn't need that many. He typically had 80 percent of his fund riding on six to eight investments—an extraordinary level of concentration. "There aren't that many great opportunities," he explains. "I was looking for low hurdles—things that other people would have bought, too, if they'd done the work."

Building on his experience in risk arbitrage, he developed an expertise in "special situations" that most investors overlooked, including corporate spin-offs, restructurings, and "orphan equities" that were emerging from bankruptcy. He also invested in small stocks with liquidity constraints, since most institutional investors were too big to buy them. He remarks, "It's easier to find bargains off the beaten path or in extraordinary situations that other people aren't looking at."

Greenblatt had the latitude to prospect in these "offbeat places" because he never let his fund become bloated. "We could have raised whatever amount we wanted, but you lower your returns," he says. In 1994, when Gotham's assets reached about $300 million, he returned all of the outside capital. As a result, the fund remained nimble enough to venture anywhere.

Indeed, when I ask him to explain Gotham's success, the first factor he cites is that "we remained small." The second is that his portfolio was exceptionally concentrated, so "you only have to find a few ideas." The third? "We got a little lucky." Over the years, he explains, Gotham suffered remarkably few disasters, which he attributes partly to good fortune. "I also hated losing money," he adds. "So we really put the bar very high before we would buy anything."

Greenblatt's ultraselective strategy meant that he routinely rejected stocks that looked good, not great. Likewise, if it was too difficult to value a particular business, he walked away. "I want to keep it easy for myself," he says. "Maybe I'm a little lazier than most people. Or, at least, I'm trying to pursue things that are one-foot hurdles rather than ten-foot hurdles."

But on those rare occasions when the market delivered a fat pitch right in his sweet spot, he didn't hesitate to whack it with all his might. One of these precious gifts from the financial gods arrived in 1993—a dream investment, says Greenblatt, that "had pretty much everything in it."

It all began with the announcement in October 1992 that the Marriott Corporation would split in two. The company had landed itself in trouble during a real estate downturn, says Greenblatt, and "got caught with a pile of hotels that they had built and now couldn't sell." Stephen Bollenbach, a financial wizard who had just restructured Donald Trump's collapsing casino and hotel empire, parachuted into Marriott to perform another corporate rescue mission.

Marriott had two businesses: a beautiful swan and an ugly duckling. The beautiful business generated a rich and predictable fee stream by managing hotels for other companies. The ugly business, which built and owned hotels, was overloaded with debt. Bollenbach prescribed a drastic surgical procedure to separate the two businesses.

The beautiful part would be carved off into a new company, Marriott International. About 85 percent of the Marriott Corporation's value would be neatly repackaged in this pristine, debt-free spin-off. Meanwhile, the unsellable hotels and about $2.5 billion in debt would be dumped into a second company, Host Marriott—a nasty little castoff that would apparently consist of all the toxic waste that no one wanted to own. The beautiful swan (Marriott International) would be free to swim off into the sunset, leaving the ugly duckling (Host Marriott) to drown. Or so it seemed.

Greenblatt knew that almost nobody would bother to analyze Host Marriott, let alone invest in it. "It just looked horrible," he says. "It had a lot of debt. It was in a bad business. There was nothing good about it." Moreover, it was too tiny for most institutional investors to hold, even if they could tolerate the stench. Existing shareholders of the Marriott Corporation would receive stock in Host Marriott when the spin-off was completed. But Greenblatt was sure they would sell in droves. So what did he do? He zeroed in on the ugly duckling.

"The way you're going to find bargains," he says, is by searching for hidden value in assets "that other people don't want."

One clue that Host Marriott might not be as rotten as it looked was that Bollenbach ("the guy who designed this evil plan") was going to run it. Why would this canny moneymaker want to take charge of the business if it was truly destined for bankruptcy? It turned out that he was well incentivized to turn the firm around. For good measure, the

Marriott family would also own 25 percent of Host Marriott. So some savvy insiders had a powerful interest in its success.

Greenblatt studied the company in depth and discovered a surprising amount of value. Sure, there was plenty of "lousy real estate," including some unfinished hotels. But there were also some valuable assets, such as airport restaurant concessions and several debt-free properties.

Best of all, the stock was fabulously cheap at around $4 per share. His best guess was that the debt-free assets *alone* were worth $6 per share. But there was also a debt-laden subsidiary that might be valuable, too, if its fortunes ever improved. "The asymmetry was so amazing," he says. "I was buying six dollars' worth of assets with no debt on it for four dollars, plus I had the upside on the other pile of assets. If the subsidiary was worth nothing, then I just paid four dollars for something worth six dollars."

So Greenblatt loaded up, staking almost *40 percent* of his fund's assets on Host Marriott. It was a breathtakingly bold move. Here was a struggling business that was leveraged to the hilt. Yet Greenblatt saw what everyone else missed: an irresistibly unfair bet.

As Graham had taught him, what mattered most was the margin of safety. If you bought a stock for much less than its intrinsic value, other investors would figure it out sooner or later and drive up the price. In the meantime, says Greenblatt, "I didn't see how I was going to lose much money." That's precisely why he made such an aggressive bet. "You size your positions based on how much risk you're taking," he says. "**I don't buy more of the ones I can make the most money on. I buy more of the ones that I can't *lose* money on.**"

So what happened? In the fall of 1993, Host Marriott began trading as an independent company. Within four months, Greenblatt tripled his money as this ugly duckling defied its doubters and took flight. Greenblatt had never expected the wager to work out so quickly. "That was luck," he says. "But we set ourselves up to get lucky."

Now, before I get too carried away, I'll admit that the *execution* of this investment was not that simple. For a start, Greenblatt bought preferred shares, which would have given him an extra measure of protection if the company had gone bust. He also used call options to structure his bet. What's more, it required a rare combination of cold rationality, independence of mind, and sheer guts to stake so much on a widely reviled business. Still, the underlying principle could not have been simpler. Remember? *"Figure out what something is worth and pay a lot less."*

## Cheap + Good = The Holy Grail

Greenblatt's investment approach continued to evolve, partly because he saw how Buffett had updated and improved Graham's strategy of buying undervalued stocks. As Greenblatt explains, Buffett added "one little, simple twist," which "made him one of the richest people in the world: **Buying cheap is great—and if I can buy *good* businesses cheap, even better."**

In his early days, Buffett had made a fortune trading in and out of mediocre companies that he bought at a deep discount. But as his assets ballooned, he needed a more scalable strategy. Under Munger's influence, Buffett shifted to buying what he described as "wonderful businesses at fair prices" and holding them indefinitely. In 1988, Berkshire invested $650 million in Coca-Cola, paying what seemed to be an exorbitant price.* On the contrary, it proved to be a steal. Why? Because it was an exceptional growth machine with a sustainable competitive advantage and high returns on invested capital. Berkshire ended up making ten times its money in twelve years.

By studying Buffett, Greenblatt gained a clearer sense of what constitutes a wonderful business. A prime specimen presented itself in 2000 with the spin-off of Moody's Corporation, a credit-rating agency that had been part of Dun & Bradstreet. Moody's "didn't appear on its face to be cheaply priced," says Greenblatt. But in a perfect example of cloning, he and Goldstein reverse engineered Buffett's Coca-Cola purchase to figure out whether Moody's might also be worth a premium price. They concluded that it was possibly the best business they'd ever seen.

Moody's was one of two dominant players in a lucrative niche with

---

* Buffett continued to buy Coca-Cola shares until 1994, ultimately investing about $1.3 billion in what he described as "the best large business in the world."

high barriers to entry. Its revenues had grown by 15 percent a year for almost two decades. And while Coke boasted impressive returns on capital, Moody's could keep growing at a healthy clip with *no* capital investment, other than paying for a few desks and computers. Greenblatt assumed conservatively that its earnings could continue to grow by 12 percent a year for a decade. The trouble was, the stock traded at a rich multiple of twenty-one times next year's earnings. But when he considered what Buffett had paid for Coke, he realized that Moody's was "still pretty darn cheap."

Who else recognized this bargain in disguise? Buffett. He bought 15 percent of Moody's and still owns much of his stake two decades later. By 2020, shares that he originally bought for $248 million were worth almost $6 billion. By contrast, Greenblatt took a handsome profit and redeployed his money in cheaper stocks. "Pretty much everything we ever owned, we sold way too early," he says. "If you're very cheap in buying, it's hard to be as comfortable when something has doubled or tripled, even if it's still good."

As a professor and a writer, Greenblatt kept pushing himself to articulate more clearly what he'd figured out about how to invest. This process "was incredibly helpful to me in trying to boil down in a very simple way exactly what I had been trying to do," he says. "It boiled down simpler and simpler." And what he came to realize is that it all boiled down to this: **Buy good businesses at bargain prices.** This combines the purified essence of Graham and Buffett.

Greenblatt's career provided plenty of anecdotal evidence that this is a smart way to win the investment game. But he wanted to prove more rigorously that he had broken the code. So, in 2003, he launched a research project that would ultimately cost about $35 million. His mission: to demonstrate that "cheap and good" companies generate outsize returns.

He hired a "computer jockey" to crunch vast quantities of data, so he could explore how these businesses had performed historically. Greenblatt needed a shorthand measure of cheapness and quality. So he chose two metrics as a rough gauge of these essential traits. First, the company should have a high earnings yield—an indication that it generates lots of earnings relative to its price. Second, it should have a high return on tangible capital—an indication that it's a quality business that effectively converts fixed assets and working capital into earnings.*

The computer whiz then analyzed 3,500 US stocks, ranking them based on these two metrics. Those with the highest combined score should, in general, be above-average businesses trading at below-average prices. Greenblatt wanted to know what would happen if a hypothetical investor bought thirty of these stocks at the start of a year, sold them after a year, then replaced them with a fresh batch of thirty top-ranked stocks. In his study, he assumed that this process would be repeated every year, creating a systematic way of investing in cheap and good companies.†

Greenblatt was "quite amazed" by the results of the back tests. From 1988 to 2004, this strategy would have generated an average return of 30.8 percent a year, versus 12.4 percent a year for the S&P 500. At that rate, $100,000 would have grown to more than $9.6 million, versus about $730,000 for the S&P 500. Here was a stock-picking strategy that relied solely on two metrics—and it annihilated the market. It was a startling testament to the power of simplicity.

Greenblatt drew on this research to write his miniature gem, *The Little Book That Beats the Market*. In between the jokes, he laid out how to "beat the pants off even the best investment professionals" by using "just two simple tools." If you want to become "a stock market master," he explained, *"stick to buying good companies (ones that have a high return on capital) and to buying those companies only at bargain prices (at prices that give you a high earnings yield)."*

---

* In his research study, Greenblatt measured earnings yield by calculating the ratio of pretax operating earnings (EBIT) to enterprise value (market value of equity + net interest-bearing debt). In other words, EBIT/Enterprise Value. He measured return on capital by calculating the ratio of pretax operating earnings (EBIT) to tangible capital employed (net working capital + net fixed assets). In other words, EBIT/(Net Working Capital + Net Fixed Assets). For the sake of simplicity, his calculations used earnings-related figures from the latest twelve-month period.

† The data-crunching was far more arduous than it sounds. For example, Greenblatt's team measured the performance of the "magic formula" portfolios over 193 one-year rolling periods between 1988 and 2004—from January 1988 to January 1989, from February 1988 to February 1989, and so on. The tests produced many striking results, including the revelation that the magic formula portfolios beat the market in 169 out of 169 three-year rolling periods.

He dubbed this simple combination of two winning traits "the magic formula."

## Do You Believe in Magic?

There is just one problem. Most investors fail miserably to become stock market masters—even when you've done all of the hard thinking for them and presented them with a magic formula.

After *The Little Book* was published in 2005, Greenblatt began to realize how difficult it was to execute the plan he'd recommended to his readers. He and his kids tried doing it, but found it tricky to keep track of so many trades. He adds, "I got literally hundreds of emails from people saying, 'Hey, thanks for the book. Can you just do this *for* me?'" He also worried that some readers might harm themselves by using unreliable corporate data pulled from the internet or by messing up the calculations when they tried to apply his formula. What if these errors led them to choose the wrong stocks and he actually hurt the people he'd set out to help?

Greenblatt's solution was to create a free website, www.magicformula investing.com, which used reliable data and made it easy to screen for stocks that met his two criteria. He often jokes, "There ain't no tooth fairy on Wall Street." But he liked the idea of protecting regular investors. So he also set up what he calls a "benevolent brokerage firm," which allowed customers to invest solely in his preapproved list of magic formula stocks.

Greenblatt gave his brokerage clients two choices. Option 1: they could open a "professionally managed" account, which followed a predetermined process of systematically buying and selling stocks from his approved list at fixed intervals. About 90 percent of the clients chose this do-it-for-me option, which freed them from making any decisions. Option 2: they could take a DIY approach, picking a recommended minimum of twenty stocks from the same list and deciding for themselves when to buy or sell. The plucky few who opted for this DIY route presumably expected that their own judgment would add a little extra magic. Ahh, such hubris!

When Greenblatt studied thousands of clients' accounts, he was shocked to discover how much worse the DIY investors performed. Over a two-year period, this group generated a cumulative return of 59.4 percent, versus 62.7 percent for the S&P 500. By contrast, the group with professionally managed accounts enjoyed a return of 84.1 percent, trouncing the S&P 500 index by 21.4 percentage points. Amazingly, the DIY investors had squandered almost 25 percentage points of performance by *making their own decisions*. Their "judgment" had transformed a market-beating strategy into a market-trailing dud. It was a startling display of self-sabotage.

"They made all the faux pas that investors do," says Greenblatt. "When the market went up, they piled in. When it went down, they piled out. When the strategy was outperforming, they piled in. When the strategy was underperforming, they stopped doing it." In theory, they may have believed in his concept of buying high-quality businesses at low prices. In practice, they chased after stocks when they were more expensive and abandoned them when they were cheaper.

To make matters worse, the DIY investors also shunned the ugliest stocks on the magic formula list, failing to recognize that these were often the most alluring bargains. Emotionally, it was hard to buy the cheapest companies on the list because their near-term prospects looked bleak and they were frequently tainted by bad news. Fearful of this uncertainty, investors missed out when these beaten-down stocks rebounded and became some of the biggest winners.

All of this self-defeating behavior highlights one of the thorniest challenges confronting every investor. **It's not enough to find a smart strategy that stacks the odds in your favor over the long haul. You also need the discipline and tenacity to apply that strategy consistently, especially when it's most uncomfortable.**

It helps immeasurably, says Greenblatt, "if you have simple principles that you can just stick to . . . simple principles that make sense, that are unshakable." Why is this so critical? Because you need this clarity of thought to withstand all of the psychological pressures, setbacks, and temptations that can destabilize or derail you along the way. "It's a hard business and the market is not always agreeing with you," says Greenblatt. "It's the nature of the beast that stock prices are emotional, and you're going to be hit from every which way, and you're going to be reading every expert saying you're wrong."

It's particularly hard to keep the faith when you're losing money or have lagged the market for several years. You start to wonder if your strategy still works or if something has fundamentally changed. But the truth is, *no* strategy works all of the time. So these periods of financial and psychic suffering are an unavoidable part of the game. Inevitably, weaker players fall by the wayside, creating more opportunity for those with the sturdiest principles and the strongest temperaments. As Greenblatt puts it, "One of the beauties of the pain that people have to take in underperformance is that, if it did not exist, everyone would do what we do."

Greenblatt has the conviction to hold firm during those painful periods. But it's easy to see why the average investor might waiver. In a back test involving the one thousand largest companies in the United States, the magic formula generated an average annual return of 19.7 percent from 1988 to 2009, versus 9.5 percent annually for the S&P 500. That's a phenomenal margin of victory. Still, the formula trailed the index in six of those twenty-two years, and it produced brutal losses of 25.3 percent in 2002 and 38.8 percent in 2008. When you're bleeding that badly, it's hard to remain unflappable unless you share Greenblatt's deep-seated certainty in the inexorable logic of the strategy.

These experiences have led him to an important revelation: "For most individuals, the best strategy is not the one that's going to get you the highest return." Rather, the ideal is "a *good* strategy that you can stick with" even "in bad times."

In recent years, that realization has inspired Greenblatt to develop a new mousetrap—a long/short strategy that's designed to reduce risk and provide a "less painful" ride. His goal: to compound money at a reasonable rate with less violent volatility, so that investors in his funds are more likely to "make it to the long term."

It's a surprising evolution for a famed gunslinger whose concentrated approach returned 40 percent a year for two decades. But it's a reminder that most investors should shoot for solid and sustainable returns, instead of something more heroic. "When I owned six or eight names, it was not uncommon to lose twenty or thirty percent in a few days every two or three years," says Greenblatt. "It's a difficult strategy to stick with, so it's not good for most individual investors. But that's perfectly good for me. When something falls twenty or thirty percent, I don't panic because I know what I own."

Nowadays, Greenblatt's team values more than four thousand businesses and ranks them based on how cheap they are. On the long side, his funds buy hundreds of stocks that trade at a discount to his estimates of fair value. He automatically bets more on the cheapest stock than on the second cheapest. On the short side, he bets *against* hundreds of stocks that trade at a premium. Again, his position size is determined by valuation, so the most expensive stock is automatically his biggest short position. "Our underlying theme is, buy the cheapest, short the most expensive—and I do that in a very systematic way," he says. "There's no emotion involved." He knows that some bets will go against him, but he's looking merely "to be right on average."

It's no easy task to execute a complex strategy involving hundreds of long and short positions. Greenblatt built a twenty-person team of financial analysts and tech mavens to help him pull it off. Yet the principles underpinning his strategy are, as ever, so simple and robust that all of us would do well to remember them:

1. Stocks are ownership shares of businesses, which must be valued.
2. They should be bought only when they trade for less than they are worth.
3. In the long run, the market is rational and will (more or less) reflect the fair value of these businesses.

The problem is that nobody ever knows if this journey toward fair value will take weeks, months, or many years. But Greenblatt is willing to wait because he trusts that these time-tested principles will eventually hold true. "If stocks are ownership shares of businesses and I'm pretty good at valuing them—at least, on average—I'll do well over time," he says. "The laws of economics and gravity will not be repealed."

## Four Simple Lessons

When I think about everything that I've learned from Greenblatt, I'm struck above all by four simple lessons. **First, you don't need the optimal strategy. You need a *sensible* strategy that's *good enough* to achieve your financial goals.** As the Prussian military strategist General Carl von Clausewitz said, "The greatest enemy of a good plan is the dream of a perfect plan."

**Second, your strategy should be so simple and logical that you understand it, believe in it to your core, and can stick with it even in the difficult times when it no longer seems to work.** The strategy must also suit your tolerance for pain, volatility, and loss. It helps to write down the strategy, the principles upon which it stands, and why you expect it to work over time. Think of this as a policy statement or a financial code of conduct. In times of stress and confusion, you can review this document to restore your equilibrium and regain your sense of direction.

**Third, you need to ask yourself whether you truly have the skills and temperament to beat the market.** Greenblatt possesses an unusual combination of characteristics that give him a significant edge. He has the analytical brilliance to deconstruct a complex game, breaking it down into the most fundamental principles: *value a business, buy it at a discount, then wait.* He knows how to value businesses. He isn't influenced by conventional opinion or authority figures such as the Wharton professors who claimed that the market is efficient. On the contrary, he delights in proving them wrong again and again. He's also patient, even-tempered, self-assured, competitive, rational, and disciplined.

**Fourth, it's important to remember that you can be a rich and successful investor without attempting to beat the market.** Over several decades, Jack Bogle watched thousands of active fund managers try and fail to prove their long-term superiority over index funds. "All these stars proved to be comets," he told me. "They light up the firmament for a moment in time. They burn out, and their ashes float gently down to earth. Believe me, it happens almost all the time."

Bogle often argued that "the ultimate in simplicity" is to buy and hold a single balanced index fund that owns a fixed percentage of US and foreign stocks and bonds. And *that's* it. No self-destructive attempts to time the market. No fantasies of picking the next hot stock or fund.

While writing this chapter, I followed his advice and chose a single index fund for my wife's retirement account—a global fund that invests 80 percent of its assets in stocks and 20 percent in bonds. I'm sure this is not the optimal strategy. But it should be good enough, assuming that she holds on to the fund for many years and adds to it regularly. This is a simple strategy based on broad diversification, a reasonable balance between risk and reward, tax efficiency, exceptionally low expenses, and a long time horizon. It lacks boldness and panache. But as Bogle told me, "You don't *have* to be great."

Personally, I am perennially torn between the mathematical logic of indexing and the dream of beating the market. But I know this much: whichever path we choose, it pays to keep it simple.

# CHAPTER SIX

# Nick & Zak's Excellent Adventure

A radically unconventional investment partnership
reveals that the richest rewards go to those
who resist the lure of instant gratification

---

If by giving up a lesser happiness a greater happiness could
be found, a wise person would renounce the lesser for the
sake of the greater.

—The Dhammapada

Everyone then who hears these words of mine and does
them will be like a wise man who built his house on the
rock. And the rain fell, and the floods came, and the winds
blew and beat on that house, but it did not fall, because it
had been founded on the rock. And everyone who hears
these words of mine and does not do them will be like
a foolish man who built his house the sand. And the
rain fell, and the floods came, and the winds blew and beat
against that house, and it fell, and great was the fall of it.

—Matthew 7:24–27

Nick Sleep dreamed of becoming a landscape architect. He envisioned
himself designing parks and public spaces that offered a refuge from
the hurly-burly of life. So, after graduating from Edinburgh University, he took a landscaping apprenticeship at a local firm. "My romantic notion of what working there might be was completely shattered by
the reality, which was that we were working on dormer windows and
car parks," he says. A few months later, he was laid off. "The staff went

from thirty to twenty. . . . And I was one of the ten that was kicked out."

Sleep, who is English, wanted to stay in Edinburgh, since he and his future wife, Serita, had bought a small apartment in the city's suburbs. "So I just looked around to see what Edinburgh was good at," he says. A career in information technology seemed like a viable option. But he also learned that Edinburgh had a reputation for fund management. He read an obscure book titled *Investment Trusts Explained* to help him figure out what the investing business was all about. He came away intrigued: "I liked that sense of it being an intellectual investigation."

Sleep landed a job as a trainee investment analyst at a small Scottish fund company. He was not abundantly qualified for the job. At college, he had studied geology and then switched to geography—hardly the standard preparation for a stock-picking career. His employment history offered no evidence that he had yearned since birth for a career in finance. He had worked in the Harrods department store, temped at an IT firm, and secured a sponsorship deal for windsurfing. With his movie-star looks and soft-spoken charm, he didn't fit the mold of a corporate drone.

Still, as luck would have it, he had stumbled into a field that perfectly suited his idiosyncratic mind. Like all of the best investors, Sleep views the world from an unusual angle. He suspects this stems from his formative experience as a teenager at Wellington College, an English boarding school founded by Queen Victoria. Sleep was one of the few students who lived at home, which meant that he "floated free" on the periphery of school life. He even worked in a pub on weekends, while most of his classmates stayed on their four-hundred-acre campus. "I got comfortable with being different from everyone else early on," he says. "I was happy being outside the group."

When Sleep was about twenty, he fell under the spell of Robert Pirsig's *Zen and the Art of Motorcycle Maintenance: An Inquiry into Values*. This memoir-as-tutorial, which had been rejected by 121 publishers, is a strange but brilliant meditation on what it means to lead a life dedicated to "Quality." Pirsig exalts people who care so intensely about the quality of their actions and decisions that even the most mundane work becomes a spiritual exercise—a reflection of inner traits such as patience, integrity, rationality, and serenity. Whether you're mending a chair, sewing a dress, or sharpening a kitchen knife, he writes that there is "an ugly way of doing it" and "a high-quality, beautiful way of doing it."

For Pirsig, motorcycle maintenance provides an ideal metaphor for how to live and work in a transcendent way. "The real cycle you're working on is a cycle called yourself," he writes. "The machine that appears to be 'out there' and the person that appears to be 'in here' are not two separate things. They grow toward Quality or fall away from Quality together."

As you might imagine, most of the hyper-ambitious strivers on Wall Street don't have a lot of patience for mystical mumbo jumbo about motorcycles. But Pirsig's vision of a soulful, ethical, intellectually honest approach to life resonated deeply with Sleep and shaped the type of investor he would become. In an email about Pirsig's enduring impact on him, Sleep remarks, "You really want to do everything with quality as that is where the satisfaction and peace is."

But what does this mean when it comes to investing? In 2001, Sleep and his friend Qais "Zak" Zakaria created a fund called the Nomad Investment Partnership, which they viewed as a laboratory test for how to invest, think, and behave in the most "high-quality" way. In one of his eloquent and amusing letters to shareholders, Sleep would muse, "Nomad means far more to us than simply managing a fund. . . . Nomad is a rational, metaphysical, almost spiritual journey (without the sand and camels, although Zak may be happier with them)."

None of this would matter if it weren't for the stunning outcome of their peculiarly high-minded experiment. Over thirteen years, Nomad returned 921.1 percent versus 116.9 percent for the MSCI World Index.* In other words, their fund beat its benchmark index by more than *800 percentage points*. To put that another way, $1 million invested in the index would have grown to $2.17 million, while $1 million invested in Nomad rocketed to $10.21 million.

In 2014, Sleep and Zakaria returned their shareholders' money

---

* These figures exclude Nomad's performance fees. The fund's annualized return *before* fees was 20.8 percent. After fees, it was 18.4 percent, versus 6.5 percent for the MSCI World Index.

and retired as fund managers at the ripe old age of forty-five. Since then, they've managed their own money with equally striking success, approximately tripling their wealth in their first five years of retirement. Sleep, with characteristic indifference to conventional opinion, invested almost all of his fortune in just three stocks. At times, he and Zakaria have had as much as 70 percent of their money in a single stock.

Among the cognoscenti, few other investors are held in such high esteem. Bill Miller, who says he admires the "complete independence" and "clarity of their thinking," invested his own money in Nomad. Guy Spier, who is friends with Sleep, reveres him as one of the most profound thinkers in the investment world. When I asked Mohnish Pabrai for advice about which investors to interview, he told me, "Nick Sleep is exceptional. He does very deep research and has very high concentration. That's a lot of putting your nuts on the line. . . . He would be a fascinating interview, but he won't do it. He's a very private person."

Indeed, part of their mystique lies in the fact that Sleep and Zakaria have always flown under the radar. They had minimal interest in marketing their fund and even less interest in self-promotion. As a result, their story has never been told. But over the last few years, I've interviewed Sleep on multiple occasions. Then, in the fall of 2018, I spent an afternoon with him and Zakaria at their office on the King's Road in London—a bright and cheery space, which is so informal that Zakaria doesn't even have a desk. He prefers to work in a plush leather armchair, which faces a wall where their matching beekeeper suits hang together from hooks. It was there—in "Galactic HQ"—that they reflected on what they call their "adventures in capitalism."

What emerged from our conversations is a heartening morality tale in which the good guys win. It's also a story about the extraordinary advantages that accrue to investors with the discipline and patience to resist the temptations of instant gratification. In a high-speed era dominated by short-term thinking, this capacity to defer rewards is one of the most powerful contributors to success, not only in markets, but in business and life.

## A House Built on Sand

Zakaria, like Sleep, never dreamed of working on Wall Street. "To be honest, I would have loved to have done something else," he says. "I would have been a meteorologist if my parents had let me. I found it fascinating. I used to read weather reports and do my own weather reports, and my parents thought it was stupid."

Born in Iraq in 1969, he came from a relatively privileged family. His father worked for the Iraqi central bank. His mother lectured on nutrition at the University of Baghdad. But it was a perilous time, rife with political intrigue and violence. "We were purged," says Zakaria. His family fled, leaving everything behind. In 1972, a Catholic charity helped his parents find refuge in the UK, where they would raise their three children. "They pitched up here with nothing," says Zakaria. "Literally nothing except an orange Volvo, which they'd been given by someone in Turkey."

His father knocked on doors until he found a job as a junior accountant. He worked his way up, then started a successful business exporting machinery to Iraq. Zakaria's parents expected him to join the firm and eventually run it, helping to expand their cushion against the uncertainties of life. "Money is very important to them," he says. "The accumulation of money. Not necessarily spending it. It's about security and status." In 1987, Zakaria headed to Cambridge University to study mathematics. Everything seemed on track. But that same year, his father went bankrupt.

It turned out that he'd speculated in the stock market using borrowed money. He had traded hot stocks touted in dubious tip sheets and had fallen for pyramid schemes pitched by sleazy salesmen. One stockbroker "would recommend a stock based on this pyramid of who was in first and who was in last," says Zakaria. "The more money you put in, the higher you got in the pyramid. My father never got high enough, and when it all collapsed, he lost everything." The family was deluged with debt and the export business died.

For Zakaria, it was a sickening introduction to the investment business. "My father had made his money on things he understood and lost it on things he didn't understand, and he was taken to the cleaners by very unscrupulous people." These memories left Zakaria with a permanent suspicion of salespeople, get-rich-quick schemes, and the "casino" aspect of Wall Street.

After graduating from Cambridge in 1990, Zakaria entered the investing game largely by default. The family business was no longer an option. Unlike his siblings, he couldn't become a doctor because he faints at the sight of blood. And meteorology is stupid. So he took a job in Hong Kong as an equity analyst at Jardine Fleming, one of Asia's leading asset managers. It went well enough until 1996. Then his boss, a hotshot fund manager, was accused of allocating successful trades to his own account, allegedly depriving clients of profits that should have been allocated to *their* accounts. The fund manager was fired and fined millions of dollars. But with the firm's reputation in tatters, the business had to be restructured. Zakaria was laid off.

"I rang round a couple of friends and said, 'Do you have anything? I'll literally do *anything*.'" A friend who ran a stockbroking desk at Deutsche Bank took mercy and gave him a job as a "sell-side" analyst specializing in Asian stocks. It was one of life's cruel cosmic jokes. Zakaria, with his distrust for salespeople in general and stockbrokers in particular, would earn his keep by hawking stock tips to the bank's institutional clients. "I did it for four years, and it was absolute hell," he says. "Not being someone who is easily sold to, I couldn't sell to anyone."

His time at Deutsche provided Zakaria with a crash course in the ways of Wall Street. "It was a shocking place to work," he says. Moral compromises went with the territory. "My good friend and boss there said, 'You must never persuade someone not to do what they want to do, even if you think it's wrong. Just let them do it because you'll never be thanked.' And I thought, 'That's a terrible way to live.' It's awful! I mean, if you think they're making a mistake, you should *tell* them." Zakaria says he was so ill-suited to the job that he'd have been fired within a month if his boss hadn't "shielded" him. Still, there was one consolation. He met Nick Sleep.

After three years in his first investing job back in Edinburgh, Sleep had become an investment analyst at Sun Life of Canada, a financial services giant with tens of thousands of employees. "I was almost allergic to working there," he says. "Once you've worked for a feisty company, it's quite difficult to go work for something big, dull, and boring." He quit after a few months and landed in 1995 at Marathon Asset Management, where he would stay for more than a decade. It was a scrappy, high-flying investment firm in London that was "trying to outbox the big guys."

Sleep's mentor there was one of Marathon's cofounders, Jeremy Hosking, an English eccentric whose hobbies include collecting vintage steam engines. "He's naturally iconoclastic," says Sleep. "His bias is to buy just about the most despised thing he can find. . . . He likes the controversy, the difficulty." When the Asian financial crisis struck in 1997, Hosking and Sleep went scavenging for cheap stocks in the smoldering markets of Southeast Asia. Everyone else seemed to be running for cover as Asia's economic miracle turned to disaster. But the Marathon Men found an unlikely ally in an Asia-based broker who wasn't like everyone else: Zakaria.

Sleep and Zakaria talked regularly about the crazy bargains they were unearthing in places like Singapore, Hong Kong, and the Philippines. Most brokers focused on popular assets that were easy to sell. But Zakaria was excited by reviled stocks trading at fabulous discounts. "Zak was a rubbish stockbroker because what would appeal to him would appeal to us and would appeal to nobody else," says Sleep. "So it had no commercial value. You couldn't sell it to anybody else." But Zakaria's eye for discarded jewels was precisely what made him valuable to Marathon. Hosking told him, "When you can't sell a stock to anyone else, call us."

During the miracle years, investors had been so bullish about Asia that they had bet on stocks trading at three times the replacement cost of their assets. During the crisis, you could buy those same stocks for *one-quarter* of the replacement cost of their assets. In less than a year, Marathon invested about $500 million in Southeast Asia and made a killing as the region rebounded. Part of the credit went to Zakaria. "He was exactly the analyst we needed in the Asian crisis," says Sleep. "He was just a salesperson working for an investment bank, but he wasn't really doing a salesperson's job because he wasn't selling what they wanted him to sell." This sense that Zakaria was swimming (somewhat desperately) against the tide was about to intensify.

If you were a satirical novelist looking to write about Wall Street at its worst, you might choose a golden age of greed such as late 1999 and early 2000. It was a time when the mania for tech and internet stocks mangled the minds of bankers, brokers, fund managers, and regular investors. Millions of people were consumed by a desire for instant riches, and their only apparent fear was the fear of missing out.

Deutsche and its rivals profited handsomely by taking half-baked companies public at inflated valuations, ignoring whatever doubts they may have harbored about whether these businesses would endure. Research analysts at supposedly reputable brokerages acted as shameless stock promoters.* And brokers like Zakaria felt obliged to sell this dreck to investors who either knew no better or dreamed of getting rich before the frenzy faded. This was the ultimate casino. Yet Zakaria refused to play. "The IPOs were all absolutely awful, and I'd *tell* people they were awful. And, of course, you wouldn't sell any, and it was all very miserable."

One deal etched forever in his mind involved a Taiwanese tech start-up, GigaMedia Ltd. It was less than two years old and profits were nothing but a distant dream. Undeterred, Goldman Sachs and Deutsche Bank decided to take it public on Nasdaq in February 2000 at the peak of the bubble. Zakaria says one of his colleagues—"your archetypal perfect salesperson"—phoned a fund manager in Paris and told him, "I think you should buy it." The fund manager placed a $150 million order. There was just one problem. This exceeded the total assets in his fund. Still, nobody seemed to care, since it was all a game. The fund manager was betting that the bank would grant him a fraction of the shares he requested and that the stock would surge.

Lo and behold, GigaMedia's stock shot up from $27 to $88 on the day of the IPO, giving this money-losing minnow a valuation of more

---

* The research department at Merrill Lynch was particularly cynical, positioning itself as a relentless cheerleading team that helped to attract lucrative investment banking clients to the firm. Henry Blodget, Merrill's star internet analyst, issued buy recommendations for companies that he described privately as "dogs," a "piece of shit," and "falling apart." In 2003, regulators fined Blodget $4 million and banned him permanently from the securities industry. I'm not writing this to single him out, but to give you a flavor of that euphoric period and a keen sense of why we need to be perennially wary of *anything* that Wall Street is powerfully incentivized to sell.

than $4 billion. But it was all an illusion. When the dot-com bubble burst a few weeks later, GigaMedia lost 98 percent of its value.

For Zakaria, it was all too much—the irrationality, the lack of substance, the willingness to do whatever it took to make a quick buck regardless of who got hurt. "I suffer from anxiety, and I needed something that was more grounded," he says. "My time at Deutsche Bank was just so bad for me healthwise because there's nothing grounded in being a stockbroker. You turn up in the morning and you have no idea how your day is going to develop, whether your client is going to like you or hate you, or whether you're going to be sacked or not. It was all so unstable."

He was rescued by Marathon. In April 2000, when the dot-com darlings were getting smashed to pieces, Zakaria escaped from Deutsche to work with Sleep as an analyst at Marathon's office in London. In May, they traveled together to Omaha for Berkshire Hathaway's annual meeting. "It was wonderful," says Zakaria. Warren Buffett and Charlie Munger spoke about companies they expected to own for decades. They weren't rolling the dice on the latest idiotic IPO or scheming to line their pockets at other people's expense. "Oh, my God," thought Zakaria. "This is nothing to do with a casino! This is about real businesses!"

Sleep kept nagging his bosses to let him launch a concentrated fund within Marathon, with Buffett serving as his model. Buffett struck him as the embodiment of quality. It wasn't just the depth of his thinking about businesses, but the honorable way in which he treated Berkshire's shareholders, beginning with his modest salary of $100,000 a year. At one extreme, says Sleep, "you've got Buffett being as principled as you can possibly be." At the other extreme, "there are marketing-driven companies that happen to be selling investment funds, but could be selling cars or washing machines. . . . They couldn't give a toss about their clients."

When Sleep's bosses gave him the green light to start the Nomad Investment Partnership in 2001, he asked Zakaria to join him as comanager of the fund. "It was obvious that we were always going to do something a little bit odd," says Sleep. Indeed, from the start, they regarded Nomad as an act of rebellion against what he calls "the sin and folly" of the investment industry. "We wanted to prove that there's another way of investing and another way of behaving," says Sleep. "You don't have to go and do all of the Wall Street bollocks."

## Never Mind the Bollocks*

Sleep and Zakaria had no interest in building a colossal fund that would shower them with fees. They didn't fantasize about appearing as market gurus on CNBC or being fetishized on the cover of *Forbes*. They had no desire to buy themselves castles, airplanes, or yachts. Their ambition was simple. They wanted to generate superb long-term returns.

Specifically, their target was a tenfold increase in Nomad's net asset value. Sleep, who has three daughters and a godson, framed this mission in somewhat whimsical terms: If they ever asked him, "What did you do during the war?," he wanted to reply, "We turned one pound into ten pounds."

Anyone looking to achieve stellar returns would do well to study what Sleep and Zakaria figured out about where to focus their attention—and, equally important, what they ignored. Sleep cites a line from the philosopher William James: "The art of being wise is the art of knowing what to overlook." He and Zakaria rejected a slew of standard practices. "We were just getting rid of all the things we didn't like," says Sleep. "We were signed-up members of the awkward squad."

For a start, they disregarded all of the ephemeral information that distracts investors from what matters. Sleep notes that information, like food, has a "sell-by" date. But some of it is *especially* perishable, while some has "a long shelf life." This concept of shelf life became a valuable filter.

---

* In the unlikely event that you're wondering about the origin or meaning of this elegant phrase, it's a reference to the 1977 punk album *Never Mind the Bollocks, Here's the Sex Pistols*. The word *bollocks*—a British term for testicles—was deemed so offensive that many stores refused to carry the album. But the *Oxford English Dictionary* says the word has been in use since at least the thirteenth century. The Sex Pistols emerged triumphant from their obscenity trial after an expert witness noted that *bollocks* even made an appearance in early translations of the Bible. The controversy helped to launch the career of Richard Branson, who'd released the album on Virgin Records.

For example, when I spoke with Sleep and Zakaria again in May 2020, the financial news was full of speculation about the near-term impact of the COVID-19 virus on consumer spending, corporate profits, unemployment, interest rates, and asset prices. An article in the *Financial Times* even debated whether a US economic recovery might resemble the letter *V*, *U*, *W*, *L*, or a "Nike swoosh." To Sleep and Zakaria, this fleeting news coverage was all part of the daily "soap opera" of the market—too superficial, short-lived, and unreliable to hold their attention. They couldn't predict how the economic news would unfold. So why waste mental energy on the unknowable?

Similarly, they ignored the flood of short-term financial data and recommendations gushing out of Wall Street. Brokerage firms, which have an incentive to spur activity among investors, crank out unreliable estimates of the next quarter's earnings per share for thousands of companies. Sleep refers dismissively to the "quarterly EPS junkies" who crave this information, which will already be "worthless" in twelve weeks. As he sees it, the "short-term crowd" responds constantly to "false stimuli," whether it's the latest economic data point or the trivial news that a company has beaten analysts' expectations. "You need to be wired not to believe the bullshit, to not be listening."

One practical way of extricating themselves from this muck was to discard all of the sell-side research excreted by Wall Street. "We put it in a pile," says Zakaria. "Every month or so, you start looking through, thinking, 'I'm bored.' So the whole lot would go in the bin. . . . It really was all just gossip and bits of nonsense, and we became very happy with the idea of not hearing it." Likewise, Sleep and Zakaria told stockbrokers that it was pointless phoning them with sales pitches since they relied on their own research to reach independent conclusions.

They also disengaged from the day-to-day action of the market by minimizing their use of a Bloomberg terminal. Fund managers often stare interminably at a wall of four monitors flashing real-time data and financial news at them. The Bloomberg, which costs about $24,000 a year to rent, is a status symbol among professional investors. But to this day, Sleep and Zakaria relegate their single Bloomberg monitor to a short side table without a chair. "It was *meant* to be uncomfortable," says Zakaria. "Nick wanted it on a low table because you could only spend five minutes without thinking, 'Oh, my back's killing me,' and you move on."

Pat Dorsey, a Chicago-based hedge fund manager, expresses a similar view. "The single best thing any investor can do is to not have a TV and a Bloomberg terminal in their office," he once told me. "That I have to walk fifty feet down the hall to look at stock prices or check the news on our portfolio is great. It's so tempting. It's like checking email obsessively: you get a little dopamine rush. But as we all know logically and rationally, it's utterly nonproductive."

This practice of *intentional disconnection* may seem perverse in a culture that prizes instant access to infinite information. But Sleep and Zakaria disavowed the standard game of ceaselessly collecting data and betting on what it might portend for stocks in the near term. They wanted to think in peace, undisturbed by the popular obsession with what Sleep termed "wiggle guessing."

It requires uncommon conviction to disregard what most of your peers consider significant. But once they'd decided to shut off the noise from Wall Street, they felt joyously liberated. "It's like a voice in your head [that's] chattering away all the time," says Sleep. "Stop listening to it and you'll be fine." So how did they spend their time? "We just read annual reports until we were blue in the face and visited every company we possibly could until we were sick of it." Sleep traveled so much that he filled every page of a supersize passport and had to order another.

When they analyzed companies and interviewed CEOs, Sleep and Zakaria probed for insights with a long shelf life. They sought to answer such questions as *What is the intended destination for this business in ten or twenty years? What must management be doing today to raise the probability of arriving at that destination? And what could prevent this company from reaching such a favorable destination?* They referred to this way of thinking as "destination analysis."

Wall Street tends to fixate on short-term outputs, favoring questions such as *What will this company's profits be over the next three months?* and *What is our twelve-month price target for this stock?* Sleep and Zakaria focused instead on the inputs required for a business to fulfill its potential. For example, they wanted to know, *Is this company strengthening its relationship with customers by providing superior prod-*

*ucts, low prices, and efficient service? Is the CEO allocating capital in a rational way that will enhance the company's long-term value? Is the company underpaying its employees, mistreating its suppliers, violating its customers' trust, or engaging in any other shortsighted behavior that could jeopardize its eventual greatness?*

It's worth noting that destination analysis is an equally handy tool in other areas of life. If, say, your goal is to be healthy in old age, you might ask yourself what inputs (in terms of nutrition, exercise, stress reduction, medical checkups, and the like) are required now to boost your odds of reaching that destination. If you want to be remembered lovingly by your family and friends, you might picture them at your funeral and ask how you need to behave today so they will cherish the memory of you. This emphasis on destinations had a profound impact on Sleep and Zakaria. "You want to look back at eighty," says Sleep, "and think that you treated your clients equitably, did your job properly, gave money away properly—not that you had four houses and a jet."

It came naturally for them to think along unconventional lines because they were two odd ducks who had landed in the investment industry by accident—a failed landscape architect and a frustrated meteorologist. As perennial outsiders, they questioned everything. Above all, they could never accept the unspoken belief that their own financial interests trumped those of their clients. As a result, Nomad's fee scheme was uncommonly fair. Sleep and Zakaria charged a tiny annual management fee that merely covered their costs, instead of the usual fee of 1 or 2 percent of assets. They also received 20 percent of their fund's investment profits, but only *after* delivering a 6 percent annual return. If they performed poorly, they would earn no fees at all.

A few years later, they stacked the deck even more heavily against themselves by deciding to place their performance fees in a holding bucket for several years. If Nomad subsequently fell short of its 6 percent annual hurdle, they would *refund* a portion of those previously earned fees to their shareholders. "We quite liked the idea that this wasn't going to be a big payday for us," says Zakaria. "We wouldn't make out like bandits as everyone else does."

Their attitude was influenced by *Zen and the Art of Motorcycle Maintenance,* which Sleep had recommended to Zakaria shortly after they met. The book reinforced their determination to resist any low-quality behavior that seemed self-serving or deceitful. "The very rapid rejection of things made life very straightforward," says Zakaria. "It was all about quality. . . . Money was secondary. It was much more about doing a good job, a *quality* job, doing the right thing. I don't think we ever took a decision which was driven by—"

"—putting money in *our* pockets. Definitely not," says Sleep, completing Zakaria's thought.

"There was something a little provocative about the whole thing," says Zakaria. "Could you set up an investment outfit which is not about the money? It's about doing everything right."

As you'd expect, the priority at most investment firms is to maximize their own profits, which creates some glaring conflicts of interest. For example, they routinely prosper by selling overpriced products that deliver lackluster returns. They also place an overwhelming emphasis on increasing their assets under management, since this generates bounteous fees with which to bankroll lavish salaries and bonuses. It's no secret that investment returns tend to deteriorate as assets expand. But money managers typically resist the logical solution of closing their oversize funds to additional investments. As the author Upton Sinclair wrote, "It is difficult to get a man to understand something, when his salary depends upon his not understanding it!"

By contrast, Nomad was conceived from the start as a vehicle for maximizing returns, not assets. "We had a different morality system," says Sleep. "If you're in the asset-gathering business, then you've got sales guys, you've got compliance guys, you've got client-holding people, you've got bureaucracy, and it becomes this big machine. If you're wanting to compound and have really good investment performance, you don't need any of that crap. . . . We just concentrated on picking good stocks and thought everything else was peripheral."

For a start, they regarded sales and marketing as a distraction. They almost never spoke to the media. They didn't care if a potential client was large or small since their priority was never to build the most lucrative commercial enterprise. They also made it clear that they'd return money to their existing shareholders and turn away new investors if Nomad's size ever became a hindrance to its performance. They repeatedly closed the fund to new subscriptions, starting in 2004 when they managed about $100 million—a paltry sum by industry standards. They reopened only when they could find sufficiently alluring opportunities to deploy additional cash.

They also took delight in turning away investors who seemed unsuitable or irritating, regardless of how rich they were. Zakaria chuckles at the memory of a comically awful meeting with a team that managed billions for heirs to the food-packaging company Tetra Pak. These financial advisers demanded access to Nomad's proprietary stock research as a condition for investing their clients' money in the fund. Zakaria says the atmosphere grew "frostier and frostier," with Sleep crossing his arms and legs in a sign of mounting annoyance. After fifteen minutes, Sleep and Zakaria showed their visitors the door.

Potential investors were also required to sign a document acknowledging that Nomad was inappropriate for anyone with less than a five-year time horizon. "I wanted it in a different psychic space than all the other investments they had," says Sleep. "We weren't just another bloody hedge fund. . . . We were tackling the whole investment problem in a different way."

Indeed, Nomad rejected all of the get-rich-quick tactics that hedge funds routinely use to pump up their short-term performance—high-testosterone strategies that Sleep dubbed "investment Viagras." For example, Nomad never used leverage, never shorted a stock, never speculated with options or futures, never made a macroeconomic bet, never traded hyperactively in response to the latest news, never dabbled in exotic financial instruments with macho names such as LYONs and PRIDEs. Instead, Sleep and Zakaria played what they viewed as "a long, simple game," which involved buying a few intensively researched stocks and holding them for years.

Their slow, patient, deliberate strategy was so countercultural that it sounds almost quaint. Investor time frames have shortened drastically over the years. When Vanguard's founder, Jack Bogle, entered the investment business in 1951, mutual funds held stocks for an average of about six years. By 2000, that figure had shrunk to about one year, provoking Bogle to warn that "the folly of short-term speculation has replaced the wisdom of long-term investing." In 2006, Sleep wrote to shareholders that Nomad's average holding period for stocks was seven years, whereas other investors held the US stocks in Nomad's portfolio (excluding Berkshire Hathaway) for an average of only fifty-one days.

Sleep and Zakaria were appalled by this cultural shift toward short-termism. "We cannot for the life of us figure out why society at large is served by having company owners swap seats every few months," wrote Sleep. "This basic building block of society is broken when those with their hands on the permanent capital change their minds with their underwear." Nomad would succeed by taking the opposite approach. "The Bible would say that you want to build your house on rock rather than sand," says Sleep. "You want to build something that has permanence."*

## A House Built on Rock

Sleep and Zakaria named their fund Nomad because they were willing to roam anywhere in search of value. They were not trying to replicate a particular index or perform well on a *relative* basis. They were gunning for outstanding *absolute* returns, unconstrained by reference to what anyone else was doing. Their quest took them to some of the least popular corners of the globe.

The fund began trading on September 10, 2001—one day before the attack on the Twin Towers. Markets cratered as investors confronted unfathomable threats of terrorism, war, and economic disruption. Adding to the gloom, many investors were still in shock from the bursting of the tech bubble. Sleep and Zakaria invested boldly amid the turmoil, targeting temporarily depressed businesses that others were too scared to own, since the future seemed so precarious.

In the Philippines, they invested in Union Cement, the nation's largest cement producer, after its stock had plunged from thirty cents to less than two cents. Pessimism was so pervasive that the market val-

* Sleep, who believes in what he describes as "nondenominational kindness," says, "I don't know whether there's a God or not, but if you change the word from *God* to *good*, I completely believe in that. . . . It's enough for me that good exists, and I believe that good things grow."

ued the business at one-quarter of the replacement cost of its assets. In Thailand, they invested in Matichon, a newspaper publisher whose stock had crashed from $12 to $1. It traded at 0.75 times revenues and was worth about three times what they paid for it. In the United States, they bought preferred shares of Lucent Technologies, a fallen telecom star that had lost 98 percent of its value. These were classic "cigar butts"—not the best businesses, but fantastically cheap. By the end of 2003, Nomad's net asset value had doubled as opportunistic bets like these paid off.

The supply of bargains dwindled as fears receded and markets revived. So Sleep and Zakaria ventured to one of the few remaining pockets of despair. In 2004, they crossed the border from South Africa into Zimbabwe. Under Robert Mugabe's despotic rule, Zimbabwe's economy was paralyzed by corruption, a currency collapse, the nationalization of many privately owned farms, and mobs of looters. Undaunted, Sleep and Zakaria bought a basket of four Zimbabwean stocks—virtual monopolies that traded as if they were almost worthless. Zimcem, a cement producer, sold on the stock exchange in Harare for *one-seventieth* of the replacement cost of its assets.

Writing to Nomad's investors about the perverse appeal of this detested market, Sleep remarked, "The clients will hate it. Compliance will hate it. The consultants will hate it. Marketing will hate it. The size of the investment opportunity is tiny. It is not part of the benchmark. . . . It's perfect."

For a while, Nomad valued its basket of bargains at zero because trading on Zimbabwe's stock exchange ceased entirely. The economy remained a catastrophe. Still, by the time Nomad sold the last of its Zimbabwean stocks in 2013, they'd risen between threefold and eightfold. As a souvenir, Sleep and Zakaria gave each Nomad shareholder a worthless banknote for 100 trillion Zimbabwean dollars, which the government had issued at the height of hyperinflation.

Nomad's appetite for reasonable businesses selling at unreasonably low prices made sense, given the opportunities available at the time. But this strategy had one drawback. When stocks like these rebounded and were no longer that cheap, they had to sell them and hunt for new bargains. But what if nothing particularly attractive was on sale when they sought to redeploy those winnings? **An obvious solution to this reinvestment risk was to buy and hold higher-quality businesses that were more likely to continue compounding for many years.**

This second strategy grew out of a costly mistake. In 2002, Nomad made its biggest wager to date, investing in Stagecoach, a debt-ridden British bus operator that had overreached disastrously while expanding overseas. The stock had crashed from £2.85 to 14p, but Sleep and Zakaria figured it could easily be worth 60p. In part, they were betting on a turnaround led by the founder, a former bus conductor who'd run the firm so adroitly in the past that he'd become one of Britain's richest people. He came out of semiretirement to streamline the business and refocus on its neglected cash cow: the UK bus operation. His strategy worked. Sleep and Zakaria cashed out at around 90p and congratulated themselves on a sixfold gain. But Stagecoach was a better business than they'd realized. In late 2007, the stock hit £3.68. "We felt like a bit of a horse's arse," says Sleep. "We had framed it in our own minds as only ever being a cigar butt."

Sleep and Zakaria started searching for other businesses run by far-sighted managers whom they could trust to keep building wealth over time. "If they're thinking rationally and thinking about the long term," says Sleep, "you can subcontract the capital allocation decisions to them. You don't have to be buying and selling shares." They also began to wonder what characteristics account for the success of companies with unusually long shelf lives, and they would reach the revelatory conclusion that one business model may be more powerful than all the rest. Their term for it is *scale economies shared*.

The company that introduced them to this model was Costco Wholesale, an American discount retailer that embodied everything they sought in a business. When they first invested in Costco in 2002, its stock had tumbled from $55 to $30 amid concerns about the company's low profit margins. But Sleep and Zakaria saw underappreciated strength in Costco's fanatical focus on delivering value to shoppers. At the time, its customers paid a $45 annual membership fee, which gave them access to warehouses filled with dependable products sold at the lowest-possible prices. Costco marked up its goods by no more than 15 percent above cost, while a typical supermarket might mark up prices by 30 percent. Members had no need to forage elsewhere for bargains because Costco treated them so fairly. The company could have jacked up its prices and boosted margins, but that would have jeopardized its members' trust.

To the skeptics on Wall Street, this generosity seemed soft and uncompetitive—the corporate equivalent of collectivism. But Sleep and Zakaria saw the long-term logic of Costco's largesse. Satisfied customers kept returning and spending more money in its stores, thereby generating enormous revenues. As the company grew, it negotiated better deals with suppliers and kept driving down its famously low costs. Costco then shared these economies of scale with consumers by lowering its prices even further. Sleep and Zakaria estimated that its members saved $5 for every $1 that Costco kept for itself. The effect of this policy of self-restraint was a virtuous cycle that Sleep sums up like this: "Increased revenues begets scale savings begets lower costs begets lower prices begets increased revenues."

Most big, successful corporations eventually lapse into mediocrity. But Costco's readiness to *share* the benefits of its scale with customers meant that size became an advantage, not a burden, enabling the company to extend its edge over rivals that boasted higher margins. Costco, which was founded in 1983, *kept growing by giving back*, instead of grabbing all of the spoils for itself. Its low margins reflected patience, not weakness. Writing to Nomad's investors, Sleep explained, "The firm is deferring profits today in order to extend the life of the franchise. Of course Wall Street would love profits today but that's just Wall Street's obsession with short-term outcomes."

Sleep and Zakaria kept adding to their investment as their reverence for Costco grew. By 2005, it accounted for one-sixth of Nomad's assets. Today, it remains one of the linchpins in their personal portfolios. During the eighteen years they've owned the stock, it's risen from $30 to about $380, while also paying rich dividends. Still, they have no intention of selling it anytime soon, given the likelihood that Costco will continue to advance toward a desirable destination.

One benefit of their inactivity is that Sleep and Zakaria had time to read, think, and talk at length about what they were learning. Sleep has the mental agility to skip lightly between different disciplines—

from business history to religion, neuroscience to sports—and to identify common themes and patterns. Zakaria, whom Sleep describes as "hugely intelligent," has less breadth, but tends to probe more deeply. One subject they often discussed was the question of which business models work best. They kept a list of them on a whiteboard in their office. What emerged from these discussions was a conviction that nothing matches the might of the scale-economies-shared model in fostering corporate longevity.

When they studied Walmart's annual reports from the 1970s, they realized that it had much in common with Costco. Likewise, durable winners such as Dell Computer, Southwest Airlines, and Tesco all followed a similar path. These formidably efficient firms kept costs low and passed most of their savings back to consumers, who reciprocated by doing more business with them.

In the same vein, GEICO and the Nebraska Furniture Mart—two of Buffett's favorite businesses—continued to drive down costs as they grew, enabling them to save their customers so much money that it became increasingly difficult for rivals to compete. Henry Ford pulled off a similar trick a century ago, harnessing the benefits of assembly-line production to drop the price of a Model T touring car from $850 in 1908 to less than $300 in 1925. "So it's not a new business model," says Sleep. "But it does need to be pursued with an evangelical zeal."

The culture of such companies is typically molded by visionary founders, not hired hands. They tend to be passionate about the smallest details, improving the customer experience, cutting costs even in good times, and investing for the distant future despite external pressures to report strong numbers now. "They have to be almost high on being iconoclastic," says Sleep. These legendary figures include Sam Walton at Walmart, Jim Sinegal at Costco, Herb Kelleher at Southwest, and Rose Blumkin at Nebraska Furniture Mart. Blumkin, a Russian immigrant who worked from the age of six until after her hundredth birthday, built America's biggest home-furnishings business by faithfully observing three commandments: "Sell cheap, tell the truth, don't cheat nobody."

Once Sleep and Zakaria understood the magic of this one business model, they made it the overriding focus of their fund. The attraction of cigar butts waned and they concentrated instead on a hand-ful of companies that shared their economies of scale with customers. They were acutely aware of how little in life we ever truly know. But they *knew* that they had uncovered a deep truth. "That's the best single thought you may have ever had in your life," says Sleep. "It needs to dominate everything because you're not going to get many insights like that. Everything else is a bit low quality, isn't it? It's a bit transitory. It doesn't make a big difference."

Sleep and Zakaria packed their portfolio with companies cut from the same cloth. They bet 15 percent of Nomad's assets on ASOS, a Brit-ish online fashion retailer with a cost advantage over traditional high street stores, and rode its stock up from £3 to £70. They invested heav-ily in Carpetright, a chain founded by Lord Harris, a British entrepre-neur with severe dyslexia who inherited his father's small business at fifteen and ended up with hundreds of stores across Europe. Nomad also became the largest foreign shareholder of AirAsia, the world's lowest-cost airline. And then there was Amazon.com—the ultimate practitioner of scale economies shared.

When Sleep first encountered Amazon in 1997, it was an upstart bookseller preparing to go public. Its founder, Jeff Bezos, gave a presen-tation in London, explaining how his profitless start-up would offer an almost infinite selection of books, how it would gain a cost advantage by avoiding the expense of physical stores, and how it would reinvest its cash flow in other businesses. Sleep raced back to his office at Mara-thon and told his boss, "This is absolutely fantastic. It could be huge. And he says, 'Yeah, okay, Nick, but what are they doing that nobody else can do?'"

It took years for Sleep and Zakaria to grasp the nature of Amazon's competitive advantage. But eventually, the penny dropped. Bezos was following in the hallowed footsteps of the Ford-Walton-Sinegal gang—and the internet would enable him to turbocharge their classic strategy.

Like them, Bezos was ruthlessly efficient about controlling costs. According to Sleep, Amazon even went so far as to save $20,000 a year by removing the light bulbs from vending machines in its offices. Bezos was obsessed with saving money and time for customers. And he invested patiently for the future, seeding new business initiatives that he didn't expect to bear fruit for five to seven years. Each year, he invested hundreds of millions of dollars in the form of discounted prices and shipping subsidies—a consummate display of deferred gratification.

True to form, Wall Street grumbled about Amazon's lack of reported profits, failing to appreciate that Bezos was patiently laying the groundwork for mind-blowing growth. Writing to Amazon's shareholders in 2005, Bezos explained that "relentlessly returning efficiency improvements and scale economies to customers in the form of lower prices creates a virtuous cycle that leads over the long term to a much larger dollar amount of free cash flow, and thereby to a much more valuable Amazon.com." Sleep and Zakaria had found their corporate soul mate.

That year, Bezos launched Amazon Prime, a membership service that offered free two-day shipping for an annual fee of $79. He would later sweeten the deal by throwing in everything from free movies and TV shows to unlimited storage of photographs. In the short run, this overabundance of benefits and savings would hurt the bottom line. In the long run, it would strengthen customer loyalty and spur even more spending. When Bezos unveiled Prime, Sleep and Zakaria recognized instantly that it was the Amazonian equivalent of Costco's annual membership fee. "Oh my God, I know *exactly* what game they're playing here," thought Sleep. "Amazon suddenly became Costco on speed."

Nomad started buying Amazon aggressively in 2005 at around $30 per share. In 2006, Sleep and Zakaria resigned from Marathon and made Nomad a fully independent fund, giving themselves even more latitude to follow their idiosyncratic convictions. They bet 20 percent of the fund's assets on Amazon and secured permission from their shareholders to go beyond that limit. A quarter of their clients yanked their money from Nomad, fearful of its overexposure to one stock.

Skepticism about Amazon continued to swirl. In the midst of the 2008 market meltdown, Sleep attended an event in New York where George Soros spoke about the threat of an impending financial apocalypse. Soros, one of the most successful traders in history, named just one stock that he was shorting as the world fell apart: Amazon.

Over lunch that day, Sleep caught up with Bill Miller, whose mutual funds owned the largest outside stake in Amazon. Miller had recognized Amazon's strengths earlier than anyone else and had bought

15 percent of the company. But he told Sleep that he'd been forced to reduce his holdings to meet redemption requests from investors fleeing from his funds. Sleep phoned Zakaria in London that evening and asked, "Are you sure we know what we're doing because everyone here is going in another direction?" They had never felt more confident about a company's eventual greatness. But what if they'd misanalyzed the business? What if they'd missed something and all the doubters were right? "Either we're brilliant," thought Sleep, "or we're really toast."

Amazon lost almost half of its market value in 2008, while Nomad fell 45.3 percent. Sleep and Zakaria held an emergency meeting in an appropriately posh location—McDonald's—to discuss the possibility that Nomad's future might be in peril if the market continued to crash. They shuddered at the thought of ending up as analysts at some shitty Wall Street firm.

Still, they didn't crack. While others panicked, they exploited the market mayhem to upgrade their portfolio, concentrating even more heavily on the highest-quality companies, including Amazon, Costco, ASOS, and Berkshire Hathaway. When the rebound came, the rewards were breathtaking. From 2009 through 2013, Nomad returned 404 percent.

In early 2014, Sleep and Zakaria dissolved the Nomad Investment Partnership. By then, it had grown to about $3 billion in assets, giving them the scale to earn astronomical sums. But that had never been the purpose of their great adventure. Many funds "start with lots of cake as their goal," Sleep writes in an email. "It's not the cake that gratifies us. What we found gratifying was the process of solving the investment problem, learning along the way and doing as good a job as we knew how—they are all internal personal goals. The cake was then a (happy) byproduct."

Zakaria, in particular, worried that the work would become repetitive. "Intellectually, we felt we had completely sucked it dry," he says. "We had thought about this from every angle, about what we thought was important, and I think I'm right saying there was nothing left." So they retired, hoping to devote the second half of their lives to supporting charitable causes. Sleep wrote a letter to Buffett, thanking him for his role in Nomad's success. Buffett replied, "You and Zak have made the right choice. I predict you will find life is just beginning."

In less than thirteen years, Nomad had gained a staggering 921 percent before fees—just short of their target of turning £1 into £10. Amazon, which had risen tenfold since 2005, had played a pivotal role. At one point, it had grown to about 40 percent of the fund's assets.

In retirement, Zakaria kept half a dozen or so of his favorite stocks from Nomad's portfolio. His biggest holding, Amazon, surpassed $3,000 per share in 2020, giving it a market value of $1.5 trillion and making Bezos the world's richest person. Zakaria, who has never sold a share of Amazon in his personal portfolio, has about 70 percent of his money riding on that one stock. The rest is almost entirely invested in Costco, Berkshire Hathaway, and an online retailer named Boohoo .com. Zakaria says he occasionally glances at his portfolio and wonders, "What would Nick do? And I think, 'Nick wouldn't do *anything*.' And I go, 'Okay, that's done for another six months.'"

As for Sleep, he invested almost all of his money in just three stocks: Amazon, Costco, and Berkshire. "There are very few businesses that are investing in the future the way they are," he says. "They don't care about Wall Street. They don't care about the trends and the fads. They're just doing the right thing long term." The volatility of a three-stock portfolio didn't bother him, given the high probability that all three businesses would reach a desirable destination.

However, by 2018, Amazon had risen so meteorically that it accounted for more than 70 percent of his net worth. Sleep began to worry. Could its market value grow to $3 trillion or $4 trillion, or were there limits even to Amazon's greatness? He wasn't sure. So, after thirteen years, he sold half of his stake in a single day for $1,500 a share. How did it feel? "I hated it," he says. "I felt horribly conflicted, and I'm not sure it's a good decision."

For a while, Sleep sat patiently on tens of millions of dollars in cash, not sure how to invest his windfall from selling those shares in Amazon. But when we spoke in 2020, he had invested the money in a *fourth* stock, ASOS—an online retailer that he'd previously owned at Nomad. Since he repurchased it, the stock had already doubled. In short, life is still sweet.

## Five Lessons with a Long Shelf Life

As I see it, there are five key lessons to be learned from Sleep and Zakaria. **First, they provide a compelling example of what it means to pursue quality as a guiding principle in business, investing, and life**—a moral and intellectual commitment inspired by *Zen and the Art of Motorcycle Maintenance*. It's easy to dismiss quality as a vague and subjective notion, but it offers a surprisingly useful filter for many decisions. For example, it was obvious to Sleep and Zakaria that a low annual management fee that merely covered Nomad's operating costs was a higher-quality option than a fatter fee that would enrich them regardless of how they performed.

**Second, there is the idea of focusing on whatever has the longest shelf life, while always downplaying the ephemeral.** This principle applied not only to the information they weighed most heavily, but also to the long-lasting companies they favored.

**Third, there is the realization that one particular business model— scale economies shared—creates a virtuous cycle that can generate sustainable wealth over long periods.** Sleep and Zakaria took this one great insight and profited massively from it by focusing on a few high-quality businesses that followed a similar path. Paradoxically, they also argued that it was less risky for them to own a small number of stocks (usually about ten) than to own hundreds—a standard strategy that would inevitably have produced less dazzling returns. "We knew that we didn't know many things," says Sleep. "So it made sense to us only to have a few shares because those were the only things we ever understood and ever *really* knew."

It was no surprise to them that the businesses they knew the best and loved the most—Amazon, Costco, and Berkshire—proved remarkably resilient even when the world was turned upside down by COVID-19. After all, their economies of scale enabled them to provide customers with exceptional value for money. "With Amazon and Costco, in particular, what you've seen is their businesses being *enhanced* by the crisis," says Zakaria. "The worse the environment gets for the economy in general, the better it gets for these cost-advantaged businesses."

Fourth, it's not necessary to behave unethically or unscrupulously to achieve spectacular success, even in a voraciously capitalistic business where self-serving behavior is the norm. During the financial crisis, Sleep wrote about the destruction caused by a culture in which "the players just have to win" and "are not too squeamish about the means." He and Zakaria wanted Nomad to embody a more enlightened form of capitalism.

This explains why they adopted a fee scheme that favored their shareholders over themselves. They were generous to each other, too. For example, Zakaria insisted that Sleep should own 51 percent of their investment firm, instead of an equal share; if a disagreement were ever to arise, Zakaria trusted Sleep to make the final decision. Sleep says it was unthinkable to abuse a partner who had "loaded a revolver, passed it across the table, and said, 'Go on, then, you can shoot me if you like!'" He adds, "There's a kindness to the relationship, which I think is important to our success." It's telling that they still share an office several years after winding up their fund. As Sleep puts it, "Good behavior has a longer shelf life."

A strong emphasis on charity is also a distinguishing feature of their gentle version of capitalism. "Once we had proved what we wanted to do running Nomad, it was very obvious to both of us that the job at hand was to give the money back to society," says Sleep. "It lowers the risk of us being bent out of shape by having too much money." Plus, "you have the joy of giving it away."

Zakaria and his wife, Maureen, support an array of charities that are oriented toward scientific research and medicine, including the London Mathematical Laboratory, the Royal Society, and the Royal Hospital for Neuro-disability. Meanwhile, Sleep spends much of his time helping OnSide Youth Zones, a charity that creates safe havens where kids in poor areas can socialize and learn new skills. He says the primary focus for him and Zakaria has shifted to "doing the maximum amount of good . . . over the very long term."

That said, Sleep hasn't renounced *all* worldly pleasures. He loves motor racing and competes regularly in his 1965 Shelby Mustang GT350 and his 1967 Lola T70. He also took part with his daughter Jess in a thirty-six-day rally from Beijing to Paris (via Mongolia and Siberia), taking turns driving his 1964 Mercedes Pagoda.

**Fifth, in a world that's increasingly geared toward short-termism and instant gratification, a tremendous advantage can be gained by those who move consistently in the opposite direction.** This applies not only to business and investing, but to our relationships, health, careers, and everything else that matters.

Deferring gratification is no easy task, given the environment in which we live. In wealthier nations, everything is available on demand—limitless food, information, bingeable TV shows, every flavor of porn, or whatever else tickles our fleeting fancy. Our attention spans are shortening under a high-speed bombardment of emails, text messages, Facebook posts, and Twitter notifications. Similarly, in the investment realm, we can now dart in and out of the market instantaneously by pushing a few keys on our mobile phones. We're all struggling in our own ways to adjust to this technological and social revolution, which is both miraculous and perilous. As pleasure-seeking creatures, we tend to be drawn to whatever feels good now, despite the price that we (or others) may have to pay later. This is evident not just in our individual lives but collectively in everything from government deficits to unconstrained energy consumption.

"It's all about deferred gratification," says Sleep. "When you look at all the mistakes you make in life, private and professional, it's almost always because you reached for some short-term fix or some short-term high. . . . And that's the overwhelming habit of people in the stock market."

Just think for a moment of the many unchecked impulses that ruin investors' returns: for example, the tendency to trade too frequently; to make emotional decisions based on alarming or alarmist news stories; to join the herd in charging after the most popular (and overpriced) assets; to dump funds that have lagged for a year or two; or to sell winning stocks prematurely, instead of leaving them to compound for years. The ability to resist such urges is "one of those big superpowers," says Sleep. "You need to give it huge weight when you're weighing what works."

Sleep and Zakaria are titans of impulse control. How else could they have held Costco for eighteen years and Amazon for sixteen years while it has soared from $30 to more than $3,000 per share? They understood the fundamental truth that we benefit by deferring gratification and prioritizing long-term outcomes. But it's not enough to grasp this principle intellectually. Equally important, they constructed an internally consistent ecosystem that *supported* such behavior.

For a start, most of their investors were nonprofits (such as college endowments) with expansive time horizons. In his shareholder letters, Sleep praised them effusively for their "gentle patience"—a tactful way of reinforcing the right mindset. Nomad also invested in businesses run by fellow nonconformists, such as Bezos and Buffett, who took an exceptionally long view. It helped, too, that Sleep and Zakaria set themselves up in a peaceful office above a Chinese herbal medicine store on the King's Road, far removed from the frenetic action in major investment hubs. They also eliminated disruptive influences by shunning sell-side analysts and financial consultants (who compulsively monitor the day-to-day performance of funds). They were so detached from all of the drama and excitement that they likened themselves to hermits or monks.

If you and I hope to achieve long-lasting success as investors, we need to follow their example by *systematically resisting the external and internal forces that push us to act impetuously*. With that in mind, I ignore all of the useless media chatter about looming market corrections and crashes. I go weeks on end without checking how my investments have performed.* My default position is to do nothing. Hence, the majority of my portfolio sits quietly in two index funds and a value-oriented hedge fund, all of which I've owned for at least twenty years. My costliest mistakes have come whenever I grew impatient or envious of other people's returns and strayed off course by gambling on private

---

* Since I first wrote this sentence, I've come to realize that it's not entirely true. In reality, I often check my portfolio several times a day during stressful periods such as the COVID-19 pandemic. It's a nervous habit that's more harmful than helpful. On the plus side, it hasn't yet driven me to make any impetuous investment moves. Still, it's unsettling to realize how easy it is for me to backslide and become addicted to such counterproductive habits.

companies or individual stocks that held the promise of a racier route to riches. The paradox here is that the slower road almost always proves to be faster in the end.

The investors I admire most tend to be heroically inactive, not because they're lazy but because they recognize the benefits of patience. Howard Marks once told me, "Our performance doesn't come from what we buy or sell. It comes from what we hold. So the main activity is holding, not buying and selling. I've always wondered if it wouldn't enhance an organization to say, 'We only trade on Thursdays.' And the other four days of the week, all you can do is sit and think."

Nobody personifies this slow-motion mindset better than Thomas Russo, who has generated market-beating returns over more than three decades at Gardner Russo & Gardner, which is based in Lancaster, Pennsylvania. "I call myself a farmer," says Russo. "Wall Street is flooded with hunters—people who try to go out and find the big game. They fell it and bring it back, and there's a huge feast and everything is fabulous, and then they look for the next big game. I plant seeds and then I spend all of my time cultivating them." His biggest holdings include Berkshire Hathaway, Brown-Forman, and Nestlé, all of which he's owned since the 1980s. A few years ago, when he was fifty-nine, I asked Russo if he expected to own Berkshire and Nestlé for the rest of his life. He replied without hesitation, "I would think so."

Like Sleep and Zakaria, Russo has built his entire career on an appreciation of the power of deferred rewards. All of the businesses he owns share one trait, which he describes as "the capacity to suffer." That's to say, they invest for "the very long haul," even when this expense requires them to stomach years of painful upfront losses. As Russo remarks, we tend to benefit whenever we "sacrifice something today" to "gain something tomorrow."

What's fascinating to me is that this timeless principle applies not only to business and investing, but to every area of our lives. We can see it when we exercise or diet, when we study hard for an exam or stay late at work, and when we save money or invest for retirement. In each case, we profit in the long run by embracing or enduring something that seems unappealing in the short run. Conversely, says Sleep, "I think it's almost always true that the things we do that make us unhappy" look appealing "in the short term." He cites an array of popular pitfalls: getting drunk, "eating too much cake," telling lies, "visiting girlie bars," and "nicking sweets from a corner shop." In the moment, he says, "all of these things seem like a good idea. They're exciting. They reward. There's a bit of a rush. But in the end, they borrow from the long term."

None of this is new. In the book of Genesis, Esau—a sucker for instant gratification—trades his precious birthright to his brother, Jacob, in return for a worthless bowl of lentil soup. By contrast, Jacob's son, Joseph—a master of deferred gratification—has the foresight to set aside vast quantities of grain during the "seven years of abundance," ensuring that Egypt survives the "seven years of famine" that follow. Thousands of years later, we're presented over and over with this same choice between the *present* and the *future*, the *instant* and the *deferred*.

For most of us mortals, it's a challenging choice. But Zakaria says he enjoyed the slightly pious feeling of donning a "hair shirt" and "rejecting instant gratification" while others succumbed to temptation. This reminds me of a marvelous Buddhist phrase that's used to describe one of the subtle rewards of resisting unhealthy or unskillful behavior: *the joy of nonremorse*. Likewise, kabbalists such as Rav Yehuda Ashlag and Rav Philip Berg teach that the only way to achieve enduring happiness, fulfillment, and freedom is to resist our negative inclinations. In his landmark book *Kabbalah for the Layman*, Rav Berg writes, "Instead of choosing the line of least resistance, the quick fix, instant gratification, the kabbalist chooses the line of most resistance." It's a profoundly important truth about the counterintuitive path to contentment.

One practical trick, says Sleep, is to "reward yourself in the short term" by relishing the prospect of all the wonderful benefits you will enjoy because you chose to override your desire for instant gratification. That way, deferral becomes associated with pleasure and "you're much more likely to embrace it." Indeed, says Sleep, "I quite *like* the overriding because you just know that it's going to make your life better."

# CHAPTER SEVEN

# High-Performance Habits

## The best investors build an overwhelming competitive advantage by adopting habits whose benefits compound over time

---

It makes no small difference, then, whether we form habits of one kind or of another from our very youth; it makes a very great difference, or rather all the difference.

—Aristotle

I think that people underestimate—until they get older— they underestimate just how important habits are, and how difficult they are to change when you're forty-five or fifty, and how important it is that you form the right ones when you're young.

—Warren Buffett

In 1990, Tom Gayner weighed 190 pounds. Nobody would have mistaken him for an Olympic gold medalist in beach volleyball. Still, he says, his weight was "within the realm of reasonableness." That year, at age twenty-eight, he took a job running the investment portfolio at the Markel Corporation, an insurance firm based in Richmond, Virginia. Investing is a sedentary sport that largely entails reading, thinking, and playing with numbers. Gayner was built exquisitely for it. Even as a boy of eight or nine, his idea of an enjoyable Friday evening was to sit in front of the TV with his grandmother and watch *Wall $treet Week with Louis Rukeyser*.

As he grew older, Gayner's talent for sitting and thinking had an unintended consequence. His weight gradually drifted above two hundred pounds. Determined to drift no more, he proclaimed to friends and colleagues that he'd lose one pound per year for the next ten years. That may sound absurdly unambitious, but some studies suggest that the average American male gains one to two pounds per year between early adulthood and middle age. Gayner, a master of compounding money, understood how small advantages—or disadvantages—add up over long periods. So he set about changing the unhealthy habits of a lifetime.

"As a kid, I had the diet of a campground raccoon," he says. For example, he reckons that he ate about two hundred doughnuts per year. Some dieters would have renounced such sinful pleasures entirely, committing (for a while) to a joyless doughnut-free existence before (almost inevitably) falling off the wagon. Not Gayner. He cheerfully confesses that he might still eat twenty doughnuts per year. Overall, though, he's done an admirable job of sticking with a healthy diet. I've eaten several meals with him over the years, including lunch at an old-fashioned club in New York (where he ordered a Caesar salad with salmon and unsweetened ice tea), two lunches at his office (more salad, more fish), and dinner at his home in the suburbs of Richmond (where he cooked a delicious pesto-flavored salmon with brussels sprouts, accompanied with wine and followed with ice cream). Nutritionally, as in other areas of life, Gayner's strategy is to be "directionally correct," not perfect. "In general," he says, "I'm a satisfier, not an optimizer."

He has taken a similar approach to exercise. "I was never very good at athletics," he says. "The peak of my athletic career was in seventh grade, with church basketball." He claims to have run less than five miles *in total* before the age of fifty. Then, while sitting on an airplane, he read a newspaper article with the headline "Do You Hate Running?" "Yeah," he thought, "I hate running." But the article laid out a twenty-eight-day program so cunningly innocuous that he decided to try it. In the first week, he was required to run for a maximum of five minutes per day. That grew to ten minutes per day in the second week, fifteen in the third week, and twenty in the fourth week. At that point, he says, "you've baby-stepped yourself into it in such a way that you've created a habit." Sure enough, more than five years later, he still runs five times a week. He typically sets off around 5:30 a.m. or 6:00 a.m., while most of us are luxuriating in bed, and jogs about three miles in thirty minutes. "I have deceptive speed," he says. "I'm even slower than I look."

Gayner, who is now the co-CEO of Markel, a financial holding company with insurance and investment operations around the world, may not set any records for the 100-meter dash. But his running habit (topped off with a little yoga and some modest kettlebell lifting) helps him to handle the physical demands and daily stress of a relentless job that involves managing about $21 billion in stocks and bonds, plus a collection of nineteen fully owned companies, not to mention around seventeen thousand employees. "If you're an executive or a money manager who has these kinds of responsibilities, you're playing the game twenty-four hours a day, seven days a week. There's no off-season. There are no days off," he says. "As a consequence, I think it's very important to be disciplined about paying attention to your well-ness, your sleep, your exercise, a little work-life balance, spending time with your wife and kids and your fellow parishioners—all these sorts of things." Such behavior "may not create the outcome that you want, but it improves your odds."

What's distinctive is the indomitable consistency of his discipline. Most people get fired up for a few days, then flame out. I own a kettle-bell and a skipping rope, neither of which I've used more than three times. The primary purpose of their existence is to make me feel guilty. Yet Gayner keeps plugging away, never perfect, but always *directionally correct*. The key, he says, is that he is "radically moderate" about every-thing he does. "If I make extreme changes, they're not sustainable. But *moderate, incremental* changes—they're sustainable."

He's also careful not to let himself slide too far in the wrong direc-tion. After a brisk walk around a lake near his office, he shows me how his Apple Watch monitors his movements to ensure that he meets his "thirty-minute daily exercise requirement." Likewise, he checks his weight every day unless he's traveling, and "if it got away from me, then I'll work out a little harder or will try to be a little more conscious of what I eat for a while. If you never let it get out of whack, it's easier to keep things centered. And that, in general, describes much of how I try to get through life."

This radically moderate and doggedly persistent strategy demon-strably works.* When I spent a day and a half interviewing him in 2017, Gayner weighed in at 194 pounds, which is not much more than he weighed twenty-seven years earlier. In terms of weight gain, I've outperformed him by a hefty margin, illustrating how minor differ-ences in day-to-day behavior compound over decades.†

All of this points to an important conclusion that applies both to investing and life. **Resounding victories tend to be the result of small, incremental advances and improvements sustained over long stretches of time.** "If you want the secret to great success, it's just to make each day a little bit better than the day before," says Gayner. "There are different ways you can go about doing that, but that's the story. . . . Just making progress over and over again is the critical part."

## "The Aggregation of Marginal Gains"

Gayner has applied the same philosophy to investing. Many investors lurch erratically from one short-term bet or promising strategy to the next, much like yo-yo dieters who bounce between fad diets without entrenching a sustainable solution. Gayner, the patron saint of steady progress, adheres to a stock-picking strategy built on four principles that haven't changed in thirty years. They point him in the right direc-tion and help him to avoid "being stupid. . . . They're like guardrails."

First, he seeks "profitable businesses with good returns on capital and not too much leverage." Second, the management team must have "equal measures of talent and integrity." Third, the company should

---

* I'm not suggesting that Gayner's way of eating and exercising would work equally well for everyone, given the complex interplay of factors such as genetics and metabo-lism. But I'm confident that his approach would work better for most of us than Buf-fett's health regimen, which includes breakfast at McDonald's on his way to the office, heartbreaking quantities of red meat, and rivers of Coca-Cola. Buffett once joked to Mohnish Pabrai's daughters that he wouldn't touch anything that he didn't eat when he was less than five years old.

† NEWS FLASH! When we spoke again in 2020, Gayner informed me, "This morn-ing, as I stepped on my scale, I was 189.6." His steady, persistent effort had paid off and he had finally returned to what he weighed thirty years ago.

have ample opportunity to reinvest its profits at handsome rates of return. Fourth, the stock must be available to him at a "reasonable" price.

Once Gayner finds a business that passes his four-part test, he looks to invest with "a forever time horizon," leaving the stock to compound indefinitely while deferring the tax consequences of selling. Berkshire Hathaway was the first stock he bought at Markel back in 1990, and his stake has snowballed to more than $600 million. Buffett made a mistake in 1965 when he acquired control of Berkshire, which was then a failing textile manufacturer destined for extinction. Still, the stock has since soared from about $15 to $330,000 as he's reinvested the company's assets in greener pastures. "What you had going for you," says Gayner, was that the person "making the reinvestment decisions was a genius." As Gayner sees it, Berkshire demonstrates that the most important of his four criteria is number three, "the reinvestment dynamic."

Gayner's second-largest holding is CarMax, which he's owned since the late 1990s. Back then, it was a small company with the novel idea of selling used cars at fixed prices, violating the tradition of haggling with and hoodwinking buyers. Gayner, a devout Episcopalian who was raised as a Quaker, recalled that the Macy's department store was founded in the 1850s by a Quaker who sold each item at a set price, eliminating any suspicion that customers would be duped by sly salesmen. Wouldn't CarMax enjoy a similar advantage, given its commitment to transparency and fair dealing? What's more, the stock was cheap and CarMax had boundless opportunities to reinvest its profits by opening new dealerships. Since he first invested, it has expanded from about eight dealerships to two hundred, and the stock has risen more than sixtyfold.

Gayner's portfolio is dominated by dependable compounding machines such as Brookfield Asset Management, the Walt Disney Company, Diageo, Visa, and Home Depot—businesses that he expects to prosper for a long time, despite the threat of creative destruction. For example, it reassures him that Diageo owns Johnnie Walker, a two-hundred-year-old brand of Scotch whisky: "That seems to me to be a pretty durable thing. So I just try to find things like that in life." He's not looking to trade them, but to sit tight as they grow: "It's been my experience that the richest people were those who found something good and held on to it. The people who seemed the least happy and the most frenzied and the least successful are those that are always chasing the next hot thing."

In all, Gayner owns about one hundred stocks, which may be overly defensive. But two-thirds of his assets are in his top twenty positions, which is moderately aggressive. His attitude toward tech stocks such as Amazon, Alphabet, and Facebook has been similarly measured. He was "very slow" to appreciate their sustainable competitive advantages, but belatedly recognized that they met his four investment criteria. Still, they weren't cheap, and he couldn't value them precisely. So he took an incremental approach. He "steadily" accumulated big (not huge) positions, dollar-cost averaging his way in to reduce the risk of overpaying. If he has blundered, it won't be disastrous.

This emphasis on disaster avoidance reminds me of a marvelous insight from Jeffrey Gundlach, who oversees about $140 billion as the CEO of DoubleLine Capital. Gundlach, a brash and brilliant billionaire known as the King of Bonds, says he's wrong about 30 percent of the time. So he asks one critical question before making any investment: "If I assume that I'm wrong on this, what's the *consequence* going to be?" He then tries to structure his bet so the outcome won't be ruinous, whatever happens. "**Make your mistakes nonfatal,**" **Gundlach tells me. "It's so fundamental to longevity. And ultimately, that's what success *is* in this business: longevity.**"

Gayner's portfolio is built to last. It would have been much more lucrative if he'd loaded up on Amazon, Google, and Facebook. But his investment decisions—much like his approach to food and exercise—are not intended to be optimal. Rather, he's attempting to be consistently and sustainably sensible. The cumulative effect of operating this way over three decades has been extraordinary because he has harnessed the power of long-term compounding without ever galloping "at such a pace" that he would heighten "the odds of some catastrophic falloff."

In the two worst years of his investment career, Gayner's stock portfolio fell 10.3 percent in 1999 (when tech stocks went berserk and he made the mistake of shorting them) and 34 percent in 2008 (when the credit crisis revealed that some of the businesses he owned were more leveraged than he'd realized). His wife, Susan, who is the CEO of a manufactured-housing business owned by Markel, says those two periods were "dark nights of the soul" for Gayner, filled with "self-doubt and despair." Gayner says the financial crisis was so stressful that he lost much of his hair. Still, he survived and eventually resumed his steady upward trajectory.

The results are remarkable. From 1990 through 2019, Gayner's stock portfolio achieved an average annualized return of 12.5 percent, versus 11.4 percent for the S&P 500. At that rate, $1 million invested in Gayner's portfolio would have grown to $34.2 million, versus $25.5 million if that money had been invested in the S&P 500. It's an impressive demonstration of how valuable it is to maintain even a modest edge over a long period.

"If you can continue to satisfy and be reasonable, there's all kinds of people that are going to fall away along the path, and it's amazing how high up in the percentile rankings you'll become," says Gayner. "I was never the number one at anything. I've always just been steady and competent and able. But as my father said, the best ability is dependability.* So to do it over and over and over and over again, it keeps you in the game. And it's amazing how you do sort of become number-oneish over time, just because the competitive field thins out so much."

Markel itself has also traveled quite a distance, and in much the same manner. When it went public in 1986, it was an obscure specialty insurer with a market value of about $40 million. The Markel family, which founded the firm in 1930, hired Gayner (who had followed

---

* Gayner's father, who was his biggest influence, was the embodiment of good-humored resilience. He grew up in the Great Depression, which bankrupted the family's glassmaking business, plunging them into poverty. In his youth, he earned cash by sneaking out of the house at night and playing clarinet in an illegal speakeasy. He fought in World War II and was shot in the knee. He later qualified as an accountant, bought a liquor store, and put together small property deals. "My father was the richest person I've ever known," says Gayner. "And it's not because he had more money than Jeff Bezos or Warren Buffett. But he had *enough*. That's a psychological statement."

the company for years as an analyst and stockbroker) to help them replicate Berkshire Hathaway's business model. Gayner took premiums from Markel's insurance operation and used that "float" to buy stocks and, since 2005, whole companies—much as Buffett invested premiums from *his* insurance operations. It was a masterful display of cloning, sustained (characteristically) over decades. Still, Gayner dislikes the term *cloning* as it might imply that he merely copied Buffett, instead of observing what worked and "recombining" it to suit his own circumstances.

How did it turn out? Gayner pulls out a copy of Markel's 1987 annual report and shows me that its total assets back then were $57.3 million. By the end of 2019, its total assets had ballooned to *$37.4 billion*. Markel's market value has grown to about $14 billion, and the company ranked 335th in the Fortune 500 list for 2020. "That's a pretty good run from there to here," says Gayner. "It's the same path. It's the same trajectory. It's the compounding."

Markel's shareholders also have reason to rejoice, including Gayner, who has more than half of his net worth in the stock. At its IPO, Markel traded at $8.33 per share. By the end of 2019, its stock had climbed to $1,143. That's a 137-fold gain.

**What Gayner's record shows is that you don't need to be extreme to achieve exceptional long-term results. On the contrary, he says, "People get themselves into trouble with extremes."** His steadfast pursuit of a radically moderate path would have met with the approval of some of the wisest thinkers in history, such as Confucius, Aristotle, Buddha, and Maimonides.

Aristotle, the ancient Greek philosopher, argued some twenty-four hundred years ago that excellence and lasting happiness depend on our ability to seek out the "golden mean"—an "intermediate" position that is "equidistant from each of the extremes." When it comes to physical pleasures such as food, wine, and sex, he taught that we should stake out a middle ground between overindulgence and abstinence. Similarly, in the face of risk, he recommended steering a judicious course between the opposing extremes of timidity and recklessness: "For the man who flies from and fears everything and does not stand his ground against anything becomes a coward, and the man who fears nothing at all but goes to meet every danger becomes rash."*

Gayner is neither cowardly nor rash. Everything he does seems reasonable and balanced—from the way he eats and exercises to the way he structures his portfolio as a compromise between diversification and concentration. The beauty of his moderate approach to investing and life is not just that it delivers bounteous rewards, but that it's *replicable* by regular human beings like you and me. Some of the famous investors I've interviewed have so much brainpower that they seem to operate in another realm, including Charlie Munger, Ed Thorp, and Bill Miller. Gayner is highly intelligent. But his real advantage is behavioral, not intellectual. Comparing himself to some of his cleverest peers, he remarks, "I compensate for the lack of intellect with more discipline and steadiness and persistence."

That said, it's easy to underestimate Gayner. Jovial and self-deprecating, he lacks the ego and glamour we often expect from the lords of high finance. He drives a Toyota Prius. ("I like getting fifty miles per gallon because I'm cheap," he says. "And if we did not need oil, I think the world would be a more peaceful place.") He lives in a pleasant but modest town house. ("It's just low maintenance.") And he describes himself as "very happily married" to his high school sweetheart—a Presbyterian minister's daughter whom he dated when he was fifteen and married at nineteen. For their first date, his parents drove them to a custard stand in the small town of Salem, New Jersey, where he grew up on a hundred-acre farm.

In short, there's nothing flashy or grandiose about Gayner. Yet it would be hard to find a better role model in the investment world. After all, his "satisfying, slow, and steady" method of building wealth relies heavily on common sense and well-chosen habits, not esoteric

---

* Lou Marinoff's illuminating book *The Middle Way: Finding Happiness in a World of Extremes* explores some fascinating parallels between Aristotle, the Buddha, and Confucius. Buddha, like Aristotle, exhorted his students to pursue the "Middle Way," avoiding two opposing and "unprofitable" extremes: "the addiction to indulgence of sense pleasures" and "the addiction to self-mortification." As for Confucius, he taught that "the superior man" follows "the path of the Mean," which leads to mental equilibrium and a harmonious social order.

skills or daredevil risks. When I ask him what regular investors should do to get rich, he offers the least exotic advice imaginable: "Live on less than you make. Invest the difference at a positive rate of return. You cannot fail if you accomplish those two tasks." He adds, "If you're living on less than your means, you're rich right now."

Gayner is remorselessly careful about controlling costs. He manages Markel's investments with razor-thin expenses and maximum tax efficiency—a cost advantage that any of us can emulate by trading infrequently and avoiding financial products with onerous fees. He's equally frugal in his personal life, a habit that he says was "hardwired" in him during his Quaker childhood. He can't bear to buy food in airports and can barely bring himself to pay for two restaurant meals a day while on vacation, even though he earns millions of dollars a year in total compensation.

If frugality is an essential ingredient of his formula for financial success, so, too, is diligence. As an undergraduate at the University of Virginia, he could get away with coasting. Now? Not so much. He typically arrives at the office by 7:15 a.m., packs his mornings with work since that's when he's most productive, and allows few distractions. "We've structured things to be quiet," he says. "We're sitting here in my office. How many times have you heard my phone ring?"

Attached to the front of his computer screen is a piece of paper bearing a quotation from Michael Jordan: "I failed over and over again in my life, and that is why I succeed." Gayner likes to remind himself that Jordan didn't make it onto his varsity basketball team as a sophomore at high school, but then harnessed his "superhuman" work ethic and "sheer willpower" to become one of the greatest players of all time. **"You cannot control the outcome," says Gayner. "You can only control the effort and the dedication and the giving of one hundred percent of yourself to the task at hand. And then whatever happens, happens."**

When I interviewed him again in 2020, the United States was in the throes of riots and a pandemic. But Gayner remained as focused as ever on controlling his own effort, sticking to his investment process, and setting an example for his employees. "Keep putting one foot in front of the other," he told me. "That's what has guided me my whole life. So why should that be different now?"

Another feature of Gayner's incremental self-improvement strategy is his deep commitment to "continuous" learning. He reads voraciously—everything from scientific books on habit formation to biographies to novels by his favorite author, Mark Twain. But he also views himself as "a node in a neural network," interconnected with many smart people who can assist in his constant quest to expand his knowledge and improve his skills.

Chuck Akre, a renowned money manager whom we'll soon meet again, helped him to refine his understanding of reinvestment as the most powerful driver of business success. Josh Tarasoff, a gifted hedge fund manager, helped him to figure out why he should own Amazon. Gayner also served for years alongside Buffett on the board of the Washington Post Company. One indelible lesson was that "persistence and endurance" are essential components of Buffett's edge: "The energy and stamina that he has is absolutely unbelievable. . . . In the morning, he's ready to go, and he's the Energizer Bunny who just keeps going and going and going. That's an athletic feat."

It's no accident that Gayner enjoys the trust of many leading investors. "One of the advantages I have is that I'm a nice guy," he says. "I try to help people. I try to do the right thing. As a consequence, what I've found is that I have this wonderful network of friends, colleagues, and associates who are rooting *for* me, rather than *against* me. And they help you. They just help you." We sometimes assume that you have to be ruthless to elbow your way to the top. But Gayner illustrates the subtler benefits of consistently looking to be kind and decent. I've come to think of this underappreciated edge as the Mensch Effect. Guy Spier, who runs the Aquamarine Fund, invests so much of his energy in helping others that he is similarly surrounded by people who wish to help him. Spier describes this phenomenon as "the compounding of goodwill."

If your goal is *sustainable* success, Gayner is convinced that it works better to behave admirably, not least because more people want to do business with you if you're trustworthy. "Sometimes people build great careers and enjoy great successes for a period of time through bluster and bullying and intimidation and slipperiness," he says. "But that always comes unraveled. Always. Sometimes it takes a while, but it does. The people you find that just keep being successful year after year after year after year, I think you find those are people of deep integrity."

When I try to identify the many reasons why Gayner has achieved so much, I'm reminded of a concept that Nick Sleep mentioned to me: "the aggregation of marginal gains." The phrase was coined by a legendary performance coach, Sir David Brailsford, who turned the British cycling team into an unstoppable force at the Beijing and London Olympics. Those triumphs stemmed not from one major innovation, but *a multitude of minor improvements*, which combined to create a crushing advantage. For example, Brailsford's cyclists raced on wheels rubbed with alcohol to enhance their grip. They wore electrically heated overshorts to maintain the right temperature for their muscles. They studied how surgeons wash their hands to reduce the risk of illness. They even brought their own pillows on trips so they were more likely to sleep well.

Brailsford, who has an MBA, was inspired by the Japanese principle of *kaizen* (continuous improvement), which had played a starring role in vaulting Toyota to greatness. Speaking with Eben Harrell at the *Harvard Business Review*, Brailsford explained, "It struck me that we should think small, not big, and adopt a philosophy of continuous improvement through the aggregation of marginal gains. Forget about perfection; focus on progression, and compound the improvements."

Sleep, who is an avid cyclist, says the best businesses share this obsession with securing even the most marginal gains. He recalls how Lord Harris, the founder of Carpetright, insisted on reusing old price tags, writing on both sides to save a penny here, a penny there. "It's not one secret sauce," says Sleep. "You just have to care about all the little things and add them all together."

If you want to understand Gayner's success, then look no further. Nobody cares more about all the little things. Individually, his day-to-day habits seem inconsequential—the equivalent of cyclists traveling with their favorite pillows. *He gets up early and arrives at the office early. He jogs and does yoga. He eats heaps of salad and a dearth of doughnuts. He works in a quiet office where he can focus. He consistently applies four time-tested principles as a filter for every investment idea. He invests in a tax-efficient manner. He keeps his investment expenses as low as possible.*

*He lives way below his means. He reads insatiably. He studies and intelligently clones other sophisticated investors. He prays, goes to church, and draws emotional strength from his faith in a higher power. He behaves in ways that inspire trust and goodwill.*

**None of these practices is earth-shattering in isolation. But remember: it's the *aggregation* of marginal gains that's so powerful. Moreover, the modest benefits generated by smart habits continue to compound over many years.** In the short run, all those tiny, incremental advances seem insignificant. But time is the enemy of bad habits and the friend of good habits. When you pound away year after year, decade after decade, the cumulative effect is stunning. Indeed, what sets Gayner apart is one indispensable trait: he is the king of constancy.

The good news, then, is that we don't need a secret sauce or a stratospheric IQ. **What we need is a selection of sensible habits that are directionally correct and sustainable—habits that give us a marginal advantage that will compound over time.** Gayner has set us on the right track. Now let's see what other high-performance habits the best investors adopt to give themselves that persistent edge.

## Bring the Heat

In 2000, I interviewed Jeff Vinik, a secretive investment superstar who, at thirty-three, had become the manager of the world's biggest and most famous mutual fund: Fidelity's Magellan Fund. Will Danoff, who succeeded him as the manager of Fidelity's Contrafund, says Vinik was "the best fund manager" of their generation at Fidelity—"an investing prodigy."

Vinik beat the S&P 500 during his four years at Magellan; left Fidelity on a sour note after an ill-timed bet on bonds; then launched a gunslinging hedge fund whose results were a wonder to behold. When we spoke, his company, Vinik Asset Management, was about to return billions to his investors, so he could manage his own riches and spend more time with his family. By then, he'd spent a total of twelve years as a fund manager and had averaged a stunning 32 percent a year.

When I asked Vinik why he'd been so successful, he offered two explanations. First, he said, "I've really used the same consistent approach to investing throughout my career, which is focusing on individual companies with good earnings outlooks that are selling at very reasonable valuations." For example, he'd recently made a fortune on "little, mundane restaurant stocks that will grow earnings twenty percent [a year] but are selling at twelve times earnings. That's the real show, and that's the way to make money." In retrospect, this seems to me a perfect example of Joel Greenblatt's notion of reducing the complexity of investing to its essence and applying the most fundamental principles over and over again.

Second, said Vinik, "There's another constant through the twelve years, and that's very, very hard work. The more companies you can analyze, the more cash-flow statements you can go through—and go through every line of—the more good ideas you're going to find and the better the performance is going to be. There's no substitute for hard work."

What was his schedule like? "I'm usually in the office at 6:45 in the morning," Vinik told me. "I go home at approximately 5:00 p.m., so I can spend a lot of time with my family. Usually, after my children go to bed, I'll do two to three hours of reading at night." He waded through heaps of corporate filings and industry publications and tried to read "all the research that Wall Street puts out." It helped that he had a phenomenal memory: "The way I operate is just to keep track in my head of what's going on in literally thousands of companies." That way, he was poised to detect subtle shifts that others would overlook—for example, the turning point when profits began to accelerate at a scorned cyclical business whose prospects were about to improve.

Danoff's investment style is different, with more emphasis on holding stocks for the long run. But his work ethic is no less intense. "Money management is all about turning over more rocks, talking to more analysts, looking at more annual reports. And the more you do, the better you're going to do," he says. "It's crazy competitive." Danoff has managed the Contrafund since 1990. Still, through some peculiar quirk in his wiring, his hunger for beating the market and adding value for his shareholders has never dwindled. "Other fund managers don't give a shit, quite frankly," he says. Many are "in it for the fees" or "the glory. . . . I *care* more."

Danoff reads me a letter he received in 1993 from a couple who had invested in his fund to save for their one-year-old son's college education: "We have enclosed his pictures so you can get a sense that there are real people out here trusting you with their hard-earned money." For Danoff, that responsibility—combined with "guilt," "fear," and the desire to "set a good example"—is a powerful motivator. He declares, "I have to bring the heat every day."*

Whatever their motivation, I think of the best investors as mental athletes. They strive constantly for an intellectual advantage—*more* information, *better* information, *faster* information, or simply a more nuanced interpretation of information that's already out there for everyone to see. All that hard-earned knowledge compounds over time and pays off in unpredictable ways.

Danoff, who meets with the management of hundreds of companies each year, shows me his notes from an April 2004 meeting with a "dying" dot-com business, Ask Jeeves. Its executives revealed that they were getting crushed by an unbeatable upstart: Google. That was the day, says Danoff, "when I first realized that Google is a special company." Primed with that insight, he met with Google's cofounder Sergey Brin and CEO, Eric Schmidt, in August 2004 and began to grasp the enormity of its potential. Google's revenues were doubling every few months, says Danoff, and it boasted 25 percent operating margins, loads of cash, and no debt: "Its financial performance was extraordinary, particularly when compared with the many unprofitable unicorns of today." Most fund managers steered clear when Google went public later that month. But Danoff's fund became one of its largest investors. Sixteen years later, the company (now renamed Alphabet) is still one of his biggest and most profitable investments.

As a marquee player at a firm with $7.3 trillion in customer assets, Danoff can gain access to almost anyone. But what distinguishes him is his determination to leverage that advantage by driving himself inces-

---

* My favorite story about Danoff's intensity comes from Bill Miller, who recalls being introduced to him at an investment conference in Phoenix about thirty years ago: "I stuck out my hand and I said, 'Nice to meet you, Will.' And he didn't hold his hand out. He just looked at me and said, 'I'm gonna beat you, man. I'm gonna beat you.'"

santly to keep turning over those rocks. On a research trip to Palo Alto in 2010, it bothered him to discover a gap in his packed schedule. "Wednesday after four thirty p.m., why aren't we seeing anybody?" he asked his colleagues. "Maybe we should see Tesla." Danoff visited the money-losing carmaker as "an afterthought," arriving late on a December afternoon when it was turning dark outside. Within minutes, Tesla's charismatic founder, Elon Musk, made an unscheduled appearance and described his vision of "making fabulous cars that America is going to be proud of again." Danoff was so impressed that he made an early—and extremely lucrative—investment, which he continues to own a decade after that auspicious trip.

It's no coincidence that Vinik and Danoff both started out as protégés of Peter Lynch, who had run the Magellan Fund for thirteen years with blazing intensity. When I interviewed Lynch two decades ago, he explained the simple logic that had driven him to study so many stocks each day. "I always thought that if you looked at ten ideas in a day, you might find one good one," he told me. "If you looked at twenty, you might find two." Recalling one of his best investments, Lynch added, "If a hundred people had visited Chrysler in 1982 with an open mind, ninety-nine would have bought it."

Once again, it's all about the cumulative effect of many minuscule advantages, which add up miraculously over years: the *one extra company* that Lynch bothered to visit; the *one empty time slot* that Danoff insisted on filling; the *two or three extra hours* of reading that Vinik pushed himself to complete after his kids went to bed. The best predictor of success is often nothing more mysterious than the unflagging fervency of a person's desire.

Early in his career, Bill Miller asked Lynch for advice. Lynch told him that the investment business is so rewarding financially and intellectually that it attracts an overabundance of intelligent people. "The only way you can beat them is to outwork them," said Lynch, "because nobody is just so much smarter than the next person." Lynch told Miller that he stayed ahead of the pack by reading investment research while he carpooled to the office at 6:30 a.m., working after dinner and on weekends, and taking no vacations for years. When Miller asked if it was possible to slow down as you got older, Lynch replied, "No. In this business, there are only two gears: overdrive and stop." Miller agrees: "That's basically right. You *have* to be focused."

In 2014, when Marty Whitman was ninety, I asked him why he'd performed so badly during and after the 2008 crash—a rare failure for one of the giants of value investing. "As I got older and richer, I got lazier," he told me. "I really knew better in 2007 and didn't act on it. I should have sold all my housing-related stocks. . . . It doesn't reflect on the investment techniques. You've got to be diligent and careful, and in 2008, I wasn't."

I admired Whitman's candor, but his confession troubled me. I'd invested with him for many years and been happy with the results, which led me to trust his firm with a major portion of my mother's savings. It hadn't occurred to me that he would become complacent. Looking back on his dismal handling of the financial crisis, Whitman remarked, "It's intellectually dissatisfying, but it doesn't make that much difference. . . . What's the difference if my kids end up with ten million dollars less and charities end up with ten million or twenty million dollars less?" I didn't have the heart to tell him that his lack of care and diligence would make a profound difference to my mother.

### "Very Few People Could Be Married to Me"

To surpass so many smart competitors, it's not enough merely to out-work them. You also have to *outthink* them. Even the most experienced investors must engage in a ceaseless process of continuing education because the world changes so drastically that aspects of their knowledge become outdated. As Munger often remarks, one of Buffett's most valuable traits is that, even in old age, he remains "a continuous learning machine." On a typical day, Buffett might read for five or six hours, frequently isolating himself in his office with the door shut.

"Buffett is a perfect example of the degree to which you can improve yourself over the years," says Paul Lountzis, the president of Lountzis Asset Management. Lountzis, who has attended Berkshire's annual meeting for three decades, is awed by Buffett's ability to keep evolving. He started out by investing in cheap stocks, then embraced better businesses, then bought whole companies, then ventured into foreign markets such as China and Israel, then invested in two industries he'd famously avoided: railroads and technology. That evolution enabled Buffett to make the most lucrative stock pick of his career in his late eighties—an investment in Apple Inc. that has so far earned a profit of more than $80 billion. "He's kept true to his discipline and principles, but he's adapted them to the particular economic and investing environment at the time," says Lountzis. "It's unbelievable. Very few people can do that."

Lountzis, too, is a consummate practitioner of continuous learning, which has helped him to haul himself out of meager circumstances and become a well-regarded money manager. Born in 1960, he grew up in a Greek immigrant family in Pennsylvania, one of five children of a bartender and a sewing-machine operator. "My dad would leave the tips on the kitchen table, and that's what my mom used to go grocery shopping," he says. "My parents just sacrificed. . . . My mom would wear shoes from friends and not buy shoes for herself." Early in their marriage, when they already had three kids, their life savings amounted to $30.

When Lountzis was eight, he started earning money by washing dishes. He later worked as a cleaner at McDonald's and paid his way through Albright College by working full-time in a hospital every weekend and vacation. It took him eight years to graduate.

On the side, he studied investing. "I immersed myself fanatically," he says. At thirteen, he read about Buffett. At fourteen, he was mesmerized by Ben Graham's *The Intelligent Investor*. He then became captivated by Philip Fisher's 1958 classic, *Common Stocks and Uncommon Profits*, which introduced him to the practice of "scuttlebutt" research as a means of gaining an informational advantage. "Those two books really created the foundation," says Lountzis. "I've read them both fifty or sixty times."

Lountzis is a warm and exuberant man who speaks effusively of his four adult children and his wife, Kelly, who has stayed by his side for almost forty years. But his life is built almost entirely around his compulsive craving for any knowledge that could make him a better investor. "I try to read four, five, six, seven hours a day, seven days a week," he says. "I have no hobbies. I have never golfed in my life. . . . It's just my personality—always trying to get smarter, to learn."

He regards social functions as a bothersome distraction: "I love people. But if I'm not learning and growing and being stimulated intellectually, I'd rather be elsewhere." Part of what he cherishes about his wife is that "she places no demands on me, and I can't tell you how important that is. . . . She understands me and lets me be me. Very few people could be married to me." Lountzis makes no apologies for his extremism: "You need a maniacal focus to really be great at anything. Anyone who tells you that you can have everything all at once, you can't. I mean, you don't become Roger Federer by not playing tennis. It *has* to be consuming."

Lountzis is a ravenous consumer of insights from the titans of business and investing. He adores books about entrepreneurs such as Nike's cofounder Phil Knight: "I could read everything ever written about him. That fascinates me." He also has a server on which he's stockpiled thousands of videos featuring financial wizards who help him to think better about investing, markets, and where the world is headed: hedge fund managers such as Mohnish Pabrai and Stanley Druckenmiller; venture capitalists such as Michael Moritz and Jim Goetz; and private equity visionaries such as Leon Black and Stephen Schwarzman. Lountzis says he has at least five hundred videos of Buffett, along with any recording he can find of Munger's infrequent public appearances. And then there are his transcripts of dozens of their annual meetings. Buffett and Munger "are not just really smart," he says. "They're geniuses."

Most days, Lountzis watches a video on his iPhone while riding a Peloton bike at his gym. Most nights, he lies in bed and watches a video on his iPad, often lulled to sleep by the sweet sounds of investment wisdom. As he listens, he keeps pondering the same underlying questions: "What am I missing? Who's doing something that no one else is doing? How can I get better?" His aim is never to replicate other investors' behavior. "You can't mimic them because you're not them," he says. "Learn it and adapt it and modify it into your own process."

There is breadth to his studies. But what makes Lountzis such a powerful learning machine is his habit of obsessive repetition. For example, he estimates that he's watched Buffett's 1998 lecture at the University of Florida fifteen times and has read the transcript at least five times.

Likewise, he's studied Berkshire's 1993 annual report with such devotion that he can recite, in order, the five main factors that Buffett said he considers when evaluating the riskiness of any stock. It's this same habit of repetition that has kept Lountzis trekking to Omaha for Berkshire's annual meeting for nearly thirty years and has led him to read the same books dozens of times. The benefit of so much repetition, he says, is that many "foundational" teachings are "etched in my brain"—not unlike the effect of repeating the same prayers or affirmations every day.

I suspect that the value of repetition is vastly underrated and that most of us would do well to find one or two books that we read so often that they become part of us. I dip into the *Zohar* almost every day, and there are other books that I return to again and again, including *Meditations* by Marcus Aurelius, *The Wisdom of Truth* by Rav Yehuda Ashlag, and *The Book of Joy* by the Dalai Lama and Archbishop Desmond Tutu.

Having ingrained many timeless investment principles so they are part of his essence, Lountzis follows his own bespoke process to assemble a portfolio of around fifteen intensively researched stocks.* He focuses on outstanding businesses with leaders who are "creative, adaptable, visionary" and have "enormous courage." Such qualities are more important than ever in an era of unprecedented disruption, which threatens even the most dominant businesses. "The problem," says Lountzis, is that *qualitative* factors such as adaptability or courage "are not measurable" in financial statements, which offer a *quantitative* record of the past.

His solution is to operate more like an investigative reporter than an accountant. "Businesses are changing very rapidly, and many of them are becoming obsolete, so you have to see around corners and get some insight beyond the numbers," says Lountzis. "You've got to go out in the field and talk to competitors, customers, former employees, and then create a mosaic that you can dovetail on top of the numbers." With that in mind, he frequently conducts in-person interviews with

---

* Lountzis, who worked for Bill Ruane as a young analyst, inherited his willingness to concentrate aggressively in a few high-quality businesses trading at attractive valuations. In 2020, Lountzis told me that he'd exploited the crash triggered by the COVID-19 pandemic to boost his stake in Berkshire Hathaway to 25 percent of his stock portfolio.

experts, such as retired CEOs, who can provide "unique, differential insights."

Laura Geritz is an equally formidable learning machine. But she has built a different type of informational advantage. While Lountzis invests primarily in the United States, Geritz is one of America's foremost investors in foreign markets. In a typical year, she spends six to nine months roaming around the world in search of the best investments. At the age of forty-eight, she's already traveled to seventy-five countries. Geritz, who is the CEO and chief investment officer of Rondure Global Advisors in Salt Lake City, Utah, feels a profound sense of duty to shareholders in her two mutual funds. But she's not that interested in piling up money for herself. She remarks, "I have enough." Above all, she's an intellectual adventurer, propelled by "the passion to learn."

In an industry overrun by alpha males, many molded by the same elite business schools, Geritz fits none of the stereotypes of her profession. She's a true original, who likens her "nonlinear" investment approach to the unconstrained poetic rhythms of free verse. From the start, she was never a conventional candidate for a career in fund management. Many of her relatives were farmers and factory workers. Her father took a position as a literature professor at a small college and moved the family to what Geritz describes as "a tiny little town in western Kansas, straight out of the opening paragraph of *In Cold Blood*." In case you don't remember the opening paragraph of Truman Capote's nonfiction novel about a quadruple murder, it begins like this: "The village of Holcomb stands on the high wheat plains of western Kansas, a lonesome area that other Kansans call 'out there.'" Geritz, a diminutive Midwesterner with a mild and unassuming manner, may not seem like a warrior. But making the journey from "out there" to where she is today required astonishing drive and determination.

Geritz studied political science and history at the University of Kansas, but she also delighted in reading the *Wall Street Journal* every day. By nineteen, she'd saved enough to invest for the first time, buying shares in a fund run by Marty Whitman. She fantasized about investing professionally, but figured that she could never break into the business unless she developed a skill that set her apart. So she did a master's degree in East Asian languages and culture, lived in Japan for a year, and became fluent in Japanese. As a result, she landed a job as a bilingual client representative at American Century Investments. A couple of years later, she won a spot as an analyst on the firm's fund management team—a position that could attract as many as twelve thousand applicants. She subsequently spent a decade at Wasatch Advisors, earning renown as a market-beating fund manager who specialized in emerging and frontier markets. She quit to create her own firm in 2016 and hired three analysts who work alongside her in one "very noisy" room.

When we first spoke in 2017, Geritz's funds were only two weeks old. But she'd already made research trips to Russia, Turkey, Japan, and South Korea. Twice a year, she screens about sixty-nine thousand stocks, which helps her to identify unloved markets that she can visit in her global scavenger hunt for great companies at good prices or good companies at great prices. "I like to go where others aren't going," she says. "If you're daring to be different, to be great, you have to go against the grain." The market that excited her most was Turkey, where she'd just met with about thirty companies. But it wasn't hard to see why so few investors shared her excitement.

Turkey's autocratic president, who had celebrated his own magnificence by building himself a palace with more than eleven hundred rooms, had recently survived an attempted military coup. He lashed back by declaring a state of emergency; jailing thousands of soldiers, police, and judges; closing media outlets; and denouncing his political opponents as terrorists. The nation's reputation was further scarred by a series of suicide bombings, including one at Istanbul's main airport. Tourism collapsed. The currency plunged. Inflation and debt soared. Foreign investors fled.

But Geritz had visited Turkey many times before, allowing her a more nuanced perspective. A few years earlier, when optimism about the country's economic future had been in full bloom, she'd attended an investment conference in Istanbul. Back then, the hotel hosting the event had wanted $1,200 a night for a room, and she'd refused to stay there. "This time, I paid seventy dollars a night for a hotel," says Geritz. "To me, that's pessimism to an extreme." The day-to-day reality also seemed nowhere near as frightening as the foreign news coverage suggested: "On the ground, I don't feel any reason to be afraid. It's one of the friendliest countries in the world."

For Geritz, that gap between reality and perception offered an ideal opportunity to invest for the long haul in three of Turkey's best businesses: its largest grocery chain, its leading defense company, and its dominant maker of candy. All three had sustainable competitive advantages, reliable cash flows, high returns on invested capital, and (most critical) strong balance sheets. Plus, they were so cheap that she was unlikely to suffer any permanent loss of capital. Given the dangers in developing markets, this unwavering emphasis on risk mitigation is crucial. Indeed, most of the companies Geritz owns have net cash, enabling them to endure terrible times when the supply of capital dries up and weak businesses wither. "I'm really investing in survivors," she says. "I buy great companies, but I like to buy them in countries that have been hit."

Geritz's willingness to travel extensively gives her a *cumulative advantage* over more parochial investors. "The more you go out into the world, the more you see the patterns," she says, including cycles of boom and bust that recur in different countries as credit expands or contracts and optimism rises or falls. This pattern recognition helps in "avoiding the massive blowups you can get in emerging and frontier markets." For example, she sold out of Brazil during a period of euphoria when foreign capital had flooded in, the government had overspent, and prices had gone crazy. The symptoms of excess looked ominously familiar. "The hotels were a thousand dollars a night, easily," she recalls. "I had spent, I think, thirty-five dollars on a piece of pizza in the airport."

She saw similar warning signs in Nigeria when foreigners piled in, convinced that it was "the best investment destination in Africa." Her wary verdict: "I've seen that movie before. I've seen it in China when valuations go high and everyone loves the market. I've seen it in Brazil."

Before each trip, Geritz creates a study program designed to enrich her understanding of the place she's visiting. "I try to read at least three books for every country I go to," she says. Typically, one book is about the economics or politics of the country or region; one is a work of literature; and one is a lighter piece of pop culture, such as a mystery or crime novel. "If we're going for a research trip to Uganda, I probably carry a tiny suitcase full of clothes and a giant backpack full of twenty books," she says. "It's a big joke." She also carries a Kindle, "but I've had it go down in a couple of countries, and I can't live without books."

Geritz and her team at Rondure meet every couple of weeks to discuss a book that they've been reading as a group: "The last book we read was *Investing the Templeton Way*, which I've read many times. But it might also be something like *Grit* or *The Creative Brain*." For the past thirteen years, she has also chosen one major subject (sometimes two) that she studies in depth throughout the year. These topics, which she selects with joyous anticipation, have included Africa, the Middle East, physics, oil, and "the literature and history of Russia." In 2019, we chatted over a sushi lunch, and I asked Geritz about her latest topic. Her reply: "Oh, it's a quirky one! I'm reading all about explorers, starting from the Vikings."

Geritz, who reads two or three books a week, seldom bothers with newspapers and ignores the minute-by-minute news on her Bloomberg terminal: "I'd rather read the *Rise of the Robots* and think about what the world might look like ten years from now than think about what the world looked like ten minutes ago." It's an unusually cerebral approach to investing, based on her belief that reading deeply and traveling widely will give her a more expansive perspective that is a significant, yet intangible, edge. "There's a limit to just sitting in an office and perusing financials day in and day out," she says. "I don't think our job is a linear one."

Geritz has even tried to institutionalize her freewheeling mindset by designating Fridays as "our creative day," which her colleagues can spend as they wish. She often uses it to sit beside a stream in Salt Lake City, where she reads in peace or writes in journals as a way of synthesizing ideas from her travels. She finds it useful to be based in Utah: "Being here, off the beaten path, allows you to think." During the coronavirus pandemic, an earthquake and several construction projects made her apartment unsuitable for "deep thinking." So she rented "a quiet house with a stream" in a remote part of Idaho and quarantined herself contentedly with forty-five books.

But Geritz also wanders farther afield to other places that are conducive to contemplation. Among them, she visits an island off the Australian coast with only eight houses: "You take a boat with your groceries and they leave you on the island. Sometimes you have cell phone communication and sometimes you don't. You don't have internet. You have some music and you have a beautiful view of the water and you have your books."

Intermittently, Geritz plants herself in a foreign location for weeks at a time, so she can immerse herself more fully in the culture, studying how the locals live, spend, and consume. She rents a cheap vacation property near the center of the market she wants to learn about and uses it as her regional base, partly "because the wear and tear of flying back and forth gets really hard," since she travels in economy class. Over the years, she has stationed herself in countries as diverse as Tanzania, Kenya, England, France, Holland, Dubai, Abu Dhabi, Thailand, Singapore, and Japan.

Several years ago, when Japanese property prices were depressed, she grabbed the chance to buy an apartment in the heart of Kyoto, the ancient imperial capital, which gives her a base from which to visit companies across Asia. It's a simple place with a bed, a sofa, a table, and a couple of chairs. It used to be a restaurant specializing in blowfish— a deadly delicacy unless the poison is skillfully extracted. Her yard is dominated by a big rock that she can't move because the locals believe it was placed there to honor "the snake god." Geritz spends at least one month a year in Kyoto. When I ask if she regards America or Japan as her home, she replies, "Honestly, Japan."

Most of us yearn to live in a place where we feel a sense of belonging and inclusion. But her natural state is to be "a complete and total outsider." For investors, she says, "one of the critical components is just to be able to observe, and that's all you can really do in Japan: be an observer. Because you'll never get embedded enough in society to be fully accepted as part of it."

To invest successfully in a country as distinctive as Japan, she must set aside her preconceptions and observe the culture on its own terms. For example, American companies typically put their shareholders' interests first. But Geritz, whose Rondure Overseas Fund has one-third of its assets in Japan, says the priority for Japanese companies is to serve their customers, followed by their employees, business partners, and society at large: "And then I think the shareholder comes last."

Activist investors from the West often try in vain to persuade Japanese CEOs to boost profits in the short term by deploying cash more productively or taking on more debt. But Geritz says the Japanese care more about building companies that survive—sometimes for centuries—despite such threats as earthquakes, tsunamis, wars, and epidemics. "It's not an instant-gratification culture," she says. Given her inclination to build wealth sustainably, their conservatism suits her.

Geritz's globe-trotting career has satisfied her limitless curiosity. But it comes at a cost. "You can't stop," she says. "If I'm pausing for any length of time, I lose my edge. . . . You owe it to your investors not to pause because it's their future." Even simple pastimes that "most normal people" enjoy "like going to the ski slopes or hanging out with friends" would be "very hard for me," she says, "because all I want to think about is stocks and countries."

What about family? "I don't have kids, and I'm really fortunate because I have a husband who I love and who knows that this is what I do [and] knows what it takes. So he has always been incredibly supportive." Her husband, Robb, an American whom she met in high school, is in international sales at a manufacturer of sporting goods. His work has given him the flexibility to tag along on many of her research trips. But their jobs require them to spend long periods apart. He mostly lives in their home in Kyoto, while she mostly lives in their home in Utah.

Geritz knew from the start that a high-pressure investment career would demand extreme focus. So she postponed any thought of raising children: "Part of it was the challenges and rigors of being a female in the business early on, recognizing that in order to keep up with the guys in the industry, that might not be the best thing to do." In those days, there were hardly any female role models at American Century. But Geritz remembers one woman in her office who couldn't work beyond 8:00 a.m. to 5:00 p.m. because she had a child: "She was told that they would never promote her to a higher level because the minimum hours they expected were a lot longer. . . . You didn't have to be told. You just emulated who was successful, and the people who were successful were those who stayed in the office from six a.m. to ten p.m. and then were there Saturday and Sunday."

Later in her career, Geritz felt ready to have a child, but by then her husband was more hesitant. "Then the time got away from us." Does she ever regret it? "Sometimes, yes." On the other hand, she says, "I love what I do so much that I don't feel like I've sacrificed."

## The Art of Subtraction

If there is one habit that all of the investors in this chapter have in common, it's this: **They focus almost exclusively on what they're best at and what matters most to them. Their success derives from this fierce insistence on concentrating deeply in a relatively narrow area while disregarding countless distractions that could interfere with their pursuit of excellence.**

Jason Zweig, an old friend who is a personal finance columnist at the *Wall Street Journal* and the editor of a revised edition of *The Intelligent Investor*, once wrote to me, "Think of Munger and Miller and Buffett: guys who just won't spend a minute of time or an iota of mental energy doing or thinking about anything that doesn't make them better. . . . Their skill is self-honesty. They don't lie to themselves about what they are and aren't good at. Being honest with yourself like that has to be part of the secret. It's so hard and so painful to do, but so important."

I think this applies to any elusive skill that we hope to master, whether it's picking stocks, healing patients, or wrestling with words. One of my heroes is the late Oliver Sacks, an eminent neurologist and a superb author, who put up a big yellow sign in his house with the word NO! written on it in block letters. In a memoir, he explained that it was his way of "reminding myself to say no to invitations, so I could preserve writing time."

Thousands of years earlier, the Taoist philosopher Lao-tzu wrote that the path to wisdom involves "subtracting" all unnecessary activities: "To attain knowledge, add things every day. To attain wisdom, subtract things every day."

**The art of subtraction is incalculably important, particularly in an**

**age of information overload when our minds can so easily become scattered.** If you expose yourself to it, there's a deafening din of discordant political news, social media notifications, robocalls, and other disruptive noise. In *World Without Mind: The Existential Threat of Big Tech*, Franklin Foer warns, "We're being dinged, notified, and clickbaited, which interrupts any sort of possibility for contemplation. To me, the destruction of contemplation is the existential threat to our humanity."

It's also an existential threat to investment success. Hence Geritz regularly disappears to sit beside a waterfall on a mountainside in Kyoto where she can read, write, and muse. The late Bill Ruane, who generated fabulous returns at the Sequoia Fund, once spoke to me from what he called "my hideaway"—a hotel suite in New York City where he worked alone, disconnected from colleagues in his nearby office. Guy Spier, who has attention deficit hyperactivity disorder, moved his family from Manhattan to a rented house in a quiet neighborhood of Zurich, where it's easier for his beautiful but distractible mind to resemble "a calm pond." Spier's office, which is a short tram-ride from his home, has a library in which he doesn't permit himself a phone or a computer. He has consciously designed his physical environment to support contemplation.

As the head of an investment team with more than $100 billion to manage, Matthew McLennan could fill every hour of every day with meetings and calls. "You can make yourself very busy," he says. "But you have to remove unproductive busyness. . . . And I think creating windows for sustained reflection is very important." He schedules no appointments in the mornings, keeps Fridays "relatively unscheduled," and is "very systematic" in carving out time away from his office during the workweek. He also exercises regularly as a way of clearing his mind and often walks in nature on weekends. McLennan explains, "Removing yourself from a frenetic environment from time to time is very helpful."

**The more distracted others become, the more of an advantage it is to subtract mental clutter, technological intrusions, and overstimulation.** But the details differ for each of us. Ruane found a calm refuge in the middle of Manhattan. Chuck Akre, who has beaten the market by a huge margin over three decades, finds it easier to think with equanimity in rural Virginia, where his firm, Akre Capital Management, is based in a small town with one traffic light. He lives in a house that looks out on the Blue Ridge Mountains. "We see deer and bears and foxes and coyotes and wild turkeys," he says. "It's a beautiful place. It's good for the soul." One benefit of being there is that he feels so distant from all "the stupidity and the nonsense" that he doesn't get "uptight about what's going on in the market and the world. . . . We just turn it off."

Instead, he focuses narrowly on owning a few well-run businesses that earn attractive returns on capital and have the ability to keep reinvesting their free cash flow at high rates of return. And then he has the restraint to "leave things well alone." He has held Markel for twenty-seven years and made more than one hundred times his money. He has owned Berkshire Hathaway for forty-two years. His largest holding, American Tower Corporation, has risen from seventy-nine cents per share to about $260 since 2002. By constructing an unhurried life in a tranquil place, Akre can "shelter" himself from the influence of other investors' "brilliant ideas" and "stay focused completely on the things that work for us." In essence, he's discovered one well-stocked pond, and he's content to fish there for the rest of his days. Or, as Akre puts it, "We can't dance with all the ladies."

All of this leads to a few practical conclusions that can help us to become wealthier *and* happier. First, to be successful and fulfilled, we need to decide what we care about most and be honest with ourselves about what we do best. Second, we need to adopt daily habits that enable us to improve continuously where it truly counts—and to subtract habits that divert us. It's worth writing down a list of beneficial habits that should be part of our daily routine. But it's equally valuable to compile a Do Not Do list, reminding us of all the ingenious ways in which we habitually distract or undermine ourselves. As Gayner suggests, the point is not to push for perfection, but to commit to habits that are sustainable and directionally correct.

Michael Zapata, a hedge fund manager who was previously a commander in an elite counterterrorist unit, SEAL Team Six, has thought hard about the necessity of focus. "You have to know what your priorities are in life," he says. "For me, it's God, family, fund—in that order."

That clarity helps him to decide how to spend his time and energy so he's "aligned" with what matters most to him. "Even this conversation is sort of outside of that alignment because it doesn't fit into the family-fund-God thing," he says. "But it's okay to have that. You just have to make sure that it doesn't throw you off your priorities . . . that it doesn't affect your life."

Is that too extreme? Maybe. But most people make the mistake of adding too much complexity to their lives. They skim the surface, pre-occupying themselves with the superficial and the extraneous. As the best investors show, sustained excellence requires us to subtract and go deep.

# CHAPTER EIGHT

# Don't Be a Fool

How to invest better, think better, and live better
by adopting Charlie Munger's strategy of
systematically reducing standard stupidities

———————————

Wherever the fool walks, he reveals to everyone that he is
a fool.

—Ecclesiastes 10:3

To be wise one must study both good and bad thoughts and
acts, but one should study the bad first. You should first
know what is not clever, what is not just, and what is not
necessary to do.

—Leo Tolstoy, *A Calendar of Wisdom*

It is remarkable how much long-term advantage people
like us have gotten by trying to be consistently not stupid,
instead of trying to be very intelligent.

—Charlie Munger

I have traveled three thousand miles for a ten-minute interview with
Charlie Munger. I arrive an hour early for my audience with him and
wait in a state of nervous excitement to be summoned. It's February 15,
2017, and he is here in downtown Los Angeles for the annual meeting
of the Daily Journal Corporation. Munger, who is the chairman of this
obscure newspaper publisher, is better known as Berkshire Hathaway's
billionaire vice chairman and Warren Buffett's partner for more than

forty years. Born in 1924, he is one-half of the greatest investment team that ever lived.

Munger has agreed to speak with me in private shortly before the Daily Journal meeting begins. So I'm standing outside a conference room in the company's nondescript headquarters, watching as the lobby fills with hundreds of his devotees, including prominent investors such as Li Lu, Mohnish Pabrai, François Rochon, Whitney Tilson, Christopher Davis, and Francis Chou. It's a running joke that almost nobody here cares about the Daily Journal. When attendees enter the building, they sign in to a book that asks how many shares they own. For almost all, the answer is zero. Like me, they have come from far and wide to bask in the caustic wit and wisdom of this ninety-three-year-old icon.

The prospect of interviewing Munger is both thrilling and unnerving, given his reputation as a fearsomely clever curmudgeon who detects flaws and failings with devastating clarity. Buffett once declared, "Charlie can analyze and evaluate any kind of deal faster and more accurately than any man alive. He sees any valid weakness in sixty seconds." Buffett has also said that Munger boasts "the best thirty-second mind in the world. . . . He sees the essence of everything before you can even finish the sentence." Microsoft's cofounder, Bill Gates, has said that Munger is "the broadest thinker I have ever encountered."

Munger's mind inspires awe among people who are not normally inclined toward hero worship. Pabrai, who claims that Munger is "a quantum leap above Warren" in terms of intelligence, chuckles at the memory of hearing him speak onstage alongside a Nobel Prize–winning scientist who was "Caltech's biggest brain. That guy looked like a shrimp who didn't know shit. You could see the contrast: dumbass on one side, *real* brain on the other." Pabrai adds that Munger's innate gifts gave him a "huge head start," which he's extended by synthesizing several books a week, roving voraciously over a multitude of disciplines. That combination of "incredible wiring" and "intense data input makes it appear like the guy has been living for three hundred years."

But there's another reason to feel trepidation as I gird myself to meet Munger. Even his most ardent admirers will admit that he can be brusque to the point of rudeness. Chou laughs as he tells me the tale of a fellow money manager who traveled regularly to Omaha and California to hear Munger speak. One day, says Chou, this friend of his ran into Munger in an elevator and exclaimed, "Charlie, you've been such an inspiration to me! I've learned so much from you over so many years!" Munger dismissed him with a single word: "So?" And then he walked away.

Bill Miller recalls running into Munger on a street in New York: "I said, 'Charlie!' And he looks at me and says, 'Who the hell are you?'" Miller introduced himself and reminded Munger that they'd once met at a behavioral finance event. "He's like, 'Oh, yeah!' And he said to his wife, 'Why don't you go on to the hotel and I'll walk around with Bill for a while. . . .' We probably walked around for an hour, just talking about stuff. But it was funny. 'Who the hell are you?'"

But my favorite story of Munger's flamboyant failures in diplomacy comes from Buffett, who shared it with Pabrai and Guy Spier over lunch in 2008. Munger, who has a glass eye, visited the Department of Motor Vehicles, where a hapless bureaucrat made the unfortunate error of asking him, "Do you still have just one good eye?" Munger replied, "No. I've grown a new one."

Pabrai had assured me that Munger is kinder and gentler than his reputation might suggest: "Charlie is a very soft, caring guy. He has a hard exterior. But once you get past it, he's a beautiful person." Munger's daughter, Molly, who is a lawyer and a philanthropist, adds that he has mellowed: "He has an acerbic edge. I think when he was younger, it was more pronounced."

Nonetheless, I took the precaution of preparing obsessively for our brief encounter. And what I began to realize while poring over decades of his speeches, writings, and other musings is that Munger adopts one practice that all of us would be wise to clone: **He strives consistently to reduce his capacity for "foolish thinking," "idiotic behavior," "unoriginal error," and "standard stupidities."**

For example, at another shareholder meeting back in 2015, he ridiculed the popular delusion in academic circles that the market is so efficient that nobody can beat it. "I knew it was bullshit," he said, adding that he also "never believed there was a talking snake in the Garden of Eden. I had a gift for recognizing twaddle. I don't have any wonderful insights that other people don't have. I just have slightly more consistently than others avoided idiocy. Other people are trying to be smart. All *I'm* trying to be is non-idiotic. I find that all you have to do to get ahead in life is to be non-idiotic and live a long time. It's harder to be non-idiotic than most people think."

It's a curious paradox that one of the smartest people on earth focuses primarily on avoiding stupidity. But as we shall see, this is an extraordinarily effective strategy in markets and life.

## The Non-idiot's Guide to Life

The door to the conference room opens and Munger greets me in a low, croaky voice: "Nice to see you. Sit down." I find myself sitting almost knee to knee with the sage. Several people are talking noisily as they leave the room, but Munger has no trouble tuning out the hubbub and focusing. He has white hair and powerful spectacles. His dark suit looks baggy on his thin and frail body. To my relief, his manner is surprisingly benevolent.

There's no time for small talk, so I cut straight to the chase. I tell Munger that I regard him as "the Grand Master of Stupidity Reduction," and I ask him why he focuses so much attention on avoiding common errors and predictable patterns of irrationality. "Because it works," he says. "It works. It's counterintuitive that you go at the problem backward. If you try and be smart, it's difficult. If you just go around and identify all of the disasters and say, 'What caused that?' and try to avoid it, it turns out to be a very simple way to find opportunities and avoid troubles."

Munger's approach of solving problems backward was influenced by Carl Gustav Jacobi, a nineteenth-century algebraist who famously said, "Invert, always invert." But Munger tells me that he also honed this mental habit of inversion with help from his friend Garrett Hardin, an ecologist who shared his fascination with the dire repercussions of shoddy thinking: "Hardin's basic idea was, if somebody asks you how to *help* India, just say, 'What could I do to really *ruin* India?' And you think through all of the things you could do to ruin India, and then you reverse it and say, 'Now, I won't do *those*.' It's counterintuitive but it really helps you to *reverse* these issues. It's a more complete way of thinking a problem through."

In 1986, Munger delivered a commencement speech at a Los Angeles prep school attended by several of his eight children and stepchildren. Instead of trotting out the usual bland platitudes about the secrets of success and happiness, he provided an inspired illustration of how to apply the principle of inversion. He gave the students a series of "prescriptions for guaranteed misery in life," recommending that they should be unreliable, avoid compromise, harbor resentments, seek revenge, indulge in envy, "ingest chemicals," become addicted to alcohol, neglect to "learn vicariously from the good and bad experience of others," cling defiantly to their existing beliefs, and "stay down" when struck by the "first, second, or third severe reverse in the battle of life."

When I ask Munger how to apply this method of thinking to practical problems such as deciding whether to get married or buy a particular stock, he recommends asking, "'Is this going to be a disaster?' instead of asking, 'Is it going to be wonderful?' Finding out what's wrong and trying to avoid it is different from finding out what's good and trying to get it. You have to do both, of course, in life. But this inversion of looking for the trouble and trying to avoid it keeps you out of a lot of messes. . . . It's a precaution. It's like a checklist before you take off in an airplane."

Similarly, if you're looking to make a thoughtful investment in a well-managed fund, you might start by asking, "How can I invest blindly in a lousy fund that's a disaster waiting to happen?" That question would lead you to list all of the pitfalls that investors routinely overlook—for example, outrageous fees, dangerous exposure to the most popular and priciest sectors of the market, and a recent streak of head-spinning returns that will almost surely prove unsustainable.

**This, then, is the first mental trick we should learn from Munger as a safeguard against stupidity: imagine a dreadful outcome; work backward by asking yourself what misguided actions might lead you to that sorry fate; and then scrupulously avoid that self-destructive behavior.** "Of course," says Munger, "a lot of people are so interested in reaching for the prize that they don't even *think* about the stupidities that might prevent them from getting it."

Buffett and Munger have used inversion to avert many predictable and unpredictable disasters. Writing to Berkshire's shareholders in 2009, Buffett discussed the art of inversion at length under the heading "What We Don't Do." For example, "Charlie and I avoid businesses whose futures we can't evaluate, no matter how exciting their products may be," sticking instead "with businesses whose profit picture for decades to come seems reasonably predictable." Berkshire also holds vast quantities of cash, negating any need to be a "supplicant" in times of economic distress. Buffett also joked that "this inversion approach works on a less lofty level: Sing a country song in reverse, and you will quickly recover your car, house and wife."

Like Buffett and Munger, all of the best investors I've encountered have extreme clarity about *what not to do*. Joel Tillinghast, who has beaten the Russell 2000 Index by 3.7 percentage points a year since 1989 as the manager of Fidelity's Low-Priced Stock Fund, has been called "the most gifted stock picker of his generation" by Jim Lowell, editor of the *Fidelity Investor* newsletter. During an interview in Boston, I asked Tillinghast to explain his winning strategy. He responded by listing everything that he avoids. For example, he steers clear of development-stage biotech stocks, knowing that they're likely to bring out the worst in him. He can't make a valid earnings forecast because their "future is so murky." Plus, biotech stocks are so volatile that they could trigger him to react emotionally. "I'm going to be crazy if I deal with biotech stocks," he says. "So I'm *not* going to do biotech stocks."

Tillinghast, a shy and timid math whiz who manages more than $40 billion in assets, has developed a plethora of defensive principles and practices, which have helped him to outperform—and outlast— almost all of his competitors. **For a start, he says, "Don't pay too much. Don't go for businesses that are prone to obsolescence and destruction. Don't invest with crooks and idiots. Don't invest in things you don't understand."**

Tillinghast also steers clear of businesses that are deeply cyclical, heavily indebted, or faddish. He views "promotional management" and "aggressive accounting" as "red flags." He shuns areas where he has no special insight or skill because nothing is more critical than "staying away from your ignorance." He also refrains from talking "too publicly or too frequently" about his holdings because that would make it harder to change his mind and admit when he was wrong. And he resists the urge to trade stocks actively, since that would generate onerous transaction costs and taxes, which would erode his returns.

What's left once he's eliminated all of those common causes of disappointment? A portfolio packed with undervalued, understandable, financially stable, profitable, and growing businesses run by honest people. His "most amazing" stock, Monster Beverage, has risen 1,000-fold.

Following Tillinghast's example, we can all benefit from understanding the most popular recipes for failure. Think about why most investors mess up and, like him, *don't do that*. "If you want to be superior, that's difficult," he says. "But what you *won't* do is easier to control and more attainable. . . . I'm not going to lose fifteen pounds. But saying no to doughnuts, that's easy for me."

Finally, it's worth noting that Munger's method of solving problems backward is also an effective way to avert self-inflicted chaos in our personal lives. Markel's co-CEO Tom Gayner offers the example of a husband who ventures out on the town without his wife. "I'm married to a lovely woman," he says. "To be in a bar without her, by myself, under the influence of too much alcohol . . . creates a different set of temptations and circumstances than would be the case with being more moderate." He recommends applying "the Munger inversion technique" by asking a simple question: "What would be a bad thing and how do I avoid that?" A reasonable answer, says Gayner, would be to have "two drinks instead of ten."

Whether your goal is to be a terrific stock picker or a terrific spouse, it's helpful to start by asking yourself how to be a terrible one. And then? *Invert, always invert.*


## The Collector of Inanities

While other billionaires collect art, vintage cars, and racehorses, Munger describes himself as a collector of "absurdities," "asininities," and "inanities." His daughter Molly recalls listening in her youth to his many cautionary tales "about people doing stupid things," which often included "a tinge of ingratitude and poor moral judgment." A typical story would feature the cosseted heir to a fortune who turned with bitter resentment against his father. Molly Munger remarks, "It's stupid at every level: ungrateful, self-sabotaging, unrealistic, egotistical."

**This habit of actively collecting examples of other people's foolish behavior is an invaluable antidote to idiocy. In fact, it's the second great anti-stupidity technique we should learn from Munger.** It's a perverse hobby that provides him with endless entertainment and insight, enabling him to catalog in his head all of the "boneheaded" moves to excise from his playbook. Anyone can benefit from this practice, he tells me, "but I don't think you get it unless you have a certain temperament. A lot of what I do is not IQ. It's something else. Temperament. Attitude. But I think it's partly inherited"—like "quick hand-eye" coordination or "a capacity in tennis."

Munger is spoiled for choice when it comes to collecting investment inanities. For example, he derides the tendency to listen to market predictions, comparing these feeble attempts at financial divination to the ancient art of inspecting sheep's entrails to foretell the future. Another common error is "to buy a cyclical company at the top of the cycle. A lot of people just do it all the time, and the investment bankers, of course, will encourage them to buy any dumb thing that will give a commission." These naive investors fail to realize that "the old cyclicality is going to come back," trusting instead that the company's upsurge "will keep going just because it's *been* going. That's a standard stupidity."

Munger also collects examples of his own idiocy. When I attended Berkshire Hathaway's annual meeting in 2017, he spoke candidly about two of the costliest mistakes of omission that he and Buffett have made. Munger confessed to the audience of some forty thousand Berkshire shareholders that "we failed you" by not buying Google. "We blew Walmart, too, when it was a total cinch."

Most of us prefer to bury our mistakes far from public view. We're not keen on admitting them to ourselves, either. But as Munger sees it, the more transparently he reviews his mistakes, the less likely he is to repeat them. **He once told Berkshire's shareholders, "I like people admitting they were complete stupid horses' asses. I know I'll perform better if I rub my nose in my mistakes. This is a wonderful trick** to learn." Indeed, it's the third trick we must learn from him in our campaign to constrain our own stupidity.

Still, Munger doesn't engage in gratuitous self-flagellation. He acknowledges his errors, learns the lessons, and moves forward without wallowing in regret. "We were active enough so we had some mistakes to remember," he says. "We learned a lot vicariously because it's so much cheaper. But we also learned a lot from unpleasant experience." Some of Berkshire's mistakes have stung, including its 1993 purchase of Dexter Shoe Co., which was annihilated by low-cost Chinese rivals. But none of those errors have been catastrophic in the grand scheme.

No investor I've met has internalized the importance of avoiding catastrophe more deeply than Fred Martin, the founder of a Minneapolis-based firm called Disciplined Growth Investors. It's a priority that pervades every area of his life—from managing money to flying his private plane. Like Munger, Martin has made it a central focus to dissect other people's errors. "You don't have to do it with a sense of thrill," he says. "It's just to learn." For Martin, this way of thinking began as a survival strategy during four years as a US navy officer in the Vietnam War—a searing experience that showed him the devastating consequences of preventable mistakes.

Martin joined the navy in June 1969 after graduating from business school at Dartmouth. That month, an American destroyer, the USS *Frank E. Evans*, collided with an Australian aircraft carrier in the South China Sea. It was 3:00 a.m. and the destroyer's commanding officer was asleep, leaving two inexperienced lieutenants in charge. The ship turned the wrong way, strayed into the carrier's path, and was cut in two. The front half of the destroyer sank in minutes, with much of the crew trapped inside. In all, seventy-four people died. Four officers were court-martialed. An investigation concluded that "the tragic event . . . can be ascribed to error in individual human judgment."

Martin still remembers the horror he felt while staring at a photograph of the vessel's severed remains: "It's a shocking picture because the ship stops about halfway. It's literally like a welder took a torch and just cut off half of the ship." But what made the catastrophe unforgettable was that it could have happened to him. Martin was promoted to lieutenant on another destroyer and became one of the most junior officers in naval history to be cleared for command at sea. At twenty-four, he was responsible for 240 lives whenever his captain was asleep. How could he forget the two luckless lieutenants on the *Frank E. Evans*—those "poor kids" whose mistakes sank their ship?

Night after night, Martin stood watch when he was exhausted from lack of sleep. The ship's radio would be blaring, the engine room would be calling him about some problem or other, and they were steaming in the dark through treacherous waters. The situation "was ripe for terrible mistakes," he says. "Man, you were tired.... You were just trying to survive." One habit that he developed was to walk out on the wing of the bridge whenever his ship was about to turn, so he could confirm with his own eyes that the course was clear. That "simple rule" that you must "look before you turn" was "not part of our training," says Martin. "But it should have been." Looking back now in his seventies, he realizes how ingrained in him that wary attitude became.

Martin left the navy in 1973. "I came out deadly serious," he recalls. The stock market had long intrigued him. He'd bought his first stock when he was twelve and even had a subscription to the *Wall Street Journal* delivered in infrequent batches to his ship. So he found a job as an equity analyst at a bank in Minneapolis. It didn't take long to discover that most members of his new profession lacked the vigilance that had protected him and his shipmates in wartime. His own father, a successful stockbroker with a talent for sales, lost half a million dollars that year when the brokerage firm that employed him went bust. He'd staked a reckless portion of the family's wealth on that one business and missed all the warning signs that it was falling apart.

Several years later, his father made a tidy profit on a stock that Martin had recommended. When they spoke about it on the phone, Martin recognized in a moment of awful clarity that his father was "a wonderful man" but "a terrible investor"—"hyperactive," "impulsive," "always looking for the quick hit.... He was too excited. So I realized that he didn't know what he was doing."

Martin's investment career began at a time of mass excitement when rationality was in short supply. Led by the Nifty Fifty, the market went nuts in 1973, and he saw that valuations had become unhinged from reality. He recalls analyzing a hot stock with no earnings and telling his boss that he saw little value there: "And he said, 'Ah, don't worry about it, Fred. It's a *faith* stock.' Of course, the stock gets destroyed." When the market collapsed in 1974, "all the hotshots" were "washed out" of the business, says Martin. But he could see that the relationship between price and value had now swung to the opposite extreme: "It was an incredible buying opportunity. . . . All you had to do was have the guts to invest." As a devout saver, he had the cash to buy a slew of bargain stocks, including FlightSafety International—"my first ten-bagger."

Those formative experiences of market folly reinforced the lesson that Martin had learned at sea. **Nothing matters more than averting obvious errors with the potential for catastrophic consequences.** But in the decades that followed, he would observe the same pattern again and again: heedless risk followed by unnecessary disaster.

For example, during the internet and telecom craze of the late 1990s, some of his clients jumped ship and invested a major portion of their life savings with Jim Oelschlager, a gunslinging tech evangelist who, at his peak, attracted more than $30 billion in assets. Oelschlager ran narrowly focused funds filled with overpriced highfliers such as Cisco Systems. When the bubble burst in 2000, Cisco lost $400 billion in market value. As Martin had feared, gung-ho investors who were overexposed to such ultra-aggressive funds were "immolated."

Another client phoned to ask if Martin could guarantee a 12 percent return "every year without fail." Martin told him that stocks are too volatile to promise that level of consistency: "And he said, 'Aww, a guy in New York—a genius named Madoff—won't tell anybody how he does it, but *he* does 12 percent like clockwork.'" So the client entrusted his savings to Bernie Madoff, operator of the biggest Ponzi scheme in history. The lesson? "If people can't tell you how they do it" and "you can't understand what they do," says Martin, "that's probably not the best spot to be in." His **"golden rule for risk management"** is simple: **"Know what you own."**

As Martin sees it, the best defense against disaster is to "understand the core principles" of investing and then have the "basic discipline" never to violate these "financial laws of gravity." The most essential law is always to maintain a margin of safety, which stems from buying assets for less than they are worth. Martin, who coauthored a book titled *Benjamin Graham and the Power of Growth Stocks*, warns, "You're *going* to screw up. The question is, Can you recover?" Graham's concept of the margin of safety helps you to "contain" your mistakes "so they're not too big. That's how you recover."

Martin isn't advocating that we avoid risk. On the contrary, "You need to take risks if you're going to achieve returns." But they should always be "considered risks." Martin, who manages $6 billion and requires a minimum of $15 million to open a separate account, specializes in a racy niche: small and midsize companies growing at a rapid rate. But he insists on investing at cheap or fair prices, based on his estimate of their intrinsic value now and in seven years. It's "an article of faith" that a company's intrinsic value and its market value will converge over time. There are "two sources of return for a stock," he says. "One is the growth in intrinsic value. The other is the truing up" between the stock price and the "real value" of the underlying business. He has no idea when that truing up will occur. But his average holding period is a decade.

Martin will buy a stock only if it's cheap enough to generate a high expected rate of return over the next seven years. For mid-cap stocks, he requires a minimum rate of return of 12 percent a year. For small caps, which have a greater risk of failure, he requires a minimum of 15 percent a year. Why does this matter? Because those standardized requirements force him *systematically* to buy stocks only when they are a sufficiently attractive proposition. **As Martin learned in the navy, "adherence to process" is an indispensable safeguard: "Always honor it because that's going to keep you out of trouble."\* This idea of adopting a few standard practices and unbendable rules is our fourth technique for reducing stupidity.** Buffett and Munger may not need formal constraints to maintain their discipline. But you and I are not them.

Martin has another rule that he observes "religiously" as a protection against calamity. He never invests more than 3 percent of his assets in a stock at the time of purchase. Typically, he owns forty-five to fifty

---

\* While it's true that Martin adheres strictly to his investment process, he adds an important caveat: "A process is not a fixed thing. It's dynamic." Every year, his team spends three days discussing how to improve their process.

stocks. Is that too conservative? Absolutely. But it hasn't prevented him from beating the indexes by a wide margin over decades, and it *has* prevented no end of misery.

Just consider the case of Bill Ackman and Bob Goldfarb, two gifted investors who made colossal bets on Valeant Pharmaceuticals. The company lost 95 percent of its value amid scandals over its deceptive accounting and obscene overpricing of drugs. Goldfarb, who had more than 30 percent of the Sequoia Fund riding on Valeant, retired ignominiously, his illustrious record ruined by one mistake. Ackman lost $4 billion. "Apparently, he's a brilliant guy," says Martin. "But, man, that was amateur hour. . . . He doesn't have to take those kinds of extreme positions." For Martin, it's especially instructive to study "financial disasters" involving "the guys that are really good" because "you want to keep reminding yourself of how difficult this business is. . . . Humility is extremely important in investing. Always, *always* think about your own limitations."

This guarded attitude toward risk extends beyond the realm of investing. Munger often preaches about the importance of avoiding behavior with marginal upside and devastating downside. He once observed, "Three things ruin people: drugs, liquor, and leverage." The category of activities that exhibit this type of dangerous asymmetry also includes drunk driving, extramarital affairs, and cheating on taxes or expense reports. Regardless of our moral views, these are foolish bets.

Martin's survival—as a naval officer, money manager, and experienced pilot—is no accident. He focuses relentlessly on the fundamental priority of "not letting your disasters kill you." These days, he flies a secondhand Gulfstream jet, which he bought after the price tumbled from about $14 million to $5.25 million. "It's just fabulous," he says. "It goes like a scalded dog." Still, he describes himself and his company's chief pilot as "the two biggest cowards in the sky."

They have one "ironclad rule" that's kept them out of trouble for many years: If either of them doesn't have "a warm and fuzzy feeling" in his stomach during a trip, "he speaks up and we don't keep going. We turn around. . . . There's no argument about it." Martin recalls postponing a critical meeting with a major client in Florida because of the danger that his plane might be running low on fuel: "I was unwilling to violate the margin of safety. . . . Being late for a meeting is one thing. Crashing the plane and dying is something completely different."

Martin has adapted that rule so that it's also integral to his investment process. He has given two trusted colleagues the power to veto any of his stock picks before he makes the purchase—another systematic safeguard against his capacity for oversight and overconfidence.

Martin's readiness to recognize his fallibility has served him well, not only protecting him from himself but positioning him to profit from other investors' failures. Several years ago, a high-fee hedge fund that had once managed billions closed after performing poorly. Martin swooped in and bought $500,000 worth of "gorgeous" office furniture from the defunct firm for $25,000. "Let's never forget," he says, "the value of being the last man standing."*

## Beware of Your Brain

One of the thorniest problems we face as investors is that the human brain is ill-equipped to make rational decisions. Our judgment is frequently torpedoed by emotions such as fear, greed, jealousy, and impatience; by prejudices that distort our perception of reality; by our susceptibility to serpentine sales pitches and peer pressure; and by our habit of acting on flawed or incomplete information. As the evolutionary biologist Robert Trivers writes in *The Folly of Fools: The Logic of Deceit and Self-Deception in Human Life*, "our marvelous organs of perception" enable us to obtain information that our minds systematically "degrade and destroy."

In the 1990s, Munger confronted this problem in three speeches about "the psychology of human misjudgment." In 2005, he wrote an expanded version for inclusion in a collection of his greatest hits, *Poor Charlie's Almanack: The Wit and Wisdom of Charles T. Munger*. His talk, which Nick Sleep hails as "the finest investment speech ever," is a

---

* Another way that Martin increases his odds of survival is by keeping costs exceptionally low at his investment firm, not least by paying himself a modest base salary of $150,000 a year. He also lives on a tiny fraction of his total income. "If I'm wrong today, I'll be right tomorrow," he says, "because I'll be *around* for tomorrow."

dazzling display of intellectual chutzpah. Munger, who'd never taken a psychology course and had read three textbooks on the subject, compiled a list of twenty-five "psychological tendencies" that cause our minds to malfunction, giving them evocative names such as Excessive Self-Regard Tendency, Twaddle Tendency, and Simple, Pain-Avoiding Psychological Denial. He even had the temerity to criticize academic psychologists for failing to understand their own subject.

Munger's compilation of "standard thinking errors" provides him—and us—with a practical checklist of pitfalls to avoid. "The trick here is to first understand them and then train yourself out of them," says Sleep. "Articulating this stuff is easy. Internalizing it is not. That's the hard work." But it's essential because "the most enduring advantages are psychological."

Munger starts with a tendency of such importance that almost all of us underestimate its significance: the role that incentives play in "changing cognition and behavior." He quotes his hero, Benjamin Franklin, who said, "If you would persuade, appeal to interest and not to reason." Munger writes, "This maxim is a wise guide to a great and simple precaution in life: Never, ever, think about something else when you should be thinking about the power of incentives."

Incentives are pivotal in every area of life, whether it's motivating employees or cajoling the most recalcitrant of adversaries: your children. Munger notes that the Soviet Union suffered from its Communist leaders' "foolish and willful ignorance of the superpower of rewards," which led them to disincentivize much productive work. He also warns about the "incentive-caused bias" of salespeople, which can lead "a pretty decent fellow" to drift "into immoral behavior in order to get what he wants." As an antidote, Munger offers this tip: "Especially fear professional advice when it is especially good for the adviser."

The financial world is so riddled with conflicts of interest that we should always be wary of the mind-warping influence of incentives on anyone peddling products or advice. If, say, you're thinking of buying a fund or an annuity, you need to know precisely how your "advisers" are rewarded for their recommendations. It's equally imperative to assess whether a fund manager's incentives are adequately aligned with *your* best interests.

In 1998, I wrote a damning article about the Kaufmann Fund, which had hit the jackpot as a small fund making big bets on tiny stocks. Stellar returns and relentless advertising transformed it into a different beast. With nearly $6 billion in assets, it could no longer focus aggressively on small caps, and its results deteriorated. Still, its two managers raked in $186 million in fees over three years, despite lagging the S&P 500 by more than 50 percentage points. One even admitted to me that he had none of his own money in the fund. *That's* misalignment. All these years later, I'm not shocked to see that the fund still charges an egregious expense ratio of 1.98 percent a year. With $7.5 billion in assets, it's a fantastic fee machine. Given the economies of scale, wouldn't it be fairer to charge less? Sure. But who would benefit? Only its shareholders.

By contrast, Martin accepted long ago that he's incapable of investing large sums in small stocks without hurting his shareholders' returns. So he closed his small-cap portfolio to new investors in 2006 when his firm's assets in that area amounted to only $400 million. That self-restraint has cost him tens of millions in fees, but it has served his existing clients admirably. It's always revealing to see how investors structure their incentives. As vice chairman of Berkshire, which has a market value of more than $500 billion, Munger receives a salary of $100,000. As chairman of the Daily Journal, he receives no salary. He profits from performance, not fees.*

Munger often remarks on how critical it is to partner with honorable and unselfish people, while avoiding those with "perverse incentives." He was appalled by the greed that precipitated the 2008–09 financial crisis, with Wall Street's best and brightest engaged in exploits such as repackaging subprime mortgages to create pestilent bonds with pristine credit ratings. It's easy to rationalize tawdry behavior, especially when it's legal and others are feeding from the same trough. But

---

* The Daily Journal, which sells legal newspapers and software for court systems, has performed decently for a publishing company. But with a market value of less than $400 million, it's a side interest for Munger, not the main event. It's his stake in Berkshire that's made him a billionaire. Still, he's nowhere near as rich as Buffett, partly because he began his investment career after a stint in law, whereas Buffett began to compound money in the womb.

Munger recommends a higher moral standard, which involves saying, "This is beneath me."

Another cognitive danger that Munger highlights in his speech is the "tendency to quickly remove doubt" by rushing to make a decision—a habit that's often triggered by stress. This Doubt-Avoidance Tendency makes evolutionary sense, given that our ancestors had to act decisively in the face of urgent threats. But mental shortcuts that lead investors to make impetuous decisions often end in disaster. To make matters worse, we also fall victim to what Munger calls Inconsistency-Avoidance Tendency, which inclines us to resist new information and insights that might challenge our conclusions, no matter how hastily we reached them.

Munger provides a vivid analogy: "When one sperm gets into a human egg, there's an automatic shut-off device that bars any other sperm from getting in. The human mind tends strongly toward the same sort of result." **The reluctance to reexamine our views and change our minds is one of the greatest impediments to rational thinking. Instead of keeping an open mind, we tend consciously and unconsciously to prioritize information that *reinforces* what we believe.**

The mistake of clinging blindly to our existing convictions can be exacerbated by several other psychological tendencies. Excessive Self-Regard Tendency leads us to overestimate our talents, opinions, and decisions. Overoptimism Tendency lures us into careless acts of financial hubris, especially when all is going well and we're feeling clever. And Simple, Pain-Avoiding Psychological Denial causes us to distort facts when "the reality is too painful to bear." That helps to explain why so many investors fool themselves into believing that they can outpace index funds in the long run, despite lacking the requisite skills, temperament, or control over costs. Munger likes to quote the ancient Greek orator Demosthenes, who observed, "Nothing is easier than self-deceit. For what each man wishes, that he also believes to be true."

If the human mind is such a dirty trickster, how can we expect to make rational investment decisions? First, we need to acknowledge that this insidious threat exists. As Ben Graham wrote, "The investor's chief problem—and even his worst enemy—is likely to be himself."

We also need to be wary of our own distinctive psychological tendencies, which can skew our judgment in predictable directions. Howard Marks, who is inclined to worry, tells me, "If your thinking is heavily colored by wishful thinking, then your probability assignments will be biased toward favorable. . . . If you're given to fear, then you'll be biased toward the negative. . . . No one is going to say, 'This is my prediction and it's probably wrong.' But you *must* say, 'This is my expectation and I have to be aware of the likelihood that it's colored by my emotional bias.' And you have to *resist* it. For me, that means not to chicken out when the going gets tough."

One way that Munger guards against irrationality is by emulating the "extreme objectivity" of scientists such as Charles Darwin, Albert Einstein, and Richard Feynman. When I ask what we can learn from them about how to think through a problem, Munger says, "They were all very hard on themselves. . . . They *worked* at reducing stupidity. They *cared* about thinking it through properly. They had long attention spans and they worked, worked, worked to avoid the stupidities."

**Munger particularly admires their unflinching determination to seek out "disconfirming evidence" that might disprove even their most cherished beliefs. This mental habit, which takes many different forms, is our fifth defense against idiocy.**

For example, Darwin refused to allow his Christian faith or the conventional wisdom among his fellow naturalists to impede his shocking conclusions about evolution. In the introduction to his 1859 book *On the Origin of Species*, he discards a sacrosanct belief drawn from the Bible, declaring, "I can entertain no doubt, after the most deliberate study and dispassionate judgment of which I am capable, that the view which most naturalists entertain, and which I formerly entertained—namely, that each species has been independently created—is erroneous."

**That willingness to welcome the discovery of our own errors is an inestimable advantage.** Munger nurtures it by applauding himself whenever he succeeds in demolishing one of his entrenched beliefs, so that "ignorance removal" becomes a source of satisfaction, not shame. He once remarked, "If Berkshire has made modest progress, a good deal of it is because Warren and I are very good at destroying our own best-loved ideas. Any year that you don't destroy one of your best-loved ideas is probably a wasted year."

One year stands out because the best-loved idea they destroyed made way for an even better idea, which would alter Berkshire's course dramatically over the next five decades. In 1972, Buffett and Munger were presented with the opportunity to acquire See's Candies, a Californian maker of chocolate, for $30 million—a premium price of almost four times net tangible assets. Munger thought it was reasonable, given the company's powerful brand, devoted customer base, and ability to raise prices. But Buffett was a cheapskate who had made a fortune investing in mediocre businesses at such low prices that he could hardly lose. He'd learned this "cigar butt" strategy from Graham, his beloved mentor. So how could he forsake it and pay for quality?

Looking back in Berkshire's 2014 annual report, Buffett recalled, "My misguided caution could have scuttled a terrific purchase. But, luckily, the sellers decided to take our $25 million bid." Munger has said that he and Buffett would have walked away from See's if the price had been $100,000 higher: "We were that dumb back then." Since 1972, See's has earned about $2 billion in pretax profits, vindicating their new belief that it's worth paying more for great businesses.

That realization changed everything, leading them to invest in world-class companies such as Coca-Cola. Their appreciation for intangible assets, including brand loyalty and exceptional management, has continued to evolve, allowing them to pay even richer premiums to acquire unique businesses such as ISCAR and Precision Castparts. In his 2014 annual report, Buffett credited Munger with curing him of his addiction to cigar butts and establishing "the design of today's Berkshire. The blueprint he gave me was simple: Forget what you know about buying fair businesses at wonderful prices; instead, buy wonderful businesses at fair prices."

None of this would have happened if Buffett and Munger weren't so committed to challenging their beliefs. Munger has always disdained "heavy ideology" in everything from investing to politics, denouncing it as "one of the most extreme distorters of human cognition." Having practiced law before Buffett persuaded him to change professions, Munger consciously trained himself to study counterarguments so he can articulate them as accurately as if they were his own views. He also makes a point of reading articles by cogent thinkers with whom he disagrees, including the *New York Times* columnist Paul Krugman. Most of us favor media sources that echo our social and political prejudices. But Munger's example led me to adopt a simple, mind-expanding practice of reading columns in the *Wall Street Journal* that counter my own biases.

Another practical way to insure that our weak ideas and lazy prejudices don't go unchallenged is to find intellectual sparring partners who aren't afraid to disagree with us. Buffett once observed, "What the human being is best at doing is interpreting all new information so that their prior conclusions remain intact. . . . That is a talent everyone seems to have mastered. And how do we guard ourselves against it?" His answer: "A partner who is not subservient and who himself is extremely logical . . . is probably the best mechanism you can have." Munger, the ideal foil, has shot down so many investment ideas that Buffett refers to him as "The Abominable No-Man."

Munger points out that one essential benefit of having a discussion partner is that it obliges you to organize your thoughts to make a persuasive case. Pabrai recalls introducing Spier to Munger and telling him, "Charlie, this is the person I bounce all my ideas off." Spier joked that he's so dumb that Pabrai might as well talk to a monkey. "And Charlie immediately says, 'The monkey would not work.' He was very serious. This was like Moses giving the Fourth Commandment. He said, 'The monkey would not work because Mohnish would *know* it's a monkey.'"

Other leading investors have found additional ways to ensure that they remain open to divergent views. Bill Nygren, a renowned fund manager at Harris Associates in Chicago, recalls meeting Michael Steinhardt, a hedge fund billionaire who "would invite two Wall Street analysts into his office: the biggest bull and the biggest bear. And the three of them would argue about an idea over lunch. He always wanted to know what the most bearish people thought of something before he would buy it, or what the most bullish people thought before he would short it."

Inspired in part by Steinhardt, Nygren conducts a "devil's advocate review" before buying any stock. One analyst on his team presents the bullish case. Another is tasked with "putting together the strongest bearish case. . . . By better understanding what we're betting against, we're more likely to make the right decision."

Nygren knows that it's even harder to think objectively about a stock once he owns it. That's partly because of the endowment effect—a cognitive bias that makes us value what we own more highly than what we don't, whether it's a stock or a beer mug. One way that Nygren counteracts this bias is by also performing devil's advocate reviews for each of his biggest holdings. At least once a year, a team member reassesses the stock in question and "is given the responsibility of arguing why it should be sold."

Another psychologically astute strategy is to perform a "premortem" before making any significant investment decision. That's to say, you project into the future and ask yourself a hypothetical question: "Why did this decision prove to be such a disaster?" The notion of a premortem was devised by an applied psychologist, Gary Klein, to identify problems in advance and reduce the risk of overconfidence. For investors, it's a valuable safeguard because it forces us to dwell on unfavorable facts and latent threats as a formal step in the decision-making process.

In 2016, I audited the Advanced Investment Research course at Columbia Business School, which was taught for a decade by Ken Shubin Stein, a friend who was then the chairman of an investment firm called Spencer Capital Holdings. Shubin Stein, who qualified as a doctor before becoming a hedge fund manager, instructed his MBA students to imagine themselves in three years' time, when an investment of theirs has failed, and to write a newspaper article explaining the cause of death. Another eminent investor told the class that his family office writes a premortem memo as the final precaution before making any investment. The procedure exposes such serious concerns that he rejects one-third of the investments he would otherwise have made.

Nobody I've encountered is more thoughtful than Shubin Stein about the defensive measures we can take to diminish the destructive effects of cognitive biases. It helps that his experience is so diverse. He spent two decades as a fund manager and built a holding company with more than four hundred employees. But he's also steeped in science, having done research in molecular genetics, trained as a surgeon, and cofounded the International Concussion Society. His interest in the brain is so consuming that he quit the investment business in 2018 and became a neurologist.

Shubin Stein warns that "you can't immunize yourself effectively" against cognitive biases, no matter how smart or self-aware you are. The recognition that we are all subject to them is a start, but that knowledge doesn't protect us against their unconscious influence on our thinking. Still, he offers several practical suggestions that can significantly enhance our ability to make rational decisions, despite the problematic tendencies ingrained in the human brain over millennia.

For a start, Shubin Stein recommends taking the time to rewrite the list of common cognitive errors that Munger describes in his talk on the psychology of misjudgment. Instead of quoting Munger, it's best to describe these pitfalls in your own words, so you can internalize his insights and make them your own. It's also helpful to personalize Munger's checklist by including investment mistakes you've made in the past and emphasizing the tendencies to which you're especially vulnerable. "You need to learn how your own brain works, where you're strong, and where your challenges lie," explains Shubin Stein. For example, he's highly susceptible to "authority bias," which has sometimes led him to place too much faith in stocks owned by investment luminaries whom he admires. To help counter this bias, he added two questions to his cognitive checklist: "Have I done the work? And have I independently verified everything?"

Like Munger, Shubin Stein advocates a "scientific approach" to analyzing investments. That means adopting "a mindset of falsification," always striving to "disprove" your hypothesis, and seeing "if it stands up to the assault." One of Shubin Stein's favorite questions is, "Why might I be wrong?" He also stresses the importance of analyzing "alternative competing hypotheses"—a methodology that he borrowed from Richards Heuer, a CIA veteran who wrote a classic book titled *Psychology of Intelligence Analysis*. Shubin Stein told his students that they must never forget Heuer's insight that "a single piece of evidence can support more than one hypothesis."

One of Heuer's enduring contributions to the CIA was to develop a rigorous, eight-step procedure for the "simultaneous evaluation of multiple, competing hypotheses." Few of us possess the patience to think through problems that thoroughly. But as Heuer suggests, we can't overcome our "cognitive limitations" unless we have "a systematic analytical process" that enables us to think methodically. *Devil's advocate reviews. Premortems. Conversations with a skeptical discussion partner. A cognitive checklist that reminds us of our biggest biases and our past mistakes.* These are all disciplined analytical techniques that can help us systematically to slow down, open our minds, and consider risks that we might otherwise overlook.

Similarly, Shubin Stein taught his students to perform a "bull/bear analysis" for every company they analyzed—another basic procedure that entails writing two thesis statements (one positive, one negative), each on a single page of its own. The key is to use such techniques routinely, so we consistently challenge our assumptions, contemplate counterarguments, and resist the brain's tendency to conserve energy by taking shortcuts. **This emphasis on adopting systematic analytical procedures is the sixth strategy in our epic quest to be non-idiotic.**

Finally, we need a pragmatic way to protect ourselves from our emotions, given how grievously they can compromise our ability to make rational decisions. In his talk, Munger mentions how emotions such as stress, depression, hatred, and envy can cause "dysfunctional" thinking and accentuate our cognitive biases. For example, acute stress and confusion can intensify an investor's urge to follow the crowd and abandon independent thought, especially when markets are plunging. The desire to seek safety in numbers makes evolutionary sense. But for investors, herd behavior is often disastrous, driving them to buy during bubbles and sell during panics. As Munger once remarked, "Crowd folly, the tendency of humans, under some circumstances, to resemble lemmings, explains much foolish thinking of brilliant men and much foolish behavior."

In 2015, the *Annual Review of Psychology* published a survey of thirty-five years of scientific studies about the effects of emotion on decision-making. The authors write that the "one overarching conclusion" of all that research is that "emotions powerfully, predictably, and pervasively influence decision making." For example, researchers who studied gambling decisions found that "sadness increased tendencies to favor high-risk, high-reward options, whereas anxiety increased tendencies to favor low-risk, low-reward options." In other words, our emotional disposition and moods routinely distort what we see and how we relate to risk.

Based on such research, Shubin Stein developed the precautionary habit of checking whether he's "in the right psychological and physiological state to make decisions." This habit is immeasurably valuable not only in markets but in every area of life where our decisions could have calamitous consequences.

**The scientific literature shows that hunger, anger, loneliness, tiredness, pain, and stress are common "preconditions for poor decision making." So Shubin Stein uses an acronym, HALT-PS, as a reminder to pause when those factors might be impairing his judgment and postpone important decisions until he's in a state in which his brain is more likely to function well.\* This is our seventh technique for reducing avoidable stupidity.**

During the 2008–09 financial crisis, Shubin Stein suffered an agonizing trial by fire. Many of his fund's investors bailed out when they should instead have been buying. His business was in jeopardy, and he felt a deep sense of shame as he faced the first grave setback of his career. At the same time, two of his closest friends lost their daughter in a boating accident. It was such a traumatic period that it "catalyzed" him to build a healthier lifestyle that would help him to maintain his emotional equilibrium and think more clearly even under the most stressful conditions.

**"There are four things that we *know* improve brain health and brain function," says Shubin Stein. "Meditation, exercise, sleep, and nutrition."** Determined to use every tool at his disposal, he exercised strenuously, which also helped him to sleep better. He ate more fish, vegetables, and fruit. He renounced his "worst tendencies," including a habit of handling stress by gorging on vanilla ice cream with mashed-up chocolate chip cookies. And he developed a regular meditation practice—a mission-critical habit for many successful investors.

---

\*The *Annual Review of Psychology* reaches the same conclusion that "time delay" can be a helpful strategy, since "full-blown emotions are short-lived" and "humans revert back to baseline states over time."

These "practices for sustained high performance" have "a compounding effect" when you use them consistently, says Shubin Stein. For example: "The reason you meditate is not because it's important on a specific day. The regular practice of meditation will help you handle the hard setbacks and will keep you constantly prepared for them. . . . Having that practice in place prepares you well. It's a lot like preventative medicine." This is a critical nuance that I think most of us miss. The optimal time to adopt these healthy habits isn't when we're in the throes of chaos, but *in advance*.

Once trouble strikes, says Shubin Stein, the key is to recognize that our emotional state may be "setting us up for failure." When he's stressed, upset, or overwhelmed, he tries to take a break, makes sure that he's rested and well fed, and gives himself time to return to a "neutral" state that will "allow for more mindful decision-making." Simple solutions such as clearing his schedule and sleeping on decisions for a night have also helped considerably. "The more intense things get, the less I do, both personally and professionally," he says. "I try to slow things down. I try to simplify life. . . . I look at my calendar and withdraw from a lot of activities to make sure that I'm eating well, meditating, and have structured time to think and reflect."

In 2020, Shubin Stein served as a volunteer doctor in an intensive care unit filled with dying COVID-19 patients connected to ventilators. "It literally felt like being in battle," he says. "We were doing something important, but our lives were at risk and we were putting our families at risk, which felt terrible." A few days earlier, his wife had given birth to their first child. He moved into a hotel to safeguard them.

In the midst of this nightmare, Shubin Stein drew on all of the habits that had helped him to handle his emotions during his investment career, including a nutritious diet, exercise, and "small doses of meditation"—which sometimes meant "just breathing for ten seconds" in the bathroom before returning to the ICU. Above all, he tried to remain acutely aware of his "internal state," so that emotions such as fear, anxiety, sadness, anger, and loneliness wouldn't undermine his ability to care for his patients and communicate each day with their grief-stricken relatives.

One "incredibly helpful" tool was his HALT-PS checklist. He used it constantly to gauge his emotional condition and the debilitating effect of the physical pain that he felt while wearing personal protective equipment. Once you recognize "that you're not at your best," says Shubin Stein, "you can consciously compensate." In the hospital, that meant taking additional care to double-check his decisions and pushing himself "to be extra-compassionate with patients."

The challenges that he faced were extraordinary, but the overarching lesson applies to all of us. We, too, need the self-awareness and honesty to acknowledge when our emotional state is likely to compromise our judgment and our performance, so we can proceed with heightened caution.

More broadly, we also need to construct a lifestyle that's conducive to calm resilience. Munger, for one, has spent inordinate amounts of time engaged in activities that instill a sense of balance and well-being, whether it's reading books in his library at home, playing bridge with friends, golfing, or fishing. He also keeps an uncluttered schedule that leaves him ample space for contemplation. The details differ, but we all need habits and hobbies that foster equanimity.

But the truth is, Munger doesn't struggle like most of us to keep his emotions in check. When I ask him if he agrees with Marks that all of the best investors are unemotional, he replies, "Yes. Absolutely." Does he ever fret about his investments or feel fearful? "No." So he doesn't have to work *against* those emotions because he doesn't experience them? "No."

In the absence of extreme emotional static, Munger has the freedom to focus with imperturbable detachment on whether the odds of an investment succeeding favor him overwhelmingly. When bank stocks went up in flames during the financial crisis, he concluded that Wells Fargo was so ridiculously cheap that it represented a "once-in-forty-year opportunity." He bought it on behalf of the Daily Journal at the "bottom tick" in March 2009—a perfect example, he says, of "rationality and good sense." His lack of emotion is an innate advantage that few investors share. "Warren is wired that way, too," he says. "We're quite similar in the way we're wired."

Munger has also learned to control certain toxic emotions that would corrode his enjoyment of life. "Crazy anger. Crazy resentment. Avoid all that stuff," he tells me. "I don't let it run. I don't let it start."

The same goes for envy, which he considers the dumbest of the seven deadly sins because it's not even fun. He also disdains the tendency to view oneself as a victim, and he has no patience for whining. When I ask if he has a mental process that helps him to defuse self-defeating emotions, he replies, "I *know* that anger is stupid. I *know* that resentment is stupid. I *know* self-pity is stupid. So I don't do them. . . . I'm trying not to be stupid every day, all day."

## Lessons of a Lifetime

At the end of our interview, Munger retrieves his cane and hobbles slowly across the lobby of the Daily Journal's offices toward a makeshift stage. The audience breaks into sustained applause at the sight of him. He needs help to climb the two stairs onto the stage. Breathing heavily, he takes his seat and peers out with his one good eye at a room overflowing with his admirers. Many are obliged to stand because all of the seats are filled. More people are here than in previous years, he comments wryly, because "they think it's their last chance."

Part guru, part showman, Munger revels in this opportunity to share many lessons from his life. "You're cult members," he says, with an air of affectionate amusement. "We'll stay a long time because some of you have come a long way." Over the next two hours, he fields more than forty questions, dispensing wisdom and wisecracks about everything from markets to marriage.

Asked for career advice, he opines: "You have to play in a game where you've got some unusual talents. If you're five foot one, you don't want to play basketball against some guy who's eight foot three. It's just too hard. So you've got to figure out a game where you have an advantage, and it has to be something that you're deeply interested in."

Asked about China, he marvels at its economic transformation, but laments that too many Chinese "like to gamble, and they actually believe in luck. Now, that is stupid. What you don't want to believe in is luck. You want to believe in odds." Munger has no interest in gambling at casinos or racetracks. "If the odds are against me," he says, "I just don't play."

Asked about the crash of 1973–74, when his investment partnership lost more than 50 percent, he notes that Berkshire's stock price has also halved on three occasions: "If you're going to be in this game for the long pull, which is the way to do it, you better be able to handle a fifty percent decline without fussing too much about it. And so my lesson to all of you is, conduct your life so that you can handle the fifty percent decline with aplomb and grace. Don't try to avoid it. It will come. In fact, I would say if it doesn't come, you're not being aggressive enough."

Asked about diversification, he describes it as a fine "rule for those who don't know anything." But his preferred strategy is to wait for rare opportunities where the probability of gain vastly outweighs the probability of loss. When they arrive, he grabs them with "gumption." Munger confides that his family's ten-figure fortune rides almost entirely on three investments: Berkshire, Costco, and a portfolio of Chinese stocks selected by Li Lu. The chances that any of those three bets will fail is "almost zero," says Munger. "Am I securely rich? You're damn right I am."

Asked about index funds, he talks about the misery they've inflicted on much of the investment profession. The vast majority of active fund managers will fail to beat the index over time, which means they are scraping off fees as a reward for providing no added value. "The honest, sensible people know they're selling something they can't quite deliver," says Munger. "Most people handle that with denial. . . . I understand that. I mean, I don't want to think of my own death."

The crowd disperses after the shareholder meeting draws to a close. But Munger stays put. A couple of dozen faithful followers gather around him, and he spends two *more* hours answering questions. For sustenance, he opens a box of See's peanut brittle. He chomps on it joyously, crumbs flying everywhere, then shares the box with his delighted fans. I stand a few feet from his chair, observing him closely and occasionally asking questions of my own. What impresses me most is not just the range and agility of his mind, but the generosity of his spirit. I find it moving to see the patience, care, and kindness that this ailing master displays to his disciples.

As Munger looks back on his financial adventures, it becomes clear that what he cherishes most is not the scale of his victory, but the manner in which he has won it. He recalls a time when he and Buffett gladly rejected "the best deal we ever saw"—the chance to acquire a manufacturer of snuff. There was just one hitch: The company made a fortune hawking an addictive product known to cause cancer. Undeterred, the Pritzker family bought this ugly gem and made a profit of about $3 billion. Still, Munger has no regrets. "We are way better off *not* making a killing off of a product we knew going into it was a killing product," he says. "Why should we do that?"

For Munger, the goal has never been to win at all costs. "Money was very important to him," says his daughter Molly. "But to win it by cheating or win it and lose the battle for life, that was never what he was about." In the foreword to *Damn Right!*, a biography of Munger by Janet Lowe, Buffett writes, "In 41 years, I have never seen Charlie try to take advantage of anyone. . . . He has knowingly let me and others have the better end of a deal, and he has also always shouldered more than his share of the blame when things go wrong and accepted less than his share of credit when the reverse has been true. He is generous in the deepest sense. . ."

Munger embodies an enlightened form of capitalism that is infused with old-fashioned values. For example, he disapproves of mean-spirited tactics such as "brutalizing" suppliers by paying them late. "My theory of life is win-win," he says. "I want suppliers that trust me and I trust them. And I don't *want* to screw the suppliers as hard as I can." But how does he reconcile his faith in fairness with the reality that many fortunes have been built in a less honorable manner?

Munger responds by speaking about the multibillionaire media tycoon Sumner Redstone—a famously shrewd and "hard-driven tough tomato" who amassed controlling stakes in Viacom and CBS. "Almost nobody ever liked him, including his wives and his children," says Munger. "Sumner Redstone and I graduated from Harvard Law School about a year or so apart, and he ends up with more money than I did. So you can say *he's* the success. But that's not the way I look at it. And so I don't think it's just a financial game, and I think it's better to do it the other way. . . . I use Sumner Redstone all my life as an example of what I don't want to be."

When I ask Munger what we can learn from him and Buffett about how to lead happy lives, he talks about the quality of their relationships and the joy of partnering with decent, trustworthy people: "Warren has been a marvelous partner for me. I've been a good partner for him. . . . If you want to *have* a good partner, *be* a good partner. It's a very simple system, and it's worked very well." The same principle applies to marriage, too: "If you want a good spouse, deserve one."

Despite his best efforts, Munger has endured his share of suffering. His first son, Teddy, died of leukemia at the age of nine—"a miserable, slow death. And in the end, he kind of knew it was coming, and I'd been lying to him all along. . . . It was just pure agony." There was a divorce, too. And the loss of his eye. And the death of his second wife, Nancy, after fifty-two years of marriage. "The idea that life is a series of adversities and each one is an opportunity to behave well instead of badly is a very, very good idea," says Munger. "I think you take the hardships as they come. You take the blessings as they come. Have fun out of figuring out the puzzles as best you can."

It also helps to have a sense of humor. One of the highlights of the Daily Journal meeting comes when Munger recalls his romantic failures as a short, skinny boy at Omaha Central High School eight decades ago. In his freshman year, he invited a "blonde goddess" to a dance. Hoping to impress her, he pretended to be a smoker. "She was wearing a net dress, and I set her on fire," he says. "But I was quickwitted and I threw Coca-Cola all over her, and in due time the fire was out. And that's the last I saw of the blonde goddess."

Finally, after speaking for five hours straight, Munger is informed that he has another meeting to attend. I help him down from the stage, holding his arm to provide support. As he walks away, I am filled with a sense of awe. Today, I have been in the presence of greatness.

# Beyond Rich

### Money matters. But it's not the essential
### ingredient of an abundant life

_____

If all you succeed in doing in life is getting rich by buying little pieces of paper, it's a failed life. Life is more than being shrewd in wealth accumulation.

— Charlie Munger

A television reporter once asked Bob Marley, "Are you a rich man?" The musician replied warily, "What you mean rich?" The reporter clarified his question: "You have a lot of possessions? A lot of money in the bank?" Marley responded with a question of his own: "Possessions make you rich? I don't have that type of richness. My richness is life, forever."

Over the last quarter of a century, I've spent an enormous amount of time interviewing and observing many of the world's leading investors, and I've frequently found myself pondering this question of what makes a person rich. In a superficial sense, these investors are the ultimate winners. They have hit the jackpot on an almost unimaginable scale, enabling them to buy palatial properties, yachts, planes, and world-class collections of everything from art to race cars. But what does their wealth actually do for them? How much bearing does it have on their contentment? And if their physical riches are *not* the key to true abundance, then what is?

All those toys and trophies provide about as much joy as you'd expect—some, but not *that* much. Sir John Templeton once wrote, "Material assets bring comfort, but help little toward happiness or usefulness. . . . One of the real fallacies is the popular notion that happiness depends on external circumstances and surroundings." To a great extent, he was obviously right. You don't have to be an enlightened Zen monk to recognize that physical pleasures offer an ephemeral and unreliable route to happiness. Still, I would note that Templeton himself chose to live in a beautiful house in the sun-kissed Bahamas, surrounded by the superrich. His choice suggests that external circumstances do have *some* influence on our sense of well-being.

Ed Thorp, a legendary gambler and investor who exudes joie de vivre, thinks with characteristic rationality about how best to structure his life in ways that improve his odds of being happy. One of his most life-enriching decisions was to buy a waterfront house in Newport Beach, California, with sublime views of sunsets over the Pacific Ocean. It's "just a prime place to enjoy oneself," says Thorp. "Why do I want to live in a congested, madhouse city with smog and filth and terrible weather and noise and a struggle to get from one place to the next? I'll just live in a place where it's sunny and pleasant, and I can exercise outdoors, and I can enjoy a lot of beauty, and I can go on hikes, sail, and I can scuba dive."*

Thorp, who started his career as a modestly paid math professor, appreciates the luxuries that investment success has afforded him. When I ask if he has any possessions that he loves, he grins and says, "I really enjoy my Tesla. It's so much fun. It's just the greatest car." Still, he was never seduced by the fantasy that he'd become even happier if only he could amass *more* money, *more* houses, *more* cars, *more everything*. "Who you spend your time with is probably the most important thing in life," says Thorp, who was widowed after fifty-five years of marriage and has since remarried. "People who just keep piling up stuff don't get that. And they end up with a whole lot of stuff at the end, but they've spent their whole life just chasing it."

As Thorp suggests, problems tend to arise when we become so consumed by the pursuit of money and possessions that we lose sight of what matters more. During his career as a hedge fund manager, Thorp could easily have gouged his shareholders and pocketed more of the

---

* Thorp has since moved about four miles along the coast to Laguna Beach, where he's even closer to the ocean.

spoils. Instead, he asked himself what he'd consider "fair and reasonable" if *he* were the client. He then designed his incentives so he'd earn nothing unless his clients made a profit. "People who don't care about other people and are willing to do inconsistent, outrageous things and rip other people off seem to have an edge," he says. "But to me, it's maybe an edge in getting what they want. They can rip off more raw meat from the carcass of life. But they don't live well and they don't realize it. And when it's all over, they've basically wasted their lives."

All of this leads us to an important caveat. We need to be acutely aware of what we're willing and unwilling to sacrifice for the sake of money. This might include rich relationships with our family and friends; talents and ambitions that we neglect at the expense of our fulfillment; the time to relish experiences that don't advance us in a material way; or values that it's tempting (and often profitable) to violate. When I ask Thorp if he has any regrets about the choices he's made in his life, he says, "I don't regret any of the *principled* choices I made." It's a reminder that one aspect of a successful and abundant life is the self-respect that comes from trying consistently (despite all of our flaws and failings) to behave decently and avoid harming others.


### The Freedom to Work Until You're 109 Years Old


In 2015, Irving Kahn died at the astonishing age of 109. He'd lived through two world wars, the Crash of 1929, the Great Depression, the rise and fall of the Soviet Union, the invention of computers, and so much else. Benjamin Graham had been his mentor and friend, and had shared with him the secrets of intelligent investing. Kahn had drawn on that wisdom to build a respected investment firm, Kahn Brothers Group, where he worked alongside his son Thomas and grandson Andrew. Kahn was married for sixty-five years and had a busload of grandchildren and great-grandchildren. As I mentioned in a previous chapter, I typed out several questions for Kahn a few months before he died and gave them to Andrew, who wrote down his grandfather's answers over several days.

Above all, I wanted to know what had been the key to a meaningful and fulfilling life, and not just an extraordinarily long one. "It's very hard to answer this question," said Kahn. "Everyone will have a different answer. But for me, family has been very important." And what gave him the most pride and pleasure when he looked back on his life? "Having a family, healthy children, seeing what we've achieved at the firm. These have all given me great pleasure," he said. "I have also gotten pleasure from meeting people who are smarter than me and who gave me important answers. There are too many mysteries in life. At some point, you have to ask for directions."

Just think for a moment about those basic ingredients that helped to make for a richly rewarding life. *Family. Health. Challenging and useful work*, which involved serving his clients well by compounding their savings conservatively over decades. And *learning*—particularly from Graham, an investment prophet who, Kahn said, "taught me how to study companies and succeed through research as opposed to luck or happenstance."

For Kahn, much of the day-to-day pleasure of life came from intellectual discovery. He delighted in studying companies and reading about business, economics, politics, technology, and history. His sole indulgence was to buy thousands of books. He lived on a fraction of his income and never flaunted his wealth. He preferred hamburgers to lavish meals in chic restaurants and recalled with glee how, in the 1930s, he paid seventy-five cents to dine with his wife at his favorite Chinese restaurant. Even after turning one hundred, Kahn rode the bus to work several days a week. When I visited his office, I was struck by how nondescript it was. His utilitarian furniture looked tired and worn; his scuffed walls needed a coat of paint; and his most notable decoration was a bulletin board filled with dozens of family snapshots and an old picture of his teacher Graham.

"My father was interested in ideas," says Thomas Kahn, who is now president of the family firm. "Most Wall Street guys are in it for the money. They want the custom suits. . . . They buy a place in Palm Beach, get a car and driver, get a jet. The objective for them is to spend. For Irving, that was not it. . . . He was never in it for the material things." Most of all, he enjoyed "the satisfaction of being right and making good choices and doing better than others."

Yet in some ways, money mattered immensely: it allowed Kahn to live and work precisely as he pleased. As Thomas Kahn puts it, "You build capital and then you can do whatever you want because you're independent." For many of the most successful investors I've interviewed, that freedom to construct a life that aligns authentically with their passions and peculiarities may be the single greatest luxury that money can buy. Bill Ackman, a billionaire known for his bold and controversial bets, once told me, "The most important personal driver for me very early on was independence. I wanted to be financially independent. I wanted to be independent enough to say what I thought. And I wanted to be independent enough to do what I thought was right."

In his own quirky, low-key way, Kahn was true to himself. For most of us, the prospect of commuting as centenarians to an office tower in Manhattan has limited appeal. But Kahn had little interest in retirement—or, for that matter, visiting art galleries, going to the theater, or traveling for pleasure. "He enjoyed his work," says Thomas Kahn. "It was his hobby."

Equally important, Kahn's wealth gave him peace of mind. His priority was never to maximize his returns, but to preserve his capital and make sustainable progress over many decades. He set aside a hefty cash reserve, which reduced his gains but insured that he'd never be forced to sell any of his investments prematurely in times of trouble. That stable foundation, along with his modest spending habits, allowed him to withstand any amount of economic turmoil. "If the market goes down, so what? You can still eat hamburger," says Thomas Kahn. "It's a really nice thing to be able to say, 'Sure, I'm unhappy. But I'm not on the ledge like these other people.'"

That sense of deep-rooted security is a precious prize. During the global financial crisis of 2008–09, the journalism industry was eviscerated, and I lost my job as the editor of an international magazine at the same time as my investments took a shocking hit. With two kids in private school, plus the exorbitant cost of housing in London, I experienced firsthand the corrosive dread that I might be unable to take care of my family. Thankfully, I'd taken the precaution of avoiding debt. So I managed to ride out the crisis without selling any investments. Still, that traumatic period reinforced my conviction that nothing is more essential than our capacity to survive the most difficult times—not only financially, but emotionally. It's easy to forget this when everything is going well.

Money can provide an invaluable cushion, a lifeline, a critical defense against uncertainty and misfortune. But it's not enough. We also need the mental fortitude and resilience to weather those storms and rebuild in their wake. For most of us, the quality of our lives depends less on our finances than on inner attributes such as equanimity, acceptance, hope, trust, appreciation, and determined optimism. As John Milton wrote in *Paradise Lost*, which he dictated after going blind, "The mind is its own place, and in itself can make a heaven of Hell, a hell of Heaven."

### "The Ability to Take Pain"

People often assume that celebrated investors have it made, that they exist within a cocoon of wealth and privilege that insulates them from most difficulties. But I've spent enough time with them to witness up close their troubles and sorrows, including bitter divorces, sick children, and periods of overwhelming stress. Their fortunes also depend heavily on the vagaries of the financial markets, which can be fickle and cruel, dashing their dreams, punishing their hubris, and exposing their flawed thinking for all to see and mock. Mohnish Pabrai remarks that all of the best investors share one indispensable trait: "the ability to take pain."

In 2017, I met with Jason Karp in his sleek offices on the thirty-second floor of a New York skyscraper with commanding views over Central Park. Karp, then the CEO and chief investment officer of Tourbillon Capital Partners, was a rising star in the investment world. He'd graduated in the top four in his class at Wharton in 1998, become a high-flying portfolio manager at SAC Capital, and launched one of the hottest hedge fund start-ups in history. His firm scored impressive returns in its first three years and rapidly attracted more than $4 billion in assets. Handsome, charming, clever, and maniacally driven, Karp seemed destined for victory at everything he touched.

But his flagship fund lost 9.2 percent in 2016, battered in part by a failed bet that Valeant—a company sullied by scandal—would rebound once the market recognized that it wasn't *quite* as toxic as it seemed. Meanwhile, the S&P 500 returned 12 percent. It was the worst year in Karp's eighteen-year career. What's more, 2017 was off to a lousy start, and he'd finish it with a 13.8 percent loss. Karp spoke with disarming candor about the impact of his first encounter with failure. "Last year was very humbling," he said. "I took it very personally, and I got a lot of heat. . . . I felt like I was apologizing the whole year, which was sort of unusual, and there was a lot of self-doubt about what just happened. Did I just get bad? Did I get stupid? Am I losing it?"

In the past, said Karp, there had been periods when his returns were "almost unthinkably good. Everyone wants to know what your secret sauce is. Why are you so amazing? It really goes to your head." Now it felt as if he'd tumbled "from the absolute top to the absolute bottom. It was almost like they'd expected us to be immortal. . . . And then we showed our mortality."

Growing up in the 1980s, Karp had played video games so obsessively that it bordered on being "totally unhealthy." But he now regarded that misspent youth as a "very formative and helpful" preparation for his investment career. "One of the nice things about video games as a metaphor is that you die all the time," he explained. "You play, you play, you play, you die. You play, you play, you die." It's a harmless way of learning "to accept constant loss and defeat over and over again. And it doesn't bother you. You just keep doing it. And that's what investing is."

The trouble with managing money for other people, said Karp, is that "you're constantly under scrutiny. You're constantly compared to everyone else." Yet in the short term, your returns provide an unreliable reflection of your talent, your work ethic, and your long-term prospects. "You're being judged every week on something you have no control over."

That lack of control can be excruciating. Karp adhered to a logical and consistent investment process. But he started to develop a "very, *very* uncomfortable feeling" that there was no "clear linkage between process and outcome." He remarked that scientists have been known to "induce insanity" in animals during laboratory experiments by enticing them to pull a lever repeatedly and responding randomly, either with a treat or an electric shock. As an active trader in a violently volatile and irrational market, he had come to identify with those unfortunate creatures.

"There's so much randomness that it can drive you insane," said Karp. "It requires a certain type of masochistic, weirdly wired human to do this [job] for a very long period of time.... It's almost akin to subjecting yourself to torture over and over and over again. Because when you get it right, it feels great. But you get it wrong often. And you have to keep coming back."

Karp recognized that resilience is a prerequisite for success in markets and life. A competitive athlete, he'd been an Academic All-American and All-Ivy squash player in college. Then, in his early twenties, he'd developed several life-threatening autoimmune diseases and been told by his doctors that he'd lose his sight by the age of thirty. To their surprise, he recovered completely after radically altering his approach to nutrition, sleep, and stress management. Obsessed with health and sustainable excellence, he'd designed Tourbillon's offices to include a gym, a meditation room, and a kitchen stocked with nutritious food. He'd even banned soda from the premises. When it came to hiring, he specifically recruited people with a proven ability to recover from setbacks, using a former CIA interrogator to help him with the selection process.

But in 2018, Karp decided that he'd had enough. He felt that his "personal edge was gone," that he added no significant value in a market increasingly dominated by index funds and machine-driven trading. He could have kept going and collected extravagant fees for a couple more years, but he couldn't bear to be mediocre. So he closed his funds, returned about $1.5 billion to his shareholders, and quit the hedge fund business.

When I caught up with him again in 2020, Karp told me, "I was fully clinically depressed for my last few years at Tourbillon, and I was even clinically depressed when I was at the height of my success." The money, the plaudits, and the glamorous lifestyle had all failed to make him happy. "I've obviously earned enough to retire many times over," he said. "But for me, it always felt a bit hollow.... I felt that my soul was decaying." As a trader racing endlessly from one short-term bet to the next, he also sensed that his job had become an addiction. "It was just this compulsive game of winning at pushing prices around. . . . I wasn't actually building anything."

Karp had turned his life around before. In his twenties, he restored his health by embracing an "ultraclean" lifestyle free from processed food, alcohol, caffeine, and even brands of shampoo or deodorant containing chemicals. In his forties, he's reinventing himself again. Determined to create something of "enduring value," he recently unveiled his new venture—a private holding company called HumanCo, which will back and nurture businesses that "help people to live healthier lives." It's a specialized niche in which he's convinced that he has an edge. Plus, his company's focus on clean living and sustainability aligns deeply with his values.

Starting over, Karp has also left Manhattan and moved with his wife and kids to Austin, Texas—"a health-and-wellness mecca" with "better weather," "more outdoor living," "no state or city taxes," and "this positivity that the jaded New York finance crew didn't have." It turns out that what he craved most wasn't money, but a balanced and healthy life, a chance to build a "mission-driven" company that helps others, and a greater sense of control over his destiny. So how does he feel? Karp confides, "I'm the healthiest and happiest I've been in twenty years."

## Stocks and Stoics

From time to time, all of the best investors mess up or get unlucky, no matter how careful and diligent they may be. After all, the financial markets are a microcosm of life: infinitely complex and wildly unpredictable. When Joel Greenblatt launched his investment firm in 1985, the first merger deal in which he invested involved Florida Cypress Gardens, which operated a tourist attraction with exotic gardens, flamingos, and aquatic shows featuring Santa Claus on water skis. The company agreed to be acquired, and Greenblatt made what he describes as "a pretty riskless" arbitrage bet that the deal would close as planned. Then, one morning, he opened the *Wall Street Journal* to discover that the company's main pavilion had fallen into a sinkhole. The deal collapsed, and he suffered a major loss at a vulnerable time when he was "counting every nickel." Greenblatt remarks, "It would have been funny, if I hadn't been scared out of my mind."

In short, we are all subject to what Hamlet called "the slings and arrows of outrageous fortune." We cannot hope to lead happy and successful lives unless we learn to cope well with adversity. In challenging times, Pabrai attempts to clone the mindset of Marcus Aurelius, a second-century Roman emperor and Stoic philosopher whose notes to himself are preserved in *Meditations*, a book that he never intended to publish. As Marcus Aurelius saw it, "the greatest of all contests" is "the struggle not to be overwhelmed by anything that happens." But how?

The key, he wrote, is to "concentrate on this for your whole life long: for your mind to be in the right state." That includes "welcoming wholeheartedly whatever comes," "trusting that all is for the best," and "not worrying too often, or with any selfish motive, about what other people say. Or do, or think." Marcus Aurelius considered it futile to fret or complain about anything beyond his control. He focused instead on mastering his own thoughts and behaving virtuously so he would meet his moral obligations. "Disturbance comes only from within— from our own perceptions," he argued. "Choose not to be harmed— and you won't feel harmed. Don't feel harmed—and you haven't been. It can ruin your life only if it ruins your character. Otherwise it cannot harm you." He sought "to be like the rock that the waves keep crashing over. It stands unmoved and the raging of the sea falls still around it."

It's not hard to see why many top-notch investors are attracted to Stoicism—none more so than Bill Miller, who studied philosophy as a postgraduate at Johns Hopkins and announced in 2018 that he was donating $75 million to the university's philosophy department. During the financial crisis, he suffered a reversal of fortune that might have permanently derailed an investor without his reserves of Stoic endurance.

Back then, Miller was the preeminent mutual fund manager of his generation. His main fund, Legg Mason Value Trust, had famously beaten the S&P 500 for fifteen years running. But as the market crashed in 2008, he made the gravest analytical error of his career. He bet that a slew of the worst-hit financial stocks would soar once the Federal Reserve acted decisively to inject capital and avert catastrophe. He loaded up on radioactive stocks such as Bear Stearns, AIG, Merrill Lynch, Freddie Mac, and Countrywide Financial—all of which continued to melt down. In 2008, Value Trust lost 55 percent. His smaller fund fell 65 percent.

Investors fled. Miller's assets under management plunged from around $77 billion to $800 million. And as the business withered, about a hundred members of his team lost their jobs. Half of Miller's net worth had already been vaporized in his recent divorce, and he lost 80 percent of the remaining half when the market imploded, thanks to his incorrigible habit of investing on margin. Miller, who "grew up without any money" as the son of a taxi driver, remarks, "I don't really care about losing *my* money." But he was tormented by the thought of all the misery he was inflicting on others. "Laying off all those people was horrible. . . . That was the worst part of it: losing money for clients, and people losing their jobs because *I* screwed up."

Miller, who spent several years in military intelligence before becoming an investor, describes himself as "very emotionless." When stocks sink, his default mode is to remain calm and cheerful, actively welcoming the opportunity to profit from other investors' emotional disarray. But the pressure was so unrelenting during the crisis that he gained forty pounds. "When I get stressed, I eat or drink," he confesses. "I wasn't about to eat salmon and broccoli every night and drink mineral water. . . . There's only so much pain I can take, and I drew the line there."

Miller draws on philosophy in every area of his life. When I first interviewed him twenty years ago, he explained how Ludwig Wittgenstein and William James taught him to think, helping him to distinguish between perception and reality. Now, with his career, his finances, his reputation, and his peace of mind under attack, he turned for "emotional stability" to Stoic philosophers such as Epictetus and Seneca, reminding himself of their "general approach to misfortune. Basically, you can't control what happens to you," says Miller. "You *can* control your attitude towards it. Whether it's good, bad, indifferent, fair, unfair, you can choose the attitude you take to it."

Miller also reread *Thoughts of a Philosophical Fighter Pilot*, which recounts Vice Admiral Jim Stockdale's experiences as a prisoner of war after he was shot down over Vietnam in 1965. As he ejected from his burning plane and parachuted into enemy territory, Stockdale whispered to himself, "I'm leaving the world of technology and entering the world of Epictetus." He spent the next seven and a half years in captivity, including four years in solitary confinement and two years in leg chains. He was tortured fifteen times.

Epictetus, who was born into slavery, provided a path to mental freedom under any conditions. He taught that we can never be certain of controlling anything external, including our health, wealth, and social status. However, we can take total responsibility for our intentions, emotions, and attitudes. "It is *within you*," he declared, "that both your destruction and deliverance lie."

Stockdale could not prevent his jailors from torturing him until he confessed. But he fought valiantly to defend his "inner self." When marched at gunpoint to be interrogated, he chanted a mantra to himself: "Control fear, control guilt." He also insisted that American prisoners must not bow in public to their captors or accept early release. "To the Stoic, the *greatest* injury that can be inflicted on a person is administered by *himself* when he destroys the good man within him," he wrote. "You can only be a 'victim' of *yourself*. It's all how you discipline your mind."

Faced with the worst defeat of his career, Miller focused on what he could control and tried to let go of the rest. He was publicly shamed in the press and derided on social media. "I'm not happy when people write how stupid I am," he says. But as he'd learned from the Stoics, "you can't control what other people are going to say about you or think about you. You just control your reactions." His reaction was to "try to be straightforward, honest, admit mistakes," and do his best to fix what he had broken. "It certainly isn't important to me to vindicate a reputation. It was important to me basically to get my clients' money back that I'd lost them, if I could do that."

Miller had no doubt that his strategy of buying stocks "at large discounts to what they're worth . . . ought to work over time." And he'd proven to himself over two decades that he could "tell the difference between things that are cheap and things that are expensive." So he kept plugging away, first at Legg Mason, and then at a new firm of his own, Miller Value Partners. Still, he had the humility to recognize that he needed to diversify his mutual funds more broadly than he'd previously realized. "I'm much more sensitive to risk and being wrong than I was before," he says. "It's an admission that I didn't think I could be as catastrophically wrong as I was."

Investors who maintained their faith in Miller have profited richly since the financial crisis. His flagship mutual fund, Miller Opportunity Trust, ranked in the top 1 percent of all US equity funds over the following decade. Meanwhile, Miller's own fortune has also leaped to new heights. It helped that he had the gumption to buy more stocks during the meltdown, investing cash that he raised in part by selling his yacht (though not his plane, *never* his plane).

But the biggest score of all has come from his immense personal stake in Amazon, which he's owned for more than two decades. He added aggressively to his Amazon position after the dot-com bubble burst in 2001, and he then supercharged his bet by investing in options when the stock tanked again during the financial crisis. Miller believes that he's now the single-largest individual shareholder of Amazon who was never a member of the Bezos family. In 2020, Miller told me that Amazon had grown to 83 percent of his personal investment portfolio.*

Looking back on the financial crisis after all these years, Miller admits that "the pain and disappointment haven't faded at all." But he's pleased that almost all of his laid-off employees found new jobs quickly; that he didn't have so much leverage that it "would take me out of the game and cause me ruin"; and that he found the strength to continue buying cheap stocks even in the darkest days, instead of hiding "like a turtle under the shell when I lost all that money."

In personal terms, adds Miller, the crisis was "very cleansing." It's hard to remain humble when you've been "right, right, right" and "people keep telling you that you're wonderful. . . . Some of it seeps through." As a prominent investor, you're frequently invited to "pontificate about everything." But when you've been "massively wrong" and "you're getting crushed in the market, no one wants to hear about what you think.

* Miller's second-largest position is an enormous bet on Bitcoin. In short, this is not a portfolio for the faint of heart.

You're really forced to look internally and confront your mistakes and see if you can do better. And it's good for the ego."

Now that the storm has passed, Miller, who recently turned seventy, leads a radically simplified life. He oversees $2.5 billion in assets— a tiny sliver of what he once invested. But he has no desire to build a complicated business with a swarm of analysts and mountains of money to manage. He prefers to work with a handful of trusted allies, including his son. As the owner of the firm, Miller has "a huge amount of freedom," which he lacked at Legg Mason, a large public company where "the scrutiny became very intense." He no longer has to explain himself at board meetings. His standard attire is a pair of jeans and a T-shirt. His calendar is mostly empty, leaving him free to focus on the essence of his job: "trying to add value to clients every month."

Miller's wealth enables him to avoid many of the inconveniences that could distract him from that task, such as filling his car with gas, flying on commercial airlines, or figuring out how to decorate his homes in Florida and Maryland. "I control my time and the content," he says. Invited to speak at a black-tie gala, he declined, explaining that he'd thrown away his tuxedo and will never buy another one. For Miller, nothing beats being able to live and invest his own way— unconstrained, independent, beholden to nobody. "Oh, yeah," he says. "That's the best."

For me, Miller's story offers two valuable lessons. First, everyone suffers. When I'm struggling myself, it's reassuring to remember that Miller, Karp, Pabrai, and everyone else I've interviewed have been through the wringer, no matter how rich or renowned they may be. There's an old saying, sometimes attributed to Philo of Alexandria: "Be kind, for everyone you meet is fighting a hard battle." Nobody has an untroubled upward trajectory, and there are times when we all need additional support—from philosophy, spirituality, family, friends, or wherever else we can find it. If we dream that untold riches will somehow free us from mental suffering, we're setting ourselves up for disappointment. Dilgo Khyentse Rinpoche, a Tibetan Buddhist master who was a teacher of the Dalai Lama, once said, "Those who seek happiness in pleasure, wealth, glory, power, and heroics are as naive as the child who tries to catch a rainbow and wear it as a coat."

Second, there's great honor in the simple virtue of perseverance. Several years ago, I wrote to Pabrai during a painful period when he was beset with challenges on multiple fronts, including the bankruptcy of one of his largest investments, Horsehead Holdings. He replied, "Marcus Aurelius is my hero here. We cannot see it when it is happening, but facing adversity is a blessing. It eventually leads to higher highs." Pabrai's invincible optimism reminded me of a glorious line from *Meditations*: "So remember this principle when something threatens to cause you pain: the thing itself was no misfortune at all; to endure it and prevail is great good fortune."

## "I'm the Richest Guy in the World"

When I think about what constitutes a successful and abundant life, the investor who embodies it best for me is Arnold Van Den Berg. He's not a billionaire or a genius. He doesn't own a yacht or a plane. Yet there's nobody in the investment world whom I admire more. If I had to choose just one role model from all of the remarkable investors I've interviewed over the last quarter of a century, it would be him. He was dealt a terrible hand, but has defied overwhelming odds to achieve a life of prosperity that goes far beyond money.

Born into a Jewish family in 1939, Van Den Berg lived on the same street in Amsterdam as Anne Frank. The following year, Germany invaded the Netherlands and set about annihilating its population of 140,000 Jews. By 1945, only 38,000 had survived. Van Den Berg's parents hid for almost two years in the home of non-Jewish friends, Hank and Marie Bunt, who built a secret closet for them behind a double wall. But there was a terrifying risk that Arnold or his older brother, Sigmund, would make a noise if the Nazis came to search the house. If discovered, they would all be deported to concentration camps, where children were often the first to be killed. So Van Den Berg's parents took a desperate gamble. They arranged for their sons to be smuggled out of Amsterdam by the Dutch underground, using fake identity papers.

The rescue network involved three courageous families named Tjaden, Glasz, and Crommelin, who risked their own lives to protect the two boys, shuffling them secretly from one hiding place to the next. Half a century later, a Dutch woman named Olga Crommelin would write a letter recounting how she took Arnold by train and foot to a rural village where he would be hidden in a Christian orphanage along with several other Jewish children. At the time, she was about seventeen, and he was two. "I shall never forget that when the train pulled in at that station where we had to get off, there was a small group of SS men on the platform and it gave me quite a shock," recalled Crommelin. Immersed in conversation, these members of Hitler's murderous security force took no notice of the Jewish toddler and the teenage girl who dared to save his life.

Van Den Berg lived in the orphanage until he was six. For many years, he believed that he'd been sent away because his mother didn't want him. He also suffered the trauma of separation from his brother, who was given refuge by a childless couple who lived on a farm. Conditions in the orphanage were dire, with so little food and water that Van Den Berg sometimes resorted to eating plants that he found in the fields. "I almost died of malnutrition," he says. "At age six, I could barely walk. I used to crawl most of the time. . . . Truly, it's a miracle that I made it."

One day in 1944, Van Den Berg's parents ventured out of their hiding place to visit a woman from the resistance movement who could tell them how Arnold and Sigmund were faring in the countryside. An air raid siren sounded while they were on the street, and they took cover inside a butcher's shop. A Nazi collaborator working there realized that Van Den Berg's parents were Jewish and betrayed them to the police. They were arrested, interrogated, and sent to Auschwitz.

Thirty-nine members of Van Den Berg's family perished in the Holocaust. But both of his parents survived.* After the war, they reunited at the Bunts' home and traveled to the orphanage to retrieve their son. "I didn't remember that they were my parents. I didn't recognize them, and I really didn't care. I just wanted to get out of there," says Van Den Berg. "My dad said that, in another few months, I would probably have died. He was afraid to pick me up because my bones stuck through my skin so much that he was afraid he'd break them."

---

* Van Den Berg's brother, Sigmund, also survived.

A few years later, the family emigrated to a poor and threatening neighborhood in East Los Angeles. "I was a very weak, skinny kid," says Van Den Berg. "There's a lot of bullying that goes on if you're the weak one. You're the prey." When he started at his new school, his mother dressed him impeccably in lederhosen and long socks, landing him in several fights on his first day. Another formative experience came when he was shoved into a young thug who demanded that they fight in the bicycle yard at their high school. "I wouldn't have been any more scared if they'd put me in front of a firing squad," says Van Den Berg. "He beat the hell out of me till he got tired of hitting me. I literally didn't offer any resistance."

Back home, he washed the blood off his face and appraised the damage. "I had an epiphany. I thought, 'My God! I've been so afraid of this, and this is not that bad. Just think if I would have fought back. It couldn't have got any worse. . . . Immediately, I got rid of all my fears of fighting. It was just gone. It was an amazing transformation."

Determined to stand up for himself, he learned to box and soon discovered the benefits of throwing the first punch. He had so much rage in him—against the Nazis, against the bullies at school, against the anti-Semites who targeted him as he walked home, and against his parents—that he became a fearsome fighter. His three best friends were tough kids from violent homes, who leaped to each other's defense in countless battles. His mother yelled at them and sprayed them with a hose. But they would all soften with age, and they remain close in their eighties.

Van Den Berg gradually built his strength by climbing ropes, which was an Olympic sport in those days. After six months of practicing for two hours a day, he raced against a nemesis who had never climbed, hoping to demonstrate his new power. "He beat me so bad that I almost cried right there on the spot," says Van Den Berg. "I was so embarrassed. . . . Then something flashed in my mind: You wanted to get stronger and you are *getting* stronger. So why would you quit?"

His coach sent him to observe a champion from another school who had developed an innovative climbing technique. Van Den Berg was mesmerized. For months, he rose in the middle of the night and mimicked those movements compulsively in front of a mirror until they became embedded in his mind and body. He kept repeating to himself, "I am the number one man in the league." In the years that followed, he transformed himself into a star athlete, breaking school records by scaling a twenty-foot rope in 3.5 seconds, becoming the league champion three times, and competing nationally against climbers who were already in college. It was his first taste of success, his first hint of what he could achieve with relentless work and single-minded belief.

Academically, he was still a disaster. He was emotionally troubled, couldn't concentrate in class, and found it difficult to learn. "I was showing signs of not being too bright, I guess, so my mom hired one of the top psychologists because she thought maybe something happened because of the war," says Van Den Berg. He overheard the psychologist speculating that all those years of malnutrition may have damaged Van Den Berg's brain during a critical stage in his early development.

"So I always had this image of myself as not very smart," says Van Den Berg. "Look, if I was to send you my high school report card, you would have a big laugh. I had two periods of auto shop my last year. Two periods of gymnastics. A study hall. For what? I used to do my isometrics exercises in my study hall. Then I had a cappella, and I have such a bad aptitude for singing that my a cappella teacher would make me just move my mouth during performances because he didn't want me to throw the whole team off. . . . I don't have any innate talents for anything. No. Everything I've ever accomplished has taken more effort than anybody else."

Van Den Berg's father, a scrupulously honest but hard man who hit him until he finally hit back, made his sons pay for their own food, clothes, and entertainment once they turned thirteen. Van Den Berg mowed lawns, washed cars, delivered newspapers, pumped gas, worked in a garbage truck, then landed a job in a wood factory for four hours a day after class.

At sixteen, while saving for a car, he sold flowers with such success that he earned the right to hawk them on the most prized street corner. That day, it poured torrentially. Drenched, miserable, and stunned by his bad luck, he still refused to stop selling. A stranger who was driving past bought all of his flowers, so he would get out of the rain before catching a cold. She drove him to her home, gave him a dry shirt, and made soup to warm him up. "I've never forgotten her," says Van Den Berg. "That woman touched my heart.... When someone touches your heart, you're never going to be the same."

Having barely scraped through high school, Van Den Berg didn't bother with college. He worked in a printing store, where he was promoted to supervisor, joined an insurance company, where he peddled policies door-to-door, and later sold mutual funds for a financial services firm. Along the way, he married his high school girlfriend, but she left him for another man. During a period of deep depression that lasted for several years, Van Den Berg began to see a psychiatrist. He knew that he was lucky to be alive, since so few Jewish children from Holland had survived the war. But he was trapped inside his own head. "I was the personification of anger," he says. He was furious at his ex-wife and tormented by the Holocaust.

For years, he had struggled to understand why that teenage girl in Amsterdam had saved him. How could she have been "willing to sacrifice her life" for "somebody she didn't even know?" And how could her parents have allowed her to embark on such a "suicide mission?" Van Den Berg's psychiatrist told him, "It's simple. If your life is more important than your principles, you sacrifice your principles. If your principles are more important than your life, you sacrifice your life." That insight "had a profound effect on me," says Van Den Berg. He developed an intense desire "to do something with my life" and to live it by principles that were worthy of his saviors.

During the years when he was selling funds, Van Den Berg became captivated by the stock market and began to explore why some investors performed better than others. That led him to study Ben Graham's books. The concept of buying assets at a steep discount resonated instantly. Van Den Berg's mother, a shrewd businesswoman who had survived in Auschwitz by trading goods and paying guards to provide her and her husband with extra bread, had always stressed that it was dumb to buy anything for the full retail price. It seemed natural to apply her rule to stocks. After a dishonest colleague was honored as Man of the Month, Van Den Berg quit his job and decided to launch his own investment firm. It was 1974. He was thirty-five years old. He had no college degree, no relevant experience, no business plan, no office, no clients.

But he approached his new vocation with the same all-consuming commitment that he'd applied to rope climbing. His psychiatrist told him that he had triumphed back then by adopting mental strategies that professional athletes used routinely—setting clearly defined goals, visualizing themselves performing flawlessly, and repeating affirmations that crowded out all doubts and fears until they were replaced with unshakable self-belief. Van Den Berg became obsessed with such techniques for harnessing the power of the subconscious mind, making himself a human guinea pig in an experiment that has never stopped. He learned to hypnotize himself every day as a way of focusing his scattered thoughts. He flooded his mind with uplifting affirmations, gradually ridding himself of the debilitating belief that he was incapable and unworthy. And he devoured inspirational works by authors such as James Allen, returning again and again to a 1901 book that he came to regard as his bible: *From Poverty to Power*.

Allen, a freethinker steeped in Christianity and Buddhism, convinced Van Den Berg to take responsibility for his own mental state; to forgive everyone who had hurt him, including the Nazis, thereby liberating himself from his own anger; and to reform the world by focusing first on reforming himself. "By your own thoughts you make or mar your life, your world, your universe," Allen preached. "As you build within by the power of thought, so will your outward life and circumstances shape themselves accordingly. . . . The soul that is impure, sordid, and selfish is gravitating with unerring precision toward misfortune and catastrophe; the soul that is pure, unselfish, and noble is gravitating with equal precision toward happiness and prosperity."

Desperate to improve his circumstances, Van Den Berg made a total commitment to improve his character. He became a lifelong explorer of wisdom from many spiritual paths, vowing to pursue the truth wherever it led him. Honesty and integrity became guiding principles, and he took to heart Allen's assertion that "the rich man who is barren of virtue is, in reality, poor." Van Den Berg no longer allowed negative thoughts about himself or others to linger in his mind and drain his energy. Where once he'd been consumed by resentment and hostility, he now rebuilt himself from the inside by constantly repeating positive phrases such as "I am a loving person."

He had none of the skepticism or cynicism of a college-educated intellectual snob. He believed absolutely that he could create a golden future by consciously reprogramming his mind. What set him apart was his unflagging persistence and his insatiable desire to make himself a better man. "I always want to be working on self-improvement until the day I die," he says. "After it's all said and done, these are the three most important things to me. Never compromise what you believe in. Never be satisfied with what you are, only with what you can be. And never give up."

Van Den Berg cut out a photograph from *Barron's* of an eminent investor standing confidently beside his desk while dressed immaculately in a three-piece suit. He gazed at that image every day, using it to help visualize himself as a successful money manager. He set himself a target of averaging 15 percent a year without losing more than 15 percent in any year—a goal that he actually achieved over the next three decades. He removed the clutter from his studio apartment, placed a desk in the middle, and surrounded himself with investment books. He gave up chess, which he loved, because it divided his attention. He played golf just once and concluded, "This is a game I won't get into because it will shackle my mind." When a girlfriend asked if she could cook him dinner, he informed her that he had to study. She accused him of behaving like a monk.

Van Den Berg developed a consistent investment methodology that was infused with common sense. Among other things, he analyzed hundreds of acquisitions to construct a record of what sophisticated private buyers would pay for various types of business. He then formulated a few practical rules of thumb that he refused to violate. For example, he wouldn't invest in any stock unless it traded for at least 50 percent less than its private market value. And whenever a stock rose to 80 percent of its private market value, he insisted on selling.

His unswerving discipline and rigorous focus on valuations kept him on the right track. Most investors shunned stocks in the aftermath of the 1974 crash. But prices were so low that he didn't hesitate to buy, enabling him to generate powerful returns during his first decade in the business. Then, when prices surged in the bubble of 1987, he could find nothing cheap enough to replace the stocks that his ironclad rules required him to sell. Before long, his growing roster of clients had half of their assets in cash. Many were livid. Still, he never flinched, telling himself, "You're doing the right thing to stick to your discipline. . . . Now, you may go out of business, but you're doing the right thing. And that immediately brought me comfort." Soon afterward, the market crashed 22.6 percent in one day. "Everyone was panicking, and I was like a kid in a candy store."

It took more than a decade for Van Den Berg's firm, Century Management, to become solidly profitable. During those lean years, he fell in love and remarried. At the time, he was $20,000 in debt and could hardly support himself, let alone his new wife, Eileen, and her two young kids. Before long, they had a third child. They crammed into a fifteen-hundred-square-foot house in LA, using the garage as an extra bedroom. Then they bought a modest home in Austin, Texas, for about $350,000 and have lived there ever since. "I wouldn't sell it," says Van Den Berg. "We love it."

As his business expanded, Van Den Berg became wealthier and more renowned than he'd ever envisioned. He was featured in a book titled *The World's 99 Greatest Investors*, which hailed him for the rare feat of averaging 14.2 percent annually over thirty-eight years. A string of major asset managers sought to buy his company. He could probably have cashed out for more than $100 million. But how could he trust these smooth-talking corporate suitors to act in his clients' best interests, instead of their own? When four emissaries from a bank tried to convince him to sell his firm, he told them, "I'm not selling at any price. I'd close it down before I'd sell it."

In truth, he had never yearned to become seriously rich. Starting out, his aim was to build a nest egg of $250,000—enough to support himself for ten years. "I didn't care if I made millions," he says. "I just wanted to be financially independent and not take any shit off anybody. . . . The luxury is not having to worry about money or a bill or a financial setback."

For a person in his position, his lifestyle is decidedly understated. "I've never had any need for material things," he says. "I have no interest in anything like a big home. . . . That turns me off." A vegetarian teetotaler with a passion for yoga, he prefers to sip beetroot smoothies in his book-filled office than to feast in elegant restaurants. "I'm really not into clothes," he adds. "I have three suits." For many years, he drove a Nissan Maxima because "it was the best value you could get in a car." When one of his children asked why he didn't buy a Mercedes, he explained that he didn't want to "make a statement" by driving a flashy car: "I wouldn't want to be associated with people who think that way." A few years ago, his wife finally persuaded him to part with his ten-year-old Acura and upgrade to a Lexus. "She was so thrilled to get it for me that I didn't want to say no because she got all excited," he recalls. "I was almost embarrassed to drive it at first."

Once he felt "completely secure" about his financial future, no amount of money he could earn would make any difference to him. "I'm the richest guy in the world because I'm content with what I have," says Van Den Berg. "I feel wealthier not because I have more money but because I've got health, good friendships, I've got a great family. Prosperity takes all of these things into consideration: health, wealth, happiness, peace of mind. That's what a prosperous person is, not just a lot of money. That doesn't mean anything." He recalls a former client with $10 million "who was so eager for the money that he would call me collect" to save a few cents.

"The most important thing people need is love—and the less love they have, the more they need these material things," says Van Den Berg. "They look for money, for some accomplishment, or something external to validate them. But all they need to do is be loved and to give love. You know, my wife never knows how much money we have. She never cares and she never thinks about it other than how she could use it to spend it on somebody."

One of their favorite causes is a residential treatment center for abused and neglected children. Van Den Berg and his wife have bought books and toys for hundreds of these kids, and she worked closely with them for twenty years. He has also quietly helped many people with financial difficulties, typically assisting in small but significant ways— paying for a class that enabled them to earn a better living or footing a medical bill for a sick child. Being able to help others, says Van Den Berg, is "the greatest blessing the money has given me."

Having observed over several years how he interacts with other people, what impresses me most is the sheer joy that he takes in trying to guide, support, and inspire them. He delights in hypnotizing people (including me) and seeking to instill positive suggestions in the subconscious mind while they lie on his office floor in a state of deep relaxation. He becomes irrepressibly excited as he recalls various highlights of his adventures in hypnotism, including a time when his son, Scott, won a shot-put championship under hypnosis, despite having a sprained ankle in a cast. Van Den Berg loves giving talks to disadvantaged kids, college students, and prison inmates about the lessons he's learned from the Holocaust and his own struggles. And he is constantly gifting books that have helped him on his journey, including a special edition of *From Poverty to Power* that he paid to reprint. "I feel that the best gift I could give anybody, whether they're poor or rich, is to give them a book that could change their life," he says. "And so my hobby is giving out books."

Van Den Berg often wonders why he survived the Holocaust. "Was it just luck?" he asks. "You could say, yeah, because I'm just one of the statistics. But somehow, I've always had this feeling that there was a purpose to my life, that I was spared. And so I want to change people's lives. Not to my way of thinking. Just to make it better."

Tucked away inside the filing cabinets in his office, he keeps what might just be his most valuable possession: a copious collection of heartfelt letters from many of the people he has helped, including countless friends, clients, random strangers, and his own children. "The pleasure you get out of knowing you've made a difference in people's lives—that's something that nobody can take away from you," he says. "I could lose all my money, and I could still go to these files and say, 'Well, it's not like I lived my life for nothing. Look at the people whose lives I've changed.'" Van Den Berg points to his trove of letters and says, "That's my bank account."

# Acknowledgments

This book wouldn't exist without the extreme patience, generosity of spirit, and openness of the many remarkable investors who shared their insights and experiences with me. In some cases, we spent several days together. Others spoke with me countless times over many years. To my delight, they welcomed me into their homes and offices, allowed me to travel with them, spoke candidly about their setbacks and challenges, and (in one unforgettable case) even hypnotized me in an attempt to reprogram my subconscious mind. I'm deeply grateful to all of these investors for sharing the most valuable lessons they've learned about how to invest intelligently, think rationally, overcome adversity, and stack the odds of building a happy and fulfilling life.

There's a long list of extraordinarily insightful investors whose thinking has greatly enriched this book. In particular, I'd like to thank Charlie Munger, Ed Thorp, Howard Marks, Joel Greenblatt, Bill Miller, Mohnish Pabrai, Tom Gayner, Guy Spier, Fred Martin, Ken Shubin Stein, Matthew McLennan, Jeffrey Gundlach, Francis Chou, Thyra Zerhusen, Thomas Russo, Chuck Akre, Li Lu, Peter Lynch, Pat Dorsey, Michael Price, Mason Hawkins, Bill Ackman, Jeff Vinik, Mario Gabelli, Laura Geritz, Brian McMahon, Henry Ellenbogen, Donald Yacktman, Bill Nygren, Paul Lountzis, Jason Karp, Will Danoff, François Rochon, John Spears, Joel Tillinghast, Qais Zakaria, Nick Sleep, Paul Isaac, Mike Zapata, Paul Yablon, Whitney Tilson, François-Marie Wojcik, Sarah Ketterer, Christopher Davis, Raamdeo Agrawal, Arnold Van Den Berg, Mariko Gordon, and Jean-Marie Eveillard. Thanks also to five giants who are no longer with us: Sir John Templeton, Irving Kahn, Bill Ruane, Marty Whitman, and Jack Bogle.

I feel enormous gratitude to my literary agent, Jim Levine, who's provided a priceless combination of wise advice, boundless enthusiasm, and kindness. I couldn't have asked for a better partner. I'm also

ACKNOWLEDGMENTS

profoundly grateful to Rick Horgan, Scribner's executive editor, for his fierce intelligence, thoughtful editing, and perfectionism. It's revealing that the book Rick loves most of all is *Zen and the Art of Motorcycle Maintenance*, which explores the notion of quality as a guiding principle. Many thanks also to Scribner's Nan Graham, Roz Lippel, and Colin Harrison for embracing my book. Thanks also to the rest of the superb team at Scribner that worked on this book: Steve Boldt, Dan Cuddy, Beckett Rueda, and Jaya Miceli. It's an amazing privilege to be published by Scribner, the hallowed home to many of my favorite authors.

I've been helped, guided, and propped up by so many friends and allies that it's impossible to do them justice. But let me start by giving special thanks to Guy Spier, who's been an incredible friend and champion for many years. Guy takes delight in helping others and compounding goodwill, and I've benefited in countless ways—not least, from his introductions to Mohnish Pabrai, Ken Shubin Stein, and Nick Sleep. Special thanks also to Jon Gertner, an exceptional writer who not only gave me moral support but shared with me his brilliant proposal for *The Ice at the End of the World*, which helped me to craft my own book proposal.

For their many acts of kindness, care, support, and friendship, I'd also like to thank Michael Berg, Marcus Weston, Eitan Yardeni, Avi Nahmias, Jason Zweig, Aravind Adiga, Tony Robbins, Michael O'Brien, Cecelia Wong, DJ Stout, Gillian Zoe Segal, Nina Munk, Peter Soriano, Fleming Meeks, Richard Bradley, Laurie Harting, Amey Stone, Lory Spier, Saurabh Madaan, Nikhil Hutheesing, Chris Stone, Ramin Bahrani, Marlies Talay, Beverly Goodman, Wade Savitt, Nancy Danino, Piper Tyrsdotter, Matthew Winch, Jamie True, Craig Kravetz, Howard Donnelly, Christian Moerk, Gautam Baid, Shai Dardashti, Samuel Freedman, Denis Thomopoulos, Richard Wertheimer, David Worth, Malia Boyd, Tom Easton, Charles Cartledge, Eben Harrell, Aran Dharmeratnam, Sharon Callahan, Helen and Jim Neuberger, Kathleen Hinge, Ancela Nastasi, Joan Caplin, Josh Tarasoff, Elliot Trexler, Ralph Townsend, Stig Brodersen, Preston Pysh, Kenneth Folk, Hedda Nadler, Daniel Roth, Mark Chapman, Orly Hindi, Kabir Sehgal, Shalom Sharabi, Jelisa Castrodale, Randy Stanbury, John Mihaljevic,

254

# ACKNOWLEDGMENTS

William Samedy, Michael Scherb, David Mechner, Katherine Bruce, Scott Wilson, Lucy Wilson Cummings, Debbie Meiliken, Jacob Taylor, Richard Krupp, Ambi Kavanaugh, Karen Berg, and Rav Berg.

Many thanks also to my friends at the Aligned Center, which has given me so much more than a beautiful and peaceful place to write. Its founder, Matt Ludmer, is a role model in so many ways, and I've turned to him for insight on everything from investing to meditation. It's been a delight to spend time with everyone in the orbit of the Aligned Center, including Leticia Reyes-James, Caroline Hotaling, Faryn Sand, Jacopo Surricchio, David Janes, Alison Gilbert, Andy Landorf, Kristin Kaye, Gwen Merkin, Daniel Goleman, DeLauné Michel, and Dan Fried.

One of the great gifts of my life is to have landed in a family full of extraordinary people. Thanks especially to my big brother, Andrew Green, and his lovely wife, Jennifer Hirschl; and to my wonderful in-laws, Marvin Cooper, Johanna Cooper, Nancy Cooper, and Bruce Meltzer.

Finally, I'd like to dedicate this book to five family members who have made everything possible. My mother, Marilyn Green, has been an indomitable source of strength and support from day one, and it's fitting that she was invariably the first person to read every chapter that I wrote. My late father, Barry Green, sparked my love of language and my passion for investing. My son, Henry Green, has been an indispensable and gifted literary partner from start to finish: he helped immeasurably by feeding me background research, transcribing my interviews, checking facts, and pointing out when my prose needed additional polish. My daughter, Madeleine Green, displayed heroic patience in discussing the characters and ideas in this book. She also held me together emotionally, cheering me up and encouraging me whenever my spirits flagged. At times, I was pretty certain that she was parenting *me*. And then there's my wife, Lauren Cooper, the kindest and most caring of people. I met Lauren when I was only twenty-two years old, and everything that's best in my life stems from that one miraculous stroke of good fortune. Thank you all from the depths of my heart.

# Notes on Sources and
# Additional Resources

*Richer, Wiser, Happier* is based on my interviews with many of the world's most successful investors. I interviewed more than forty of them for this book, typically speaking with them at length on multiple occasions. For example, I traveled with Mohnish Pabrai for five days in India, visited him in California, met with him in New York and Omaha, and spoke with him over the phone for many hours. Similarly, I spent two days with Bill Miller at his home and office in Maryland, two days with Tom Gayner in Virginia, and two days with Arnold Van Den Berg in Texas. I've also drawn heavily on interviews that I conducted in the distant past with investment legends such as Sir John Templeton, Bill Ruane, Michael Price, Peter Lynch, and Jack Bogle.

One idiosyncrasy of this book is that I've focused almost exclusively on investors whom I like and admire. Several times, I began to write about brilliant investors whose personalities I find unappealing, but I soon stopped. It felt almost as if the body rejected that organ. I'm fascinated by investors who have demonstrated their financial prowess over many years, but I'm particularly drawn to those with wisdom, insights, and virtues that extend beyond an exceptional talent for making money. The investors I've spotlighted throughout this book can undoubtedly help us to become richer. But they also shed light on how to think and live.

I've written these Notes on Sources and Additional Resources in much the same spirit. My purpose here isn't to construct an exhaustive record of where I derived every fact and figure in the book, but to point you in the direction of a wide variety of resources that I hope you'll find useful in your own quest to become richer, wiser, and happier. With that in mind, I asked the investors I interviewed to recommend books that have helped to shape their thinking. In the pages that follow, you'll find an array of their recommendations, along with some of my own.

### INTRODUCTION: INSIDE THE MINDS
### OF THE GREATEST INVESTORS

xiii To learn more about Jack Bogle, who died in 2019, check out some of his timeless investment books, including the 10th Anniversary Edition of *Common Sense on Mutual Funds* (John Wiley & Sons, 2009), which warns eloquently about the difficulties of beating the market, the perils of speculation, and the devastating effect of excessive fees on investors' returns. My favorite of Bogle's books is *Enough: True Measures of Money, Business, and Life* (John Wiley & Sons, 2008), which features chapters with quirky titles such as "Too Many Twenty-First-Century Values, Not Enough Eighteenth-Century Values."

When I interviewed Bogle over the phone two decades ago, he spoke emotionally about what he'd learned from his mentor, Walter Morgan, a fund pioneer who embodied the old-fashioned values that Bogle championed, such as "discipline, honor, duty, [and] integrity." The phone went silent, and I wondered if we'd been disconnected. I eventually realized that Bogle was too choked up to speak. Finally, he said, "Excuse me. It's putting tears in my eyes. . . . I guess I loved him, and he did so much for me." Morgan left an indelible impact on Bogle because he was a "principled gentleman of very high character" who taught him that "the shareholder is king. . . . My God, a shareholder wrote him once that he didn't have a very good suit and did Mr. Morgan have one for him? And Mr. Morgan sent him one."

When I asked Bogle who else had shaped his investment philosophy, he mentioned two prominent writers. Charles Ellis wrote a "seminal" article in the 1970s titled "The Loser's Game" and later published a classic book titled *Winning the Loser's Game* (McGraw-Hill, 1998). Bogle also recommended Burton Malkiel's book, *A Random Walk Down Wall Street* (W.W. Norton & Company, 2020), which reinforced his unshakable belief in the logic of index funds.

xiii My profile of Bill Miller ("It's Bill Miller's Time") ran in *Fortune*'s December 10, 2001 issue. It depicted him plunging presciently into stocks after 9/11 as the market cratered. In those days, Miller's peers ridiculed him for investing $500 million in a profitless retailer that many expected to go bust: Amazon.com. But Miller pointed out to me that Amazon had "incredible economies of scale, which will eventually become apparent." As I wrote back then, "If he's wrong, it will be the most public failure of his career. But if he's right—and Miller still believes he is—the Amazon bet will rank as one of the great investment calls of all time." The stock has since soared from less than $10 a share to more than $3,000, and Miller has ridden it the whole way.

xvi Ed Thorp, the epitome of a rational thinker who focuses on maximizing the odds of success and minimizing the odds of disaster, initially gained fame as a gambler. He wrote a bestseller, *Beat the Dealer* (Blaisdell Publishing Company, 1962), which revealed how to win at blackjack by counting cards. More recently, he wrote an entertaining memoir, *A Man For All Markets* (Random House,

2017), which recounts his triumphs in everything from roulette and baccarat to trading options and warrants. When I asked Miller about Thorp, he remarked, "He's the best, I think. As great an investor as Buffett is, I think Ed Thorp is better because he figured out stuff nobody knew. . . . Thorp's record is just so much better and with almost no volatility, and he figured the whole thing out himself and invented statistical arbitrage."

One reason for Thorp's success is that he applied the Kelly criterion, a betting system that he says helped him to calculate "an optimal trade-off between risk and return. . . . It keeps you from betting too much." In *Fortune's Formula* (Hill and Wang, 2005), William Poundstone writes about Thorp's application of this betting strategy, which enabled him to compound wealth at a high rate with no risk of ruin. For a cautionary reminder of why that's so important, it's worth reading *When Genius Failed* (Random House, 2000), Roger Lowenstein's riveting history of Long-Term Capital Management—a hedge fund that was so highly leveraged that its death almost triggered a financial collapse. Thorp told me that he was offered the chance to invest $10 million in the fund, but steered clear because its famously clever (and fatally arrogant) managers were "taking too much risk . . . So the probability of their ruin appeared substantial to me."

Thorp also recommends *Superforecasting* (Crown Publishers, 2015) by psychology professor Philip Tetlock and journalist Dan Gardner. Tetlock's research shows how investors, economists, and other soothsayers overestimate their ability to predict the future. In reality, warns Tetlock, "the average expert was roughly as accurate as a dart-throwing chimpanzee." One enduring lesson that all of us should learn from battle-hardened investment sages such as Bogle and Thorp is that we must always guard against our own capacity for overconfidence.


CHAPTER ONE: THE MAN WHO CLONED WARREN BUFFETT

This chapter is based almost entirely on my interviews with Mohnish Pabrai. If you'd like to hear more from him, you can find dozens of his speeches, podcast appearances, and blogs at his website, chaiwithpabrai.com. I'd also recommend his book, *The Dhandho Investor* (John Wiley & Sons, 2007). True to form, he declares in the opening paragraph, "I have very few original ideas. Virtually everything has been lifted from somewhere."

2  If you'd like to learn more about the Dakshana Foundation, visit https://dakshana.org. It's hard to imagine a more cost-efficient way to help lift a family out of poverty than to give a gifted but underprivileged student the opportunity to win a place at the Indian Institutes of Technology or a government medical college. A donation of $99 per month for twenty-four months pays for one scholar to complete Dakshana's two-year program.

6  Pabrai uses the word *cloning* to describe his habit of shamelessly borrowing (and often improving upon) other people's best ideas and practices. Where can you learn more about this winning strategy for investing, business, and life? There are surprisingly few resources to recommend. But I regard Tim Ferriss as another grand master of cloning, though it's not a term I've heard him use. Ferriss's hefty book, *Tools of Titans* (Houghton Mifflin Harcourt, 2017), is stuffed

with practical advice that he's elicited from many world-class performers on subjects as diverse as morning routines, exercise, diet, productivity, and wealth creation.

His podcast, *The Tim Ferriss Show*, is an even richer resource. My favorite episodes are Ferriss's interviews with his friend Josh Waitzkin, a former national chess champion and world champion in Tai Chi Chuan Push Hands, who is also the author of *The Art of Learning* (Free Press, 2007). Waitzkin, who is now mastering the art of paddle surfing, also trains hedge fund managers and elite athletes to perform at their peak by cultivating "deep presence" and "unobstructed self-expression," which are critically important at the highest levels of mental games such as investing and writing. Pabrai, Ferriss, and Waitzkin share the ability to deconstruct what works and apply that knowledge with meticulous attention to detail.

Once you start to search for other examples of cloning, you soon realize how many towering figures throughout history consciously sought to emulate their role models and replicate their behavior. Leo Tolstoy wrote in his diary in 1884, "I have to create a circle of reading for myself: Epictetus, Marcus Aurelius, Buddha, Pascal, the New Testament. This is also necessary for all people." Marcus Aurelius begins his immortal book, *Meditations*, with a detailed list of desirable qualities that he's observed in sixteen people, including his adopted father, the Roman Emperor Antoninus Pius: "a man tested by life, accomplished, unswayed by flattery," compassionate, altruistic, diligent, never rude, "never content with first impressions," indifferent to "superficial honors," "always sober, always steady, and never vulgar, or a prey to fads." Similarly, the philosopher Seneca recommended imagining that we're being watched at all times by someone we revere and attempting to hold ourselves to that person's exemplary standards.

6 Pabrai's success is built to an astonishing degree on principles and practices that he cloned from Warren Buffett and Charlie Munger. Many years ago, Pabrai gave me a copy of *Poor Charlie's Almanack* (Donning, 2005), an indispensable collection of Munger's speeches and writings. Pabrai inscribed it "I hope you enjoy this as much as I did. Best book I ever read." If you want to learn deeply from Munger, not only about how to invest but about how to think more rationally, this is your bible. It repays countless readings.

For disciples of Buffett, the first challenge is to choose from a vast range of useful resources, including *Tap Dancing to Work* (Portfolio/Penguin, 2012) by his friend Carol Loomis and *The Warren Buffett Way* (John Wiley & Sons, 1994) by Robert Hagstrom. Personally, I return again and again to the Chairman's Letters that Buffett writes in his annual reports, which are available for free (going back to 1995) at www.berkshirehathway.com. Hardcore students who wish to go back further can delve into collections such as *Berkshire Hathaway Letters to Shareholders 1965-2019* (Explorist Productions, 2020), which is regularly updated by its editor, Max Olson. If you truly immerse yourself in Buffett's writings on business and investing, I'm not sure you'd need to read anything else on these subjects for the rest of your life. It's all there. Everything you need to know. Sitting in plain view. And a whole lot cheaper than an MBA.

21 Pabrai's belief in the benefits of unwavering truthfulness stems from *Power vs. Force* (Hay House, 2002), a book by the late David Hawkins, whose writ-

ings have also had a profound effect on Guy Spier and Arnold Van Den Berg. Hawkins, who was a psychiatrist and physician before he became a spiritual teacher, writes with illuminating clarity about the positive and negative effects of different types of behavior—and how to elevate our level of consciousness. For example, he observes that "Simple kindness to one's self and all that lives is the most powerful transformational force of all. It produces no backlash, has no downside, and never leads to loss or despair. It increases one's own true power without exacting any toll. But to reach maximum power, such kindness can permit no exceptions, nor can it be practiced with the expectation of some selfish gain or reward. And its effect is as far-reaching as it is subtle."

Hawkins, who taught his followers to pursue a path that he described as "devotional nonduality," also wrote books such as *The Eye of the I* (Hay House, 2001), *I: Reality and Subjectivity* (Hay House, 2003), and *Truth vs Falsehood* (Hay House, 2005). He intended them as guides for "the seriously committed spiritual student" who is seeking enlightenment. They're not as accessible as *Power vs. Force*, but they're extraordinary and may resonate with you on an even deeper level. Lately, I've been reading another of his books, *Letting Go* (Hay House, 2013), which offers a practical technique for surrendering negative emotions.

### CHAPTER TWO: THE WILLINGNESS TO BE LONELY

31　My conversations with Sir John Templeton took place in November 1998 at his office and his home in the Bahamas, and I later spoke with him again over the phone. My article, "The Secrets of Sir John Templeton," appeared in the January 1999 edition of *Money* magazine.

34　John Rothchild wrote a fine book, *The Davis Dynasty* (John Wiley & Sons, 2001), that recounts how Shelby Cullom Davis, his son Shelby M. C. Davis, and *his* son Christopher Davis built an investment business that has prospered over three generations. The family's wealth was built not only through shrewd stock picking, but extreme frugality. When I interviewed Christopher Davis, he told me that his grandfather, Shelby Cullom Davis, "viewed spending as immoral." Once, when Christopher was about thirteen, he was walking around Wall Street with his grandfather and had the temerity to ask for $1 to buy a hot dog. His grandfather refused, explaining how "that dollar would turn into $1,000 if I invested it like him and lived as long!" Christopher's father, Shelby M. C. Davis, inherited this disdain for such shocking displays of extravagance: "If I was dating someone my dad didn't like, he'd say, 'She's a spender.'"

37　Among his many free-thinking philanthropic ventures, Templeton funded scientific research that explored the intersection between health and prayer. For example, see "Study of the Therapeutic Effects of Intercessory Prayer in Cardiac Bypass Patients: A Multicenter Randomized Trial of Uncertainty and Certainty of Receiving Intercessory Prayer," published in the *American Heart Journal* in 2006. The Templeton Foundation continues to pursue his vision of "relentless curiosity in pursuit of infinite discovery." Its website, templeton.org, describes its funding for a multitude of intriguing projects, ranging from cutting-edge genetics research to a "Cultivating Genius Initiative" that seeks to nurture "one-in-a-million mathematical minds" to a film titled *Act Like a Holy Man* about Archbishop Desmond Tutu and the Dalai Lama. By the end of 2018, the foundation had given away $1.5 billion and still had an endowment worth almost $3 billion.

38 My description of Templeton's unconventional upbringing is based primarily on my interviews with him. But I've also drawn on the biographical accounts in two of the best books written about him: *Investing the Templeton Way* (McGraw-Hill, 2008) by Lauren Templeton and Scott Phillips and *The Templeton Touch* (Templeton Press, 2012 edition) by William Proctor.

40 To learn more about the wartime investment environment, see *Wealth, War & Wisdom* (John Wiley & Sons, 2008) by the late Barton Biggs, who was a renowned investor in his own right. Biggs writes in captivating detail of the war years, while also drawing shrewd lessons on how to preserve wealth in the most tumultuous times. For example: "Uncertainty compels diversification. Diversification is and always has been the first tenet of the Prudent Man Rule of Investing. . . . In sub-Saharan Africa, for centuries, people believed cattle were the safest repository of wealth. That was until the great drought came along." Biggs also wrote a memoir, *Hedgehogging* (John Wiley & Sons, 2006), which is full of his stylish, street-smart insights. For example: "The stock market is a sadistic, contrary, changeable beast and nothing is forever."

49 Lauren Templeton and Scott Phillips provide a detailed account of Templeton's short-selling strategy in *Investing the Templeton Way*. They point out that he protected himself against the danger of runaway losses by establishing an iron-clad rule that he'd quickly "cover" his short position if a stock rose by a certain percentage after he placed the bet. When Lauren Templeton delivered a 2017 speech as part of the Talks at Google series, she suggested that Sir John (her great-uncle) may have invested as much as $400 million shorting these stocks. She explained that his strategy was to short stocks seven days before the expiration of the lockup and to cover his short position ten days after the expiration.

50 I find myself much more open to Templeton's books now than when I first read them two decades ago. For example, *Wisdom from World Religions* (Templeton Foundation Press, 2002) now strikes me as a particularly valuable collection of two hundred "eternal spiritual principles" that Templeton considered "the set of rules by which we should live." When I read the book again a couple of years ago, I felt my face flush with embarrassment and literally groaned out loud as I realized how narrow-minded I'd been and how much I'd failed to learn from him. In the margin of Templeton's book, I wrote, "The joke is how simultaneously smart and dumb I could be—so busy analyzing Proust and thinking about Nietzsche that I missed the obvious wisdom he shared with me. I was just too obtuse and prejudiced to see what lay behind his success and joy."

52 Templeton's fascination with "thought control" dated back to his childhood. Thanks to his mother, he grew up with the teachings of the New Thought movement, which emphasized the role of "mind power" in achieving happiness, health, success, and prosperity. His writings are filled with quotes from leading figures in this movement, including the Unity Church minister Imelda Shanklin, who preached, "When you rule your mind, you rule your world." Templeton wrote the foreword to a book titled *New Thought, Ancient Wisdom* (Templeton

Foundation, 2006) by his "friend and colleague on the quest," Glenn Mosley. A key figure in this spiritual movement was Ernest Holmes, a New Thought writer whom Templeton called a genius. Holmes, a believer in "spiritual mind healing," observed, "We live in an intelligent universe which responds to our mental states. To the extent that we learn to control these mental states, we shall automatically control our environment." Holmes also predicted that "Somewhere down the path of human experience we will all awake to the realization that we ourselves are heaven or hell."

## CHAPTER THREE: EVERYTHING CHANGES

55  The quotation that opens this chapter is from *Zen Mind, Beginner's Mind* (John Weatherhill, 1970), a collection of luminous talks with Shunryu Suzuki about Zen Buddhist meditation and practice. Shortly after this quote, Suzuki explains, "When we realize the everlasting truth of 'everything changes' and find our composure in it, we find ourselves in Nirvana. Without accepting the fact that everything changes, we cannot find perfect composure."

I've written at length about the implications of impermanence for investors, but I might just as easily have focused on another critically important idea that we should also borrow from Zen: the notion of *shoshin*, or beginner's mind. Suzuki suggests that we should always strive to retain an "empty mind" that is "open to everything." He regards this receptive attitude as the secret of Zen practice, observing, "A mind full of preconceived ideas, subjective intentions, or habits is not open to things as they are. . . . You should not have your own idea when you listen to someone. Forget what you have in your mind and just listen to what he says. . . . Our mind should be soft and open enough to understand things as they are."

Mariko Gordon, one of the most thoughtful money managers I've met, says investors should also retain a beginner's mind. "That's really important," she told me. "Not making assumptions and just seeing everything as if you're seeing it for the first time [and] the ability to be not too attached to a point of view." When she starts researching a company, "I don't have any preconceived notions," adds Gordon. "In talking to management, I ask a lot of open-ended questions. So I'm not going in with an agenda of 'I'm trying to find out x, y, and z.' I go and have a conversation, and I see where the conversation takes us. I just have genuine curiosity about their business. . . . I'm happy to be the village idiot. I have no shame around not knowing."

Gordon, whose open-minded curiosity has led her in many unexpected directions, recommends reading *Hardcore Zen* (Wisdom Publications, 2015) by Brad Warner, an ordained Zen teacher who was previously the bassist in a punk band. She also likes the writings of Alan Lew, a Zen rabbi who coauthored a book titled *One God Clapping* (Jewish Lights, 2001). And she recommends *The Art of Time* (Da Capo Lifelong Books, 2000) by Jean-Louis Servan-Schreiber, which she says explores "how to think about our relationship with time not in a tactical way, but a strategic way" that is "deeper" and "more meditative."

56  T. Rowe Price's essay, "Change—the Investor's Only Certainty," appears in *Clas-*

*sics: An Investor's Anthology* (The Institute of Chartered Financial Analysts, 1989), which was edited by Charles Ellis and James Vertin. The book features essays by a host of financial giants, including John Maynard Keynes, Benjamin Graham, Philip Fisher, and Roy Neuberger. One of the best essays comes from Ellis, who writes this about the psychological challenge of sustaining our long-term commitment to stocks: "The crucial question is whether the investor will, in fact, hold on. The problem is not in the market, but in ourselves, our perceptions, and our reactions to our perceptions. This is why it is so important for each client to develop a realistic knowledge of his own and/or his organization's tolerance for market fluctuations . . ." There's also a 1984 speech by Templeton on "Worldwide Investing," which ends with this startling jolt to the brain: "If you do not fall down on your knees each day, with overwhelming gratitude for your blessings—your multiplying multitudes of blessings—then *you* just have not yet *seen* the big picture."

58　You can dip into a free archive of "Memos from Howard Marks" at www.oak treecapital.com/insights/howard-marks-memos, going back more than three decades. You can also subscribe to receive email notifications whenever he posts a new memo. Occasionally, even in the world of investing, there is a free and abundantly nutritious lunch.

58　One of my favorite investing books is *The Most Important Thing Illuminated* (Columbia University Press, 2013) by Howard Marks, which includes annotations by Christopher Davis, Joel Greenblatt, Paul Johnson, and Seth Klarman. If you're a dedicated student of markets and want to understand how to position your portfolio intelligently for "the possible outcomes that lie ahead," you should also read his second book, *Mastering the Market Cycle* (Houghton Mifflin Harcourt, 2018), which looks in depth at subjects such as the credit cycle, the debt cycle, and the "pendulum of investor psychology." It's not as light a read as his previous book, but it provides a robust framework for how to think about markets. Equally important, I'd supplement everything you can learn from his two books by religiously reading his latest memos, which lay out how he's weighing the risks and rewards in the current environment. That's especially valuable at cyclical extremes, when he can help you to avoid the opposing perils of excessive fear or greed.

59　I've quoted a couple of insights from Michel de Montaigne in this chapter, both of them drawn from Sarah Bakewell's marvelous book *How to Live, or, A life of Montaigne in one question and twenty attempts at an answer* (Chatto & Windus, 2010). Montaigne, like all of the best investors, knew the value of retreating from the world so he could think in solitude. Bakewell, who describes Montaigne's library as "a chamber of marvels" stuffed with peculiar objects and memorabilia, quotes him saying, "Sorry the man, to my mind, who has not in his own home a place to be all by himself, to pay his court privately to himself, to hide!" One chapter in Bakewell's book is about the importance of questioning everything; her subtitle, inspired by a line from Socrates, is "All I know is that I know nothing, and I'm not even sure about that."

65　The role of luck in investing and life lies at the heart of Nassim Nicholas Taleb's fiercely original book *Fooled by Randomness* (Thomson/Texere, 2004), which Marks often cites. Taleb is a brilliant and combative skeptic whose intellect scares me. I have a lingering fear of being flamed by him. But nobody can match his in-your-face talent for challenging our lazy assumptions and delusions about luck, uncertainty, and risk. For example, in *Fooled By Randomness*, he declares, "we often have the mistaken impression that a strategy is an excellent strategy, or an entrepreneur a person endowed with 'vision,' or a trader a talented trader, only to realize that 99.9% of their past performance is attributable to chance and chance alone."

None of Taleb's books unsettled me more beneficially than *Antifragile* (Random House, 2012), which pushed me to ponder a critical question that every investor should attempt to answer: How can I make my portfolio and my life less fragile? As Taleb warns succinctly, "The fragile breaks with time." In truth, all of Taleb's books contain precious insights. For example, consider this from *The Black Swan* (Random House, 2007): "This idea that in order to make a decision you need to focus on the consequences (which you can know) rather than the probability (which you can't know) is the *central idea of uncertainty*." Or mull over this from *Skin in the Game* (Random House, 2018): "*In a strategy that entails ruin, benefits never offset risks of ruin*." Like all of the savviest investors—from Ed Thorp to Warren Buffett to Howard Marks—Taleb's investment philosophy is based on the essential understanding that "survival is what matters."

80   For a much more scholarly discussion of the *Satipatthana Sutta*, it's worth reading Joseph Goldstein's book *Mindfulness* (Sounds True, 2013), which is full of wisdom for Buddhists and non-Buddhists alike. Goldstein, whose book is billed as "a practical guide to awakening," is one of the preeminent teachers of mindfulness meditation in the West. For another perspective on meditation and awakening, I'd recommend *Mastering the Core Teachings of the Buddha* (Aeon Books, 2018) by Daniel Ingram. Its subtitle—*An Unusually Hardcore Dharma Book*—is both a warning and an enticement. I was introduced to the book by Josh Tarasoff, a hedge fund manager whose meditation practice plays a central role in preserving his calm equilibrium as an investor.

## CHAPTER FOUR: THE RESILIENT INVESTOR

83   You can read more about Benjamin Graham's life in *The Einstein of Money* (Prometheus Books, 2012), a solid biography by Joe Carlen. I also enjoyed *Benjamin Graham: The Father of Financial Analysis*, a paper published in 1977 by the Financial Analysts Research Foundation. Coauthored by Graham's disciple, Irving Kahn, it's available for free online, courtesy of the CFA Institute. It includes an affectionate sketch of Graham's life, along with Kahn's reflections on his mentor's character and intellectual firepower. For example: "His speed of thought was so great that most people were puzzled at how he could resolve a complicated question directly after having heard it. . . . He had another extraordinary characteristic in the breadth and depth of his memory. This explains why he could read Greek, Latin, Spanish, and German. Even more remarkable, without having studied Spanish formally, he was able to translate a Spanish novel into literary English so professionally that it was accepted by an American publisher."

Graham's magnum opus, *Security Analysis* (The McGraw-Hill Companies Inc., 1934), which he coauthored with David Dodd, is a hefty and intimidating tome. Tom Gayner, the co-CEO of Markel, recommends the 1934 edition because "that was truly Ben Graham's voice and his point of view," infused with the author's passion for Greek and Roman literature and his worldly perspective on "why people do the things they do in periods of triumph and despair."

Graham's other great work, *The Intelligent Investor*, is more accessible. It's available in a revised edition (Harper Collins, 2003) with new commentary by Jason Zweig. There's also a collection of Graham's shorter writings (plus several interviews) titled *Benjamin Graham: Building a Profession* (McGraw Hill, 2010), which was edited by Zweig and Rodney Sullivan.

97   Matthew McLennan's fascination with ancient and modern history bolsters his belief that we must "accept uncertainty" and consciously limit our financial exposure to unexpected chaos. "One book of history that informed me greatly," he says, is the *History of the Peloponnesian War* (Penguin Classics; Revised Edition, 1972) by Thucydides, which recounts how the rise of Sparta ("a very traditional, austere, military culture") threatened the might of Athens ("a thriving, America-like society") in ways that "produced insecurity" and led to war. McLennan sees similar destabilizing forces at play in the rise of China, which threatens the dominance of the United States, much as the rise of Germany in the early 1900s threatened Great Britain in a period when it was "peaking out." These historical patterns are "not necessarily a template of what will happen," but they are a reminder never to become complacent about the geopolitical and economic risks that may be building. McLennan adds, "Incidentally, Thucydides owned his own gold mine, apparently. So he was no stranger to the merits of having a potential hedge."

100  McLennan's strategy of owning "persistent businesses" that are relatively resistant to disruption and destruction stems partly from his study of physics and the principle of entropy increase, which helps to explain his belief that "things tend toward disorder over time." He has also borrowed from biology. For example, he views the economy as a Darwinian ecosystem in which all businesses are on a path to fade or die, just as most species eventually become extinct.

To explore this idea further, see Robert Hagstrom's book, *Investing: The Last Liberal Art* (Texere, 2000), which draws lessons from fields as diverse as physics, psychology, and philosophy. In a chapter titled "Biology: The Origin of a New Species," Hagstrom applies an evolutionary framework to investing. This leads him to observe how difficult it is to find a strategy that will continue to work, given that financial markets constantly change and adapt. "As more agents begin using the same strategy, its profitability drops," he writes. "The inefficiency becomes apparent, and the original strategy is washed out. But then new agents enter the picture with new ideas. . . . Capital shifts and the new strategy explodes, which starts the evolutionary process again." As Paul Lountzis points out in chapter seven, part of Buffett's genius is that he keeps evolving, instead of sticking with the same strategy as the economic environment changes.

McLennan was also influenced by Stephen Wolfram's 1197-page monster of a book, *A New Kind of Science* (Wolfram Media, 2002). Wolfram, whom he describes as "a pioneering thinker in the field of complexity," performed millions of computer experiments involving cellular automata, which consist of lines of cells, each colored black or white. Wolfram applied some simple rules that, over time, produced patterns of immense complexity. His book, which is filled with pictures of these unpredictably complex (and often seemingly random) patterns, gave "intellectual backbone" to McLennan's belief that we should expect and "respect uncertainty."

105   When I asked McLennan how he handles uncertainty in his own life, he replied that he finds it "very valuable" to study Stoic philosophers such as Seneca and Marcus Aurelius, who cause "you to reflect on what's disrupting your equilibrium." McLennan added, "Heraclitus had this expression, 'panta rhei,' and I think it was referring to this notion of everything being in flux. And I've often thought about it. What I observe in the world is that, if you can accept that stuff exogenous to you is in a state of flux, you can focus on your own endogenous equanimity. And what I see out there is most people doing the opposite. They're trying to control that exogenous flux. They're trying to predict. They're trying to be positioned for it. And that causes a state of inner turmoil. So I think part of it is almost a very simple behavioral switch. It's saying, am I philosophically willing to accept flux, complexity, and uncertainty, or not? And if you say, yes, I am, then I think it's extremely freeing in terms of your ability to focus on your own equanimity."

In practical terms, what might that entail? As someone who has focused a lot of attention on trying to build my own equanimity, I'd like to venture a few rudimentary suggestions. Like McLennan, I've also found solace and perspective in Stoic philosophy, particularly the writings of Seneca, Epictetus, and Marcus Aurelius, which we'll return to shortly.

I've also found mindfulness meditation immensely helpful. One approach that resonates for me is taught by George Mumford, a former heroin addict who later became a meditation teacher to Michael Jordan and Kobe Bryant. Mumford has a terrific course on the consistently excellent Ten Percent Happier app, which also features meditation courses with teachers such as Joseph Goldstein and Sharon Salzberg. I also like Mumford's book, The Mindful Athlete (Parallax Press, 2015), which shares various techniques that can help you to connect to "that centered place in yourself in which you're able to find space between stimulus and response, the calm eye in the center of the hurricane." The ability to remain calm and centered amid the maelstrom of life seems to me as essential for top-notch investors as for professional athletes.

The type of "loving-kindness" meditation that Salzberg and many others teach can also have hugely positive effects on its practitioners' emotions and even the wiring of their brains. If you don't believe me, read Happiness (Little, Brown and Company, 2003) by Matthieu Ricard, who abandoned his career in cellular genetics to become a Buddhist monk. "As influential as external conditions may be, suffering, like well-being, is essentially an inner state," writes Ricard. "Understanding that is the key prerequisite to a life worth living."

Books such as Altered Traits (Avery, 2017) by Daniel Goleman and Richard Davidson explore the science of mindfulness, showing the far-reaching effects of these ancient practices on the mind, brain, and body. Similarly, Kristin Neff, an associate professor at the University of Texas at Austin, studies the psychological benefits of self-compassion, a concept that she borrowed from Buddhism. She and Christopher Germer wrote *The Mindful Self-Compassion Workbook* (The Guildford Press, 2018), which draws on this scientific research to explain how self-compassion can be harnessed to build inner strength, resilience, and emotional well-being.

### CHAPTER FIVE: SIMPLICITY IS
### THE ULTIMATE SOPHISTICATION

110   Joel Greenblatt has written three books about investing. I'd start by reading *The Little Book That Beats the Market* (John Wiley & Sons, 2005), which distills a lifetime of rational thinking about the art of stock picking into its essence. The book is a model of simplicity.

Greenblatt's next book, *The Big Secret for the Small Investor* (John Wiley & Sons, 2011) wasn't as successful, but it shares some uncomfortable truths that anyone who hopes to beat the market would do well to ponder. "For most investors, figuring out the value of a business is simply out of the question—to do a good job is just much too tough," he writes. "What about getting an expert to do it for us? Sorry. . . . Due to fees and the way the investment business works, most active mutual fund managers underperform the market." Greenblatt's solution for most investors is to index, but he cautions that the garden variety of market-cap-weighted index funds own too many overpriced stocks and too few bargains.

Earlier in his career, Greenblatt also wrote *You Can Be a Stock Market Genius* (Fireside, 1999), a sophisticated but entertaining guide to investing in specialized niches such as spin-offs, mergers, and bankruptcies. For investors with the analytical skills to navigate these deep waters, it's an invaluable book. A friend of mine who studied at Harvard Business School and has run a successful investment firm told me, "I personally made $10 million because of that book." When my wife heard this, she pointed out that I'd failed to derive the same benefit from reading it.

111   Greenblatt's interest in giving back to society has mostly involved education reform. He helped to start Success Academy, a large (and politically controversial) network of not-for-profit charter schools, which you can read more about at www.successacademies.org. He sits on its board of trustees, alongside other prominent money managers such as Daniel Loeb, John Petry, and Yen Liow. In his latest book, *Common Sense: The Investor's Guide to Equality, Opportunity and Growth* (Columbia Business School Publishing, 2020), Greenblatt writes that the premise behind these charter schools was to provide a model of high-performing schools that could be replicated in many other low-income areas: "it would help show that—with the right supports—poor, low-income and minority students could achieve at the highest levels."

How has it worked out? In 2019, writes Greenblatt, students from the Success Network's forty-five schools performed so well in state math and English exams that their "results made Success # 1 for student achievement in all of New York, outperforming every wealthy suburban school district in the state." That's all the more impressive when you consider that the Success Academy schools are mostly located in the poorest areas of New York City and that 75 percent of the students come from economically disadvantaged backgrounds.

126 For the definitive account of the 1980s junk-bond scandal that led to Michael Milken's imprisonment, read James Stewart's *Den of Thieves* (Simon & Schuster, 1992) and then decide whether Milken deserved the presidential pardon that years of lobbying finally won him in 2020.

130 For a more technical discussion of how to invest rationally in high-quality businesses such as Coca-Cola, see *Value Investing From Graham to Buffett and Beyond* (John Wiley & Sons, 2001) by Bruce Greenwald, Judd Kahn, Paul Sonkin, and Michael van Biema. More specifically, Roger Lowenstein's first-rate biography, *Buffett* (Random House, 1995), includes a detailed explanation of why Buffett "staked a fourth or so of Berkshire's market value" on Coca-Cola, investing more in it "than in any previous stock." Lowenstein observes that it was a simple business with pricing power, a protective moat, and unique name recognition. And even though the stock *seemed* expensive, the company's earning power was so strong that "Buffett thought he was getting a Mercedes for the price of a Chevrolet." As Greenblatt points out, the fundamental secret of intelligent investing is simple: "Figure out what something is worth and pay a lot less."

## CHAPTER SIX: NICK & ZAK'S EXCELLENT ADVENTURE

140 As Nick Sleep and Qais Zakaria discovered, Robert Pirsig's *Zen and the Art of Motorcycle Maintenance* (William Morrow and Company, 1974) is surprisingly relevant to the patient investor—and to anyone who is trying to create something of enduring value, whether it's a fund, a business, a work of art, or a philanthropic venture. Early in his book, Pirsig explains how he plans to explore his subject: "I don't want to hurry it. That itself is a poisonous twentieth-century attitude. When you want to hurry something, that means you no longer care about it and want to get on to other things. I just want to get at it slowly, but carefully and thoroughly . . ."

Sleep recalls, "That book woke me up to the whole subject of thinking about how to think, and it just changed everything." For example, it led him to ask questions such as, "How can I make myself a better investor by thinking properly? Thinking about how to think: *that's* the job." As Sleep puts it, Pirsig is dedicated to the pursuit of what is "true," "important," and "intellectually honest," and he sheds light on what it means to behave in a "high-quality" way.

Another unexpected book that has inspired Sleep's approach to investing and life is Michael Pollan's *A Place of My Own* (Penguin Books, 2008). It tells the story of Pollan's quest to design and construct ("with my own two unhandy hands") an enchanting building in the woods behind his house "as a place to read and write and daydream." Sleep remarks, "What I love about that is the gentle, quiet contemplation of building something really properly, doing it quietly on his own, and he's reading about it and enjoying the process. But it gets expressed in this beautiful building that is almost like a little karmic temple for him. It's got this lovely, calm philosophy to it. And it occurs to me now, it's kind of how Zak and I behaved, although I wasn't conscious of that at the time."

Sleep also recommends *The Book of Joy* (Avery, 2016), which grew out of a week-long conversation between Archbishop Desmond Tutu and the Dalai Lama. It's suffused with their life-affirming wisdom, mischievous humor, and joyous resilience. Speaking of his exile from Tibet, the Dalai Lama says, "So, personally, I prefer the last five decades of refugee life. It's more useful, more opportunity to learn, to experience life. Therefore, if you look from one angle, you feel, oh how bad, how sad. But if you look from another angle at that same tragedy, that same event, you see that it gives me new opportunities. So, it's wonderful. That's the main reason that I'm not sad and morose. There's a Tibetan saying: 'Wherever you have friends, that's your country, and wherever you receive love, that's your home.'"

149 Sleep and Zakaria placed their Bloomberg terminal on a low table without a chair, so that it was physically uncomfortable to expose themselves to a ceaseless influx of short-term news and moment-to-moment data. The best writer I've encountered on this subject of how to focus and actually *think* in an era of constant digital distraction is Cal Newport, a computer science professor at Georgetown University. He's the author of *Deep Work* (Grand Central Publishing, 2016) and *Digital Minimalism* (Portfolio/Penguin, 2019). Explaining his "Deep Work Hypothesis," Newport writes, "The ability to perform deep work is becoming increasingly *rare* at exactly the same time it is becoming increasingly *valuable* in our economy. As a consequence, the few who cultivate this skill, and then make it the core of their working life, will thrive." That describes all of the most successful investors—from Buffett and Munger to Sleep and Zakaria.

167 One of the secrets of financial success is the capacity to resist the lure of instant gratification—for example, by setting aside money for the distant future and holding investments for the long term instead of trading them frenetically. The same principle also applies to corporations. As Charlie Munger remarked at Berkshire Hathaway's annual meeting in 2001, "Almost all good businesses engage in 'pain today, gain tomorrow' activities."

The importance of delaying gratification also crops up in many of the morality tales that we read as children. After I discussed this subject with Thomas Russo, he wrote to me, "Less jam today for more jam tomorrow, the three little piggies, etc, are childhood tales that inculcate thoughtful people with the message of deferred gratification. Society has, however, created endless reasons why decision makers mistakenly prefer more jam today even at the expense of jam tomorrow. Much investment opportunity arises from being able to take the other side of the short termism bet. I have been blessed with investors who permit me to take the longer view."

The ability—or inability—to delay gratification is also a popular topic in psychology. Most famously, the Marshmallow Test was a 1960s experiment in which hundreds of kids were presented with a treat and an excruciating choice: Either they could eat it immediately or wait several minutes until a researcher returned, at which point they could eat *two* treats. A team of psychologists from Stanford watched through a one-way observation window as these preschoolers wrestled with temptation. Walter Mischel, who designed the experiment, explores its implications in *The Marshmallow Test* (Little, Brown and Company, 2014). He found that "those who had delayed longer in preschool" were more able as adults "to pursue and reach long-term goals," "reached higher educational levels, and had a significantly lower body mass index."

Maria Konnikova, who studied under Mischel at Columbia, wrote about him in a 2014 article for the *New Yorker* ("The Struggles of a Psychologist Studying Self-Control"). "Mischel has consistently found that the crucial factor in delaying gratification is the ability to change your perception of the object or action you want to resist," she writes. "The key, it turns out, is learning to mentally 'cool' what Mischel calls the 'hot' aspects of your environment: the things that pull you away from your goal." One of his cooling techniques involves mentally moving the object of desire to a safe distance in your imagination. Another way to control your impulses is to reframe the object—for example, by "picturing the marshmallows as clouds not candy."

### CHAPTER SEVEN: HIGH-PERFORMANCE HABITS

170 What else should you read if you're looking to form more positive habits? The most useful book I've studied on this subject is *The Power of Habit* (Random House, 2012) by Charles Duhigg. Drawing on research into the neuroscience and psychology of habit formation, Duhigg writes, "This is how new habits are created: by putting together a cue, a routine, and a reward, and then cultivating a craving that drives the loop." For example, "If you want to start running each morning, it's essential that you choose a simple cue (like always lacing up your sneakers before breakfast or leaving your running clothes next to your bed) and a clear reward (such as a midday treat, a sense of accomplishment from recording your miles, or the endorphin rush you get from a jog). . . . Only when your brain starts *expecting* the reward—craving the endorphins or sense of accomplishment—will it become automatic to lace up your jogging shoes each morning. The cue, in addition to triggering a routine, must also trigger a craving for the reward to come."

Mohnish Pabrai and Guy Spier are enthusiastic cyclists, and they often use Facebook to share videos, photographs, and statistics from their long outdoor rides. I've often wondered why they bother. But I realize now that it's a way of creating a psychological reward for themselves, which reinforces their desire to keep working on their fitness. Similarly, when COVID-19 led me to spend most of my time at home, I became unexpectedly obsessed with my Peloton bike and took part in a competition involving dozens of teams around the world. One of the highlights of each day came when my teammates and I shared charts detailing our heroic accomplishments.

172 Tom Gayner writes about the same four investment principles every year in Markel's annual report. Repetitive? Absolutely. But that's the point. His edge as an investor stems largely from his consistent application over three decades of the same sensible, disciplined, time-tested process. You can find an archive of his annual reports at www.markel.com. They're worth reading each year because they're characterized by Gayner's steady commitment to qualities such as humility, integrity, long-term thinking, continuous improvement, and service. I suspect that we benefit by osmosis from keeping the company of someone who operates this way.

176 Gayner's standard approach to everything from investing to exercise to nutrition is to be "radically moderate," instead of adopting a more extreme strategy that would be less sustainable. His mindset is reminiscent of Aristotle's ancient teaching that enduring happiness comes from maintaining a harmonious balance known as the "golden mean."

Lou Marinoff's book *The Middle Way* (Sterling Publishing Co., 2007) explains that Aristotle's study of Euclidean geometry, combined with his appreciation for the beauty of nature, persuaded the Greek philosopher that "human behaviors ought also to be based on 'correct' proportions." According to Aristotle, "Both excessive and defective exercise destroys the strength, and similarly drink or food which is above or below a certain amount destroys the health, while that which is proportionate both produces and increases and preserves it. So too is it, then, in the case of temperance and courage and the other virtues."

Marinoff contends that Aristotle, Buddha, and Confucius all "recognized that extremism is anathema to happiness, health, and harmony: yours and everyone else's." Applying the wisdom of these sages to our own era, Marinoff writes, "Materialists who pursue pleasure and profit above all else remain unhappy. Religious fanatics who pursue denial of modernism above all else remain unhappy. . . . Buddha's Middle Way helps us avoid these extremes, by the practice of moderation in our own lives, and of compassion for the sufferings of others."

There's a great deal of practical wisdom in Gayner's philosophy of radical moderation. But by most people's standards, he's still pretty extreme. After hearing about it from Gayner, I watched *The Last Dance*, a mesmerizing documentary series about Michael Jordan and the Chicago Bulls. It wasn't hard to see why Gayner was inspired by Jordan, whose relentless work ethic and overpowering will to win made him an unstoppable force. Investing, like basketball, is so competitive at the highest levels that talent alone simply isn't enough. As Peter Lynch told Bill Miller, "The only way you can beat them is to outwork them."

## CHAPTER EIGHT: DON'T BE A FOOL

201 During my interview with Charlie Munger, I asked him to recommend a couple of books that I could give my children that would teach them how to avoid the "standard stupidities" that ruin many people's lives. "Well," he replied. "You've got *Poor Charlie's Almanack*." There's no question that this compendium of Munger's "wit and wisdom" is a priceless resource for anyone who's serious about reducing their vulnerability to "unoriginal error." It includes the dazzling 1986 commencement speech in which he shared his "prescriptions for guaranteed misery in life."

Munger also mentioned to me the influence of the late Garrett Hardin, who helped him to develop the mental habit of "inversion." Like Munger, Hardin solved problems backward by focusing first on what could go wrong, then trying to avoid that disastrous outcome. Hardin, who was a human ecologist, wrote numerous books, including *Filters Against Folly* (Viking, 1985). In weighing the risks of various calamities, such as a failure of the power grid, Hardin writes that "the only thing we can really count on in this uncertain world is human unreliability itself."

For another take on the theme of our tragicomic fallibility, see *The Folly of Fools* (Basic Books, 2011) by Robert Trivers, a leading theorist in the field of evolutionary biology. It's a disconcerting exploration of our capacity for self-deception. Trivers argues that we store false information in our minds so we can use it to manipulate others. As he puts it, "we lie to ourselves the better to lie to others." Like Munger and Hardin, Trivers pushes us to acknowledge how prone we are to error and how wary we ought to be of our own minds. If you're still inclined to trust your judgment, you might also want to read *The Logic of Failure* (Metropolitan Books, 1996) by Dietrich Dörner, a psychologist who writes about the predictable and avoidable ways in which we mess up when faced with complex decisions. The cover of my copy features an old photograph of two elegantly dressed gentlemen inspecting a train that has tumbled off the tracks.

203 If you want to learn more about Munger's way of thinking, the logical starting point is Tren Griffin's *Charlie Munger* (Columbia University Press, 2015). It's a concise book filled with clear-headed insights about how to behave rationally in markets and life. Serious Munger aficionados should also do battle with Peter Bevelin's idiosyncratic books, starting with *Seeking Wisdom* (PCA Publications, 2007), which is dense and difficult but worth the effort, followed by *All I Want to Know is Where I'm Going to Die So I'll Never Go There* (PCA Publications, 2016).

204 Joel Tillinghast, who has generated superb returns over three decades as the manager of Fidelity's Low-Priced Stock Fund, is also the author of *Big Money Thinks Small* (Columbia University Press, 2017). It's a helpful guide for the regular investor, with plenty of common-sense advice on how to succeed by "avoiding mistakes." Tillinghast closes his book with a simple insight that might just as easily have come from Munger, Pabrai, Greenblatt, or Marks: "Above all, always look for investments that are worth a great deal more than you are paying for them." Their investment styles may differ, but they are all united by this underlying principle.

213 Munger has deeply immersed himself in Benjamin Franklin's writings, including his *Autobiography*. As a self-proclaimed "biography nut," he's also well-versed in books about Franklin by authors such as Carl Van Doren and Walter Isaacson. When I asked Munger what he'd learned from Franklin about how to reduce folly, he replied, "Ben Franklin I learned a lot from: the self-control; not showing off how smart you are; not being so argumentative. Now, he learned it better than I [did]. I still offend people in a way that Ben Franklin got over."

When I read Franklin's book *Poor Richard's Almanack*, I could see throughout it aspects of Munger's philosophy of business and life. For example, Franklin writes, "Tricks and Treachery are the Practice of Fools, that have not Wit enough to be honest." And "A rich rogue, is like a fat hog, who never does good til as dead as a log." And "He that lies down with Dogs, shall rise up with fleas." And "An empty Bag cannot stand upright." And "Glass, China, and Reputation are easily crack'd, and never well mended." And "If you would be loved, love and be loveable." And "If your Riches are yours, why don't you take them with you to the t'other World?" And "The noblest question in the world is *What Good may I do in it?*"

In his home, Munger has a bust of Franklin, along with one of Lee Kuan Yew, who "may have been the best nation builder that ever lived." But in learning from the "eminent dead," Munger isn't only interested in their virtues and achievements. He's also fascinated by their flaws and mistakes, which can be even more instructive. For example, says Munger, Franklin "failed in his relationship with his only surviving son," who remained "loyal to the crown. That rupture never healed. It was just too much. . . . He didn't even talk to his son at the end. That's interesting. Franklin was capable of having more resentment than I have. I've conquered resentment better than Franklin did. I'm not that mad about the people I disapprove of."

## EPILOGUE: BEYOND RICH

239 Bill Miller's habit of drawing on philosophy to help him in every area of life makes him a particularly fertile source of book recommendations. He introduced me to the Stoics and left me with an enduring admiration for *Thoughts of a Philosophical Fighter Pilot*, (Hoover Institution Press, 1995) a splendidly titled book by a splendidly named man of action, Vice Admiral James Bond Stockdale. Thanks to Miller, I also discovered the bracing wisdom of *Meditations* by Marcus Aurelius, *The Discourses* by Epictetus, and *Letters from a Stoic* by Seneca. Likewise, I enjoyed another of Miller's favorite books, Bryan Magee's *Confessions of a Philosopher* (Random House, 1998), which is an autobiographical journey through Western philosophy.

Two decades ago, Miller also introduced me to the philosopher William James, whose works are collected in editions such as *Pragmatism and Other Writings* (Penguin Books, 2000). James, who pioneered the teaching of psychology at Harvard, was a groundbreaking observer of the ways in which we misperceive reality—a critical challenge facing every investor.

In the 1890s, James delivered a talk titled "On a Certain Blindness in Human Beings." He recalled visiting North Carolina, where he was shocked by the "unmitigated squalor" of a cabin in the mountains: "The forest had been destroyed; and what had 'improved' it out of existence was hideous, a sort of ulcer, without a single element of artificial grace to make up for the loss of Nature's beauty." Later, a mountaineer helped James to understand how differently the locals perceived this ravaged landscape. For them, "the cabin was a warrant of safety for self and wife and babes" and the clearing was "a symbol redolent with moral memories and sang a very paean of duty, struggle and success. I had been as blind to the peculiar ideality of their conditions as they certainly would also have been to the ideality of mine, had they had a peep at my strange indoor academic ways of life at Cambridge."

To Miller, the moral was clear. We must constantly guard against our prejudices—and seek to profit from opportunities that arise when others fall into this mental trap. When he spoke to me in 2001 about why he'd bought 15 percent of Amazon, he explained how James helped him to see beyond the biases that blinded his peers to the potential of this profitless bookseller.

To learn more about James, read Louis Menand's *The Metaphysical Club*

(Farrar Strauss and Giroux, 2001) which explores the beliefs of four great thinkers: James, Charles Sanders Peirce, Oliver Wendell Holmes, Jr., and John Dewey. Menand writes, "They all believed that ideas are not 'out there,' waiting to be discovered, but are tools—like forks and knives and microchips—that people devise to cope with the world in which they find themselves."

243 Since we first met in 2015, Arnold Van Den Berg and I have gifted each other many books. Concerned about my sloth, he also sent me a trampoline. I have a stack of his favorite titles beside me now in my study, including *The Wisdom of Your Subconscious Mind* (Prentice-Hall, 1964) by John Williams, *The Biology of Belief* (Mountain of Love Productions, 2008) by Bruce Lipton, *Core Healing* (Heart of the Golden Triangle Publishers, 2007) by Joyce Fern Glasser, *Right is Might* (Humanetics Fellowship, 1991) by Richard Wetherill, and a complete collection of James Allen's writings titled *Mind Is the Master* (Penguin Group, 2010).

A common theme that runs insistently through many of the books that have shaped Van Den Berg is the belief that our consciousness determines our reality. He has spent half a century experimenting with different techniques to change his thoughts, influence his subconscious mind, and transform himself from within. Everything comes back to what he learned from his favorite book of all, *From Poverty to Power*. As Allen wrote 120 years ago, "It matters little what is without, for it is all a reflection of your own state of consciousness. It matters everything what you are within, for everything without will be mirrored and colored accordingly."

# Index